Utility Theories: Measurements and Applications

Studies in Risk and Uncertainty

edited by W. Kip Viscusi
Department of Economics
Duke University
Durham, North Carolina 27706

Previously published books in the series:

1. Luken, R.: ENVIRONMENTAL
    REGULATION: TECHNOLOGY,
    AMBIENT AND BENEFITS-BASED
    APPROACHES
2. Shubik, M.: RISK, ORGANIZATIONS
    AND SOCIETY

Utility Theories: Measurements and Applications

Edited by
Ward Edwards
Social Science Research Institute
University of Southern California

Kluwer Academic Publishers
Boston / Dordrecht / London

658.403
U89

Distributors for North America:
Kluwer Academic Publishers
101 Philip Drive
Assinippi Park
Norwell, Massachusetts 02061 USA

Distributors for all other countries:
Kluwer Academic Publishers Group
Distribution Centre
Post Office Box 322
3300 AH Dordrecht, THE NETHERLANDS

Library of Congress Cataloging-in-Publication Data

Utility theories: measurements and applications/edited by Ward
  Edwards.
     p.   cm. — (Studies in risk and uncertainty)
     Includes bibliographical references and index.
     ISBN 0–7923–9226–4 (hardback: acid-free paper). — ISBN
0-7923-9227-2 (pbk.: acid-free paper)
     1. Utility theory.   2. Decision-making.   I. Edwards, Ward.
  II. Series.
  HB201.U88   1992
  658.4'03—dc20   92-4915

For
Elaine Corry
Assistant Director for Administration
Social Science Research Institute
University of Southern California

Elaine Corry has been the Assistant Director for
Administration of the Institute of which I am
Director since 1976. Every bit of scientific output
of the Institute over that period has her mark on
it, usually in ways much too subtle to be visible
or to be adequately appreciated. By being a
consummately skilled and utterly dedicated
administrator of science, she has enabled all of
us in SSRI to be effective scientists. Thank you,
Elaine.

Contents

Contributing Authors

Colin F. Camerer
University of Chicago
Graduate School of Business
Chicago, IL 60637

Ward Edwards
Social Science Research Institute
University of Southern California
University Park
Los Angeles, CA 90089-1111

Thomas Eppel
Krannert School of Management
Purdue University
Krannert Building
West Lafayette, IN 47907

Stuart Eriksen
13341 Eton Place
Santa Ana, CA 92705

Ronald A. Howard
Department of Engineering—Economic Systems
Stanford University
Stanford, CA 94305

Ralph L. Keeney
Safety and Systems Management
University of Southern California
University Park
Los Angeles, CA 90089-0021

L. Robin Keller
Graduate School of Management
University of California, Irvine
Irvine, CA 92717

Irving H. LaValle
A.B. Freeman School of Business
Goldring/Woldenberg Hall
Tulane University
New Orleans, LA 70118-5669

R. Duncan Luce
Irvine Research Unit in Mathematical Behavioral Science
University of California, Irvine
Irvine, CA 92717

David Matheson
Strategic Decisions Group
2440 Sand Hill Road
Menlo Park, CA 94025-6900

John M. Miyamoto
Department of Psychology
University of Washington
Seattle, WA 98195

Rakesh K. Sarin
Anderson Graduate School of Management
University of California, Los Angeles
405 Hilgard Avenue
Los Angeles, CA 90024-1481

Uzi Segal
California Institute of Technology
Department of Humanities & Social Sciences
Baxter Hall, Room 215
Pasadena, CA 91125

George Wu
Graduate School of Business Administration
Harvard University
Boston
MA 02163

Preface

The Conference on "Utility: Theories, Measurements, and Applications" met at the Inn at Pasatiempo in Santa Cruz, California, from June 11 to 15, 1989. The all-star cast of attendees are listed as authors in the Table of Contents of this book (see p. V), except for Soo Hong Chew and Amos Tversky.

The purpose of the conference, and of National Science Foundation Grant No. SES-8823012 that supported it, was to confront proponents of new generalized theories of utility with leading decision analysts committed to the implementation, in practice, of the more traditional theory that these new theories reject. That traditional model is variously identified in this book as *expected utility* or *subjectively expected utility maximization* (EU or SEU for short) and variously attributed to von Neumann and Morgenstern or Savage.

I had feared that the conference might consist of an acrimonious debate between Olympian normative theorists uninterested in what people actually do and behavioral modelers obsessed with the cognitive illusions and uninterested in helping people to make wise decisions. I was entirely wrong. The conferees, in two dramatic straw votes at the opening session, unanimously endorsed traditional SEU as the appropriate normative model and unanimously agreed that people don't act as that model requires. (These votes had a profound impact on my thinking; detail about them and about that impact is located in Chapter 10.) This unexpected agreement left the conferees free to explore the normative, prescriptive, and descriptive implications of the new utility models creatively and without tension, which they did. Afterwards, we all went home and rewrote (or, in my case, procrastinated and then wrote) our papers based on what had occurred at the conference. The book you have in your hand is the result.

What will you find here? With minor procrustean discomfort, the chapters of this volume can be grouped into five parts. The first, "Review", contains a splendid overview by Robin Keller of the axiomatic and empirical issues associated with the new utility theories. Keller's chapter was extensively rewritten after the conference, and as a result, highlights and puts the other chapters in context. Those not steeped in the new utility theories should welcome this relatively easy way to catch up; those already obsessed will find this chapter indispensable for explaining that obsession to others.

I have labelled the second group of chapters "The Old Time Religion and Its Implementation". The old time religion of course, is SEU maximization as a normative theory. I first gave it that name in my Ramsey Award speech; attendees at the conference liked it, and Ron Howard put it into the title of his chapter. That chapter is a definitive summary of the tenets of the old time religion and a persuasive argument for their normative necessity. Howard sees the violations of SEU that have led to new utility theories as being simply errors; the business of decision analysis is to help decision makers avoid them. Ralph Keeney's chapter notes that the old time religion, though indispensable to decision analytic practice, is not enough. He proposes prescriptive rules to help implement the normative ones. He also examines the topic of equity, a difficult one for the normative theory. Cognoscenti and close readers will extract from their chapters a dignified side debate between Howard and Keeney on how to think about equity issues in decision analyses. John Miyamoto, in a most ingenious chapter, proposes what he calls generic utility theory, a version of SEU that applies only to subsets of options. The purpose of generic utility theory is to provide a formal basis for getting on with various applied tasks, such as application of gamble-based elicitations in multiattribute utility measurements, in spite of the possibility that the SEU model needed to interpret such elicitations may not be descriptively valid. One way of looking at his chapter is as an operationalization of the notion that descriptively useful decision theories will be "close" to SEU in some sense. That notion is central to my own chapter, though my suggested operationalizations are different.

The third group of chapters I have called "Generalized Utility Is Not Normative". The focus of these chapters is on what Savage called *small worlds*, and on the reduction of compound lotteries axiom. Irving LaValle's chapter asks what properties a technologically useful decision theory must have and goes on to show not only that generalized utility theories do not have these properties, but also, that any kind of utility theory that does is essentially forced to be SEU. The crux of the issue is whether the historical path by which one arrives at a decision point is allowed to have an impact (other than via information leading to changes in probabilities or via changes in, say, total wealth) on the decisions from then on. A negative answer leads to SEU; a positive one leads to a variety of normative difficulties. Rakesh Sarin's chapter reaches the same conclusion from much the same set of considerations and goes on to examine what decision analysts and decision theorists should do about psychological inputs to decisions such as regrets, hopes, and fears. Uzi Segal's chapter, written from an economist's perspective, explores axiomatically different ways to reduce multistage lotteries to one-stage lotteries. His argument is an attempt to replace the reduction of compound lotteries axiom in normative theorizing. He does not discuss the technological issues with which LaValle and Sarin were concerned.

If the conferees had not started by agreeing that the new utility models are not normative, it would have been interesting to see if the arguments by LaValle and Sarin would have led them to that conclusion. I find those arguments so compelling that I can see no remaining hope at all for SEU-like theories that are simultaneously normative and descriptive.

The fourth group of chapters I have labelled "What Should Descriptive Decision Models Look Like? What Do they Describe?" R. Duncan Luce's chapter is an exposition of the rank-and-sign-dependent utility model that he is developing, set in the context of its axiomatic relation to SEU and to other models. Colin Camerer's chapter is a summary of the confrontation between various generalized utility theories and an ingenious set of experiments that mainly looks for experimentally derived indifference curves in the two-dimensional Marschak triangle that represents three-outcome gambles. Camerer's conclusion is that no existing model really fits the data well, but that Prospect Theory does best. My own chapter is an attempt to find a new point of departure for descriptive decision theory based on the straw votes taken at the conference. Its key idea is that people draw on principles of good decision making evolved from past experience, training, and analysis when they must make significant decisions. These principles, which may or may not be normatively valid and which often conflict with one another (unnoticed by the decision maker), are recalled and used in subsets as seems appropriate. What makes them even vaguely successful is that ordinal dominance is always conformed to as a principle of choice when perceived. That fact leads to behavior close to, but not identical with, the prescriptions of SEU. I have almost nothing to suggest about how the principles are retrieved or combined to make decisions.

The last group of chapters, "Discussion," contains a single chapter.

I invited five graduate students and recent PhDs, identified by their mentors, to participate in the conference as discussants, on the theory that they are the audience most affected by any conclusions to which the conference might come. They listened, contributed, and have collectively prepared a wonderful discussion chapter based on what they heard and read. It weaves together all of the themes that I have reviewed in this Preface, plus many more. It even reports on a questionnaire that the discussants used to elicit from the other conferees their views about each item on Howard's list of desiderata for a normative decision theory. If, after reading the rest of this book, you want to put what you have read into a structured perspective, you should find this discussion exceedingly helpful.

This book is not difficult to read. Yet, any book concerned with profound issues and written by researchers as farseeing as these is bound to demand real effort from its readers. Savage's advice about sitting bolt upright with paper and pencil in hand and being willing to read slowly and retrace steps, applies. Most of these authors have written with good humor, grace, and a willingness to be merciful to readers not steeped in utility theory and not particularly comfortable with axiomatic treatments. An occasional impish crack or allusion will give the attentive reader reason to smile.

The best aspirations that I had for the conference are more than fulfilled in this book. It answers, in my view definitively, the central question about normative implications of new utility theories that led to the conference. In addition, it brings a number of related questions into sharp focus and reports theoretical and empirical progress of several important kinds.

Ward Edwards

Acknowledgments

My most profound gratitude is owed to the conferees who made the conference what it was and this book what it is. Their work speaks for itself. I especially thank Thomas Eppel who was entirely responsible for organizing and managing the efforts of the discussants.

I am grateful to the National Science Foundation's Decision, Risk, and Management Sciences Program for awarding Grant No. SES-8823012, which paid for the conference. Letty Baz of the University of Southern California found the site, made the arrangements, and has been deeply involved in every step of shepherding this book through to publication. She and Silvia Edwards also managed to divert us from incessant talk about utility theory for as much as five minutes at a time out of each 24 hours. Zachary Rolnik of Kluwer Academic Publishers has helped the book through teething troubles and delays.

Refereeing is a thankless, crucial chore. Every chapter in the book was anonymously refereed by at least two people, more often three. At least one referee for each chapter did not attend the conference. Referees and authors responded nobly; each chapter was improved very substantially as a result of referee inputs. For their refereeing efforts I thank:

Phillipe Delquie	Irving LaValle
Thomas Eppel	Lola Lopes
Baruch Fischhoff	Mark Machina
Peter Fishburn	Barbara Mellers
David Grether	John Pratt
Robin Hogarth	Paul Slovic
Michael Intriligator	Richard Thaler
Ralph Keeney	Amos Tversky
Robin Keller	Detlof von Winterfeldt
David Krantz	Rand Wilcox
Howard Kunreuther	

I REVIEW

1 PROPERTIES OF UTILITY THEORIES AND RELATED EMPIRICAL PHENOMENA

L. Robin Keller

Introduction

Expected utility theory, probably the most widely accepted normative theory for decision making under risk, has several required properties. Since different sets of axioms can be combined to result in the expected utility model, the term *property* can refer to either an axiom or a characteristic resulting from combinations of axioms. Since most properties are seen as appropriate components of a normative theory of choice, they could be referred to as *principles* or *desiderata* to emphasize their normative status (see Howard, 1992). But, not all properties hold consistently in choices made by experimental subjects. The resulting conflict between the normative appeal of expected utility theory and its shortcomings as a descriptive model of choice has been a motivating force in the development of generalized utility theories which relax the requirement that various properties hold.

The purpose of this chapter is to provide an overview of the properties and related experimental phenomena and their link with developments in generalized utility theories. The chapter thus serves as an introduction for the issues raised by the remaining chapters in this volume. The chapter is

W. Edwards (ed.), UTILITY THEORIES: MEASUREMENTS AND APPLICATIONS.
Copyright © 1992. Kluwer Academic Publishers, Boston. All rights reserved.

organized as follows. The second section briefly describes expected utility theory and lists a number of generalized utility theories. The third section contains some key properties of expected utility theory, with high-lights of related experiments and generalized utility theories not requiring those properties. The fourth section continues the discussion of con-sequentialism, dynamic consistency, and substitution property violations. A summary follows in the last section.

Expected Utility and Generalized Utility Theories

This section contains a brief discussion of expected utility and generalized utility theories. Fishburn (1988) and Machina (1987b) present details on the different theories, and reviews are in Fishburn (1989), Machina (1987a), Sarin (1989), and Weber and Camerer (1987).

Expected Utility Theory

von Neumann and Morgenstern (1947) axiomatized expected utility theory by showing that, if a set of apparently normatively appealing axioms hold, alternative actions can be ranked by their expected utilities. The expected utility of an alternative action is the weighted average of the utilities of the possible outcomes where the weights are the objec-tive probabilities of each outcome. Savage's (1954) subjective expected utility model allows the derivation of a decision maker's own subjective probabilities for events, which are then used to compute the subjective expected utility of each alternative. Edwards (1955, 1962) and other psychologists have experimentally investigated a model wherein a person makes choices as if he or she transforms the objective probabilities into subjective probabilities, then computes expected utility via the resulting subjective probability weighting function. Many prescriptive applications of expected utility theory have been carried out, especially for problems with multiple attributes in which multiattribute utility theory is used (Keeney and Raiffa, 1976). Keeney (1992) discusses the choice of axioms to guide prescriptive decision analysis, along with other prescriptive issues.

A fairly large body of experimental evidence, stimulated by the paradox introduced by Allais (1953), shows that subjects systematically make choices that violate properties required by expected utility. This evidence shows that expected utility is not a fully valid descriptive model of choice under risk. Representative experimental studies are cited later in the third section, throughout the discussion of utility properties. Also, a few recent experiments have gone further and actually assessed subjects' expected utility to determine the percentage of choices correctly predicted. The preliminary evidence shows that assessed and/or fitted expected utility functions predict choices moderately well compared to generalized utility models, but with room for improvement. Currim and Sarin (1989, 1990) compared experimental subjects' assessed expected utility models with their prospect theory, weighted utility, and lottery dependent utility models; and Daniels and Keller (1990) assessed expected utility and lottery dependent utility models. Overall, expected utility did about as well as the generalized utility models in predicting choices on a hold-out sample of paired comparison choices, even when the problems were structured to induce expected utility property violations. However, the potential for improved predictive performance by generalized utility models may still be achieved. For example, Daniels and Keller (1992) have explored a choice-based assessment mechanism in which lottery dependent expected utility appears to perform better than expected utility. Also, Shafir et al. (1989) proposed an advantage model of choice that outperformed two special cases of expected utility.

There are at least three different categories of responses to the descriptive violations of expected utility. One is to argue that expected utility theory's purpose is normative and to reclarify conditions under which expected utility is an appropriate model for prescriptive use and when it is not, such as when distributional equity is involved. Keeney (1992) and Howard (1992) discuss the use of expected utility in prescriptive applications, and Keeney discusses its inapplicability in portions of problems requiring equity considerations.

Another response to descriptive violations, followed in Keller (1985a,b), is to develop prescriptive techniques, such as visual problem representations, to aid decision makers to conform with expected utility theory. The stream of research attempting to develop unbiased utility assessment procedures also follows this general approach. Keller (1989b) contains a discussion of the problems of descriptive violations of expected utility when it is to be used as a prescriptive model.

A final response is to develop new models, including the generalized utility models, that may be descriptively valid and that might be used prescriptively in special settings. Miyamoto (1992) introduces his generic utility theory, designed as a general framework for descriptive multiattribute utility modeling.

Generalized Utility Theories

Many generalized utility theories have been recently proposed as variants of expected utility theory. Weber and Camerer (1987, see Figure 10) provide a concise summary of the relationship of expected utility with the various generalized theories. Some of the theories are described in chapters of this volume. Representative theories include prospect theory (Kahneman and Tversky (1989)); weighted utility (Chew and MacCrimmon (1979a,b)), (Chew (1983)) and the related skew-symmetric bilinear utility (Fishburn (1983, 1984)) and regret theory (Bell 1982)), Loomes and Sugden (1982)); lottery dependent utility (Becker (1986), Becker and Sarin (1987)); approximate expected utility (Leland (1988)); expected utility with rank dependent probabilities (Quiggin's (1982) anticipated utility); Yaari (1987), Luce and Narens' (1985) binary

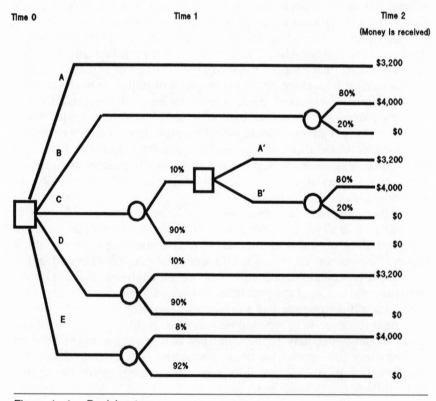

Figure 1–1.   Decision tree.

rank dependent (or dual bilinear) utility; general quadratic utility (Chew, Epstein, and Segal (1988), Machina (1982, see note 45)); implicit expected utility (Chew (1985), Dekel (1986)); and ordinal independence (Segal (1984), Green and Jullien (1988)).

Since their development was primarily motivated by descriptive violations of expected utility theory properties, most generalized theories are designed to account for these violations. Thus, they generally have the potential to describe choices that have been observed in laboratory settings. This potential is usually first demonstrated theoretically by showing that the model is mathematically able to match nonexpected utility choices. Next, new data are collected for existing or new questions to show the preference patterns the new models are theoretically capable of predicting; for example, Chew and Waller (1986) followed this approach to evaluate weighted utility theory. LaValle (1992) discusses some limitations on the use of generalized utility theories in prescriptive analysis, and Keller (1989b) discusses the role of generalized utility theories in descriptive, prescriptive, and normative decision analysis.

Properties of Expected Utility Theory

This section contains a discussion of properties required by expected utility theory. Some properties serve as axioms in certain axiomatic developments of the theory, others result from combinations of axioms or from the expected utility model in general.

Substitution

The *substitution* property of expected utility theory requires that whenever some lottery A is preferred or indifferent to a lottery B, then the compound lottery $pA + (1 - p)Z$ must be preferred or indifferent to the compound lottery $pB + (1 - p)Z$, which is formed by substituting B in place of A in the compound lottery. The compound lottery $pA + (1 - p)Z$ is constructed by having a p chance of getting lottery A and a $(1 - p)$ chance of getting lottery Z, for any probability values p ranging from 0 to 1. This property is also called *common-ratio* (Kahneman and Tversky, 1979) and *independence* (Segal, 1992).

Figure 1–1 contains a decision tree with a set of alternative actions that will be used to illustrate examples in this chapter. A decision maker who prefers the sure \$3,200 in option A in the figure over the risky option

B (with an 80 percent chance of $4,000 or else $0) also must prefer *D* over *E*, according to the substitution property. This is because *D* and *E* are formed by substituting lotteries *A* and *B*, respectively, into an otherwise identical lottery with a 10 percent chance of *A* or *B* and a 90 percent chance of *Z* (where *Z* is the degenerate lottery of getting $0 for sure). Most people choose *A* over *B* and *E* over *D*. This most common response pattern violates the substitution property, and thus expected utility. Substitution property violations have been shown by, for example, MacCrimmon and Larsson (1979), Kahneman and Tversky (1979), and Keller (1985a).

Luce (1992) points out that most tests of the substitution property confound *monotonicity* with an assumed *accounting equivalence*. The monotonicity property requires that "if a consequence in a gamble is replaced by a more preferred consequence (where this more preferred consequence may itself be a gamble), then the resulting gamble is preferred to the original one" (Luce, 1992). The hidden assumption above (and in experimental tests of the property) is the simultaneous application of monotonicity and an accounting equation requiring that a person equates the compound lottery (that has a 10 percent chance of *B* ($4,000, 80 percent; $0, 20 percent) or else $0) with the corresponding simple lottery *E*, ($4,000, 8 percent; $0, 92 percent). This accounting equation can be called the *reduction of compound lotteries* property or the *economic equivalence* property (Sarin, 1992). Keller (1985b) found evidence of violations of the reduction of compound lotteries property.

Generalized utility theories usually allow the substitution property to be violated and usually retain some of the other properties required by expected utility. Segal (1992) argues, however, that the independence (substitution) property could be retained in a generalized utility model, if the reduction of compound lotteries property were relaxed.

Sure-thing

The *sure-thing* property of expected utility requires that whenever some lottery *D*, formed by reducing the compound lottery $pA + (1 - p)Z$, is preferred over *E*, the reduced compound lottery corresponding to $pB + (1 - p)Z$; then *D'* must be preferred over *E'*, where *D'* and *E'* are formed by replacing the common consequence *Z* with a new "sure-thing" consequence *Z'*, which is commonly received in both *D* and *E*, respectively. The Allais (1953) Paradox is the prototypical example of sure-thing property violations. Howard (1992) argues that violating the sure-thing property is not rational. Sure-thing (or *common consequence*) principle violations have been shown by, for example, MacCrimmon and Larsson (1979), Kahneman and Tversky (1979), and Keller (1985a). LaValle (1992) examines the role of this "sure-thing substitution" property in utility theories.

Linearity in Probabilities

Expected utility is *linear in probabilities*, since the expected utility of a compound lottery $U(pA + (1 - p)B)$ is equal to $pU(A) + (1 - p)U(B)$. For this reason, it is sometimes called *linear expected utility*. In a Marschak triangle diagram graphically representing the set of all possible alternative actions with probability distributions over three fixed outcomes (see Machina (1987b)), this means that indifference curves for expected utility are linear and parallel. (The substitution property leads to these parallel straight lines.) Nonparallel indifference curves violate expected utility. The predominant patterns of choices violating the substitution and sure-thing properties can be represented by preference models that allow indifference curves to fan out (Machina (1982)).

Fanning-in indifference curves correspond to violations of the sure-thing property, but not in the most common response pattern. Camerer (1989) examined sets of choices to gather evidence on subjects' indifference curves and found evidence of both fanning out and fanning in of indifference curves. No one existing theory could explain all the preference data, but prospect theory and the fanning-out hypothesis matched most of the data. Camerer (1992) provides details of tests of generalized utility theories conducted by himself and others.

Betweenness

The *betweenness* property states that if lottery A is preferred over B, then the compound lottery $pA + (1 - p)B$ is "in-between" the original lotteries in the preference ordering. Camerer (1992) discusses betweenness, showing that it is a special case of the substitution property in which Z is fixed at A or B. Betweenness implies indifference curves that are straight lines. Coombs (1969, 1975) and Coombs and Huang (1970) found violations of betweenness by observing orderings of original gambles and the simple lottery formed by reducing the compound lottery (assuming the reduction of compound lotteries property holds). They then proposed portfolio theory as a preference model that can capture betweenness violations. Camerer (1992) reports on other betweenness tests.

First-order stochastic dominance preference

Expected utility orderings are consistent with *first-order stochastic dominance* rankings. Assume that more is better of the attribute (for example, money), and that outcomes are labeled in ascending order of preference, so x_i is less than or equal to x_{i+1} and y_i is less than or equal to y_{i+1}, for all i. Then alternative X dominates alternative Y in the table below if x_k is preferred to y_k for some k and x_i is preferred or indifferent to y_i for the remaining i not equal to k.

	Probabilities of States				
	p_1	p_2	p_3	$\cdots$	p_n
Alternative X	x_1	x_2	x_3	$\cdots$	x_n
Alternative Y	y_1	y_2	y_3	$\cdots$	y_n

More generally, X, dominates a different alternative Y by first order stochastic dominance, if the probability of getting an outcome less than w with alternative X (this probability is the sum of the probabilities p_i for all i's such that x_i is less than w) is less than or equal to the corresponding probability for alternative Y, for all possible levels of w (Fishburn (1988) and Bunn (1984)). This can be generalized to alternatives specified by any continuous probability distribution over outcomes. Luce (1992) suggests the term *likelihood dominance* to generalize stochastic dominance to cases when probabilities of events are unknown.

Luce points out (personal correspondence) that first-order stochastic dominance covers two generally nonequivalent concepts that need to be distinguished. First, monotonicity requires that a gamble formed by replacing a less preferred consequence with a more preferred one is preferred over the original gamble. Second, in the context of a two-outcome gamble, if a new gamble is formed by making the better consequence more likely, then the new gamble should be preferred over the original one. A theory can violate one of these concepts and not the other.

The original version of prospect theory may violate the normatively compelling property of *first-order stochastic dominance preference* (Machina

(1989, see note 17)), which is satisfied by expected utility and some generalized utility models. (A new rank-dependent form of prospect theory is under development that does not violate stochastic dominance.)

Ambiguity Indifference

Expected utility requires *ambiguity indifference*. This means that indifference must hold between two risky options that are identical except that one option has a non-vague subjective probability p for an event, and the other has the same subjective probability for a corresponding event, but the probability p is ambiguous; see Ellsberg's (1961) Paradox. Aversion to ambiguity in probabilities has been demonstrated in experiments and models have been proposed (Sarin, 1992) to accommodate nonindifference to ambiguous probabilities. Howard (1992) presents an argument that ambiguity aversion is irrational and that decision makers should be ambiguity indifferent.

Fixed Reference Level

Under expected utility theory, the status quo (or perceived reference level) is assumed to remain fixed throughout the period or epoch (see Howard, 1992) in which the model is to be used. For example, a single attribute utility function over a monetary attribute might be assessed over total assets, and the function would not be allowed to change from day to day, even though total assets change. Specifically, expected utility is not modeled as a function of changes in assets from the status quo. However, experiments show that people often react quite asymmetrically to incremental changes that are perceived as gains or losses with respect to the current perceived status quo or some target or reference level. This asymmetry has motivated the development of generalized utility models that treat gains and losses differently (for example, Kahneman and Tversky's (1979) prospect theory, which is a type of rank and sign dependent utility function; see Luce, 1992).

Note that an expected utility function can have different risk attitudes in the gain and loss domains, but the reference level must remain fixed. An S-shaped function, with a point of inflection at a target or reference level can represent risk aversion (concavity) in the gain domain and risk proneness (convexity) in the loss domain. However, some people (especially economists) argue that a person should retain either risk aversion, proneness, or neutrality over both gain and loss domains. Even if expected utility is represented with an S-shaped function, the reference level must remain fixed throughout the decision period. A reasonable prescription is to limit the number of times a decision maker resets the reference level, thus requiring a new decision model, as suggested by von Winterfeldt and Edwards (1986, pp. 373–377).

An issue not directly addressed by expected utility theory is the choice of risk attitude. Under expected utility theory, a person is labeled risk averse if a sure monetary amount (such as the $3,200 in Option *A* in figure 1–1) is preferred over a lottery (such as Option *B*) whose expected monetary value is equal to that sure amount. This labeling scheme is misleading because it mixes attitude toward risk with strength of preference for different outcomes. For example, suppose a student feels the increase in value of getting a grade of A rather than a B- is equal to the increase in value of getting a B- rather than a C. Thus, the strength of the preference increase in going from a C to a B- is the same as from a B- to an A for this student. Then, if the person is indifferent between a B- for sure or a 50 percent chance of an A and a 50 percent chance of a C, (s)he displays relative risk neutrality (Dyer and Sarin (1982), Keller (1985c)). This is because (s)he is risk neutral, relative to her/his strength of preference for outcomes. But, following the conventional labeling of risk attitude, the student is indicating risk aversion since, using the standard 4.0 grading scale, the expected grade points of the risky option are 0.5(4.0) + 0.5(2.0) = 3.0, which is equivalent to a B grade. The person preferred a B- over an option with the expected grade points = B, so (s)he is seen as giving up a risk premium of from B to B- to avoid the risk. However, aversion to risk might have not entered into this student's thinking, since B- was seen as halfway in between an A and a C in value, but not in the underlying grade point scale. Risk attitudes and strength of preference notions have not been clarified for most generalized utility theories. However, the value function in Kahneman and Tversky's (1979) prospect theory is usually interpreted as a strength of preference function measuring preferences under certainty.

An unresolved question is whether risk attitude should be a by-product of assessment judgments (as it is in expected utility theory assessment procedures) or it should be a conscious decision. For example, a person might choose to be relatively risk neutral over a certain range of outcomes. Expected utility theory can accommodate either approach since only the assessment procedures need to be modified to guarantee a specific risk attitude prior to the calibration of the utility function.

Since the choice of whether to frame the current decision problem's outcomes as gains or losses with respect to the reference level can alter the choice prescribed by a utility model, framing issues are of considerable practical concern. A related question is the choice of the temporal beginning point of the problem, as modeled by a decision tree. Should you frame your life decisions as being at the actual current decision point or at the initial life planning point (say at age 12)? LaValle (1992) addresses this issue. Also, when to stop elaborating the decision tree into the future (LaValle, 1989, 1992) and must be decided. LaValle suggests replacing the standard terms such as *consequences* or *outcomes* for the endpoints in the tree with the term *Positions*, to emphasize that an endpoint today is "the first day of the rest of your life." Howard (1992) prefers the term *prospect*. Thus, the determination of the appropriate small-world (in Savage's terms) for the current decision problem is a key problem and can be more critical for generalized utility models than for expected utility.

Separability

Expected utility preferences are *separable* across mutually exclusive events (Machina, 1989), in the sense of *replacement separability* (the contribution of each outcome x_i and its probability p_i to the overall expected utility of an alternative action is independent of the other outcome/probability pairs) and *mixture separability* (the contribution of each outcome/probability pair to the overall expected utility can be broken down into the utility of x_i, multiplied by p_i). LaValle (1992) discusses problems for generalized utility theories that are nonseparable if they are to be used for normative or prescriptive uses.

Dynamic Consistency

In a dynamic (multiple-stage) setting, expected utility theory has the property of *dynamic consistency*, that is, if a person has option C at time 0 in figure 1–1, the planned choice between A' and B' made at time 0 should agree with the actual choice made at time 1. Notice that the planned choice of CA' (C then A') is strategically equivalent to D and the choice of CB' is equivalent to E (Machina, 1989). By the substitution property, if the actual choice is A' over B', then D is preferred over E, so the planned choice will be CA' over CB'. Howard (1992) emphasizes in his related notion of *sequential consistency* that thoughts during this current epoch about planned actions should be consistent, but he says that at the future time the person is free to make any choice.

Consequentialism

Expected utility also satisfies *consequentialism* (Machina (1989), Hammond (1988)). At any point in time we can focus on the consequences from now on (choices, states, probabilities, and outcomes), and we do not need to know where we've come from or what other probability or choice branches were previously available. Thus, the analysis of the expected utility of alternative actions can be carried out by "folding back" a decision tree representation of the choices and states and by computing the maximum expected utility, based on the options and states remaining at any one point in time. Sarin (1992) uses the term *principle of optimality* to refer to consequentialism, emphasizing the notion that at the current choice point our preference order over current options does not vary with the probability that we would have ended up at this choice point.

Some generalized utility models are criticized because their analysis procedure does not allow folding back the decision tree as is possible under expected utility (LaValle and Wapman, 1986). However, Becker and Sarin (1989) show how their generalized utility model, lottery dependent utility, can be used in a modified folding back procedure. It might be possible to modify their approach for other generalized theories.

Equivalence of Extensive and Normal Forms of Decision Tree

Reducing a multiple-stage extensive-form decision tree to one in normal form with a set of options from which to choose, followed by a single chance stage with a set of possible states, will not lead to different decisions under expected utility. This is a result of applying the reduction of compound lotteries property. But, with generalized utility theories, different choices may result with the normal and extensive forms. Thus, expected utility has the property of *invariance* (LaValle, 1992), that is, the way the tree is drawn should not affect the optimal choice as long as the same real options are present and the same use of information is made. In other words, *strategically equivalent* representations should have the same preference rankings. Luce (1992) discusses the implications of this *required indifference between formally equivalent framings of a gamble*.

Transitivity

Many preference theories, including expected utility, require that if A is preferred over B and B over C, then, by *transitivity*, A should be preferred over C. Fishburn (1988) discusses nontransitive nonlinear utility theories. Luce (1992) summarizes key experimental evidence of transitivity violations, including the preference reversal phenomenon (Grether and Plott, 1979; Lichtenstein and Slovic, 1971). However, these studies assume equivalence between judged and choice indifferences, which is now being questioned (Bostic, Herrnstein and Luce, 1990; Tversky, Sattath and Slovic, 1988). MacCrimmon (1965), finding that business executive subjects sometimes violated transitivity, verbally pointed out their intransitive orderings, and many chose to readjust their orderings and become transitive. However, subjects often wish to persist in violations of other expected utility properties, especially substitution, sure-thing, and ambiguity indifference.

Discussion of Consequentialism, Dynamic Consistency, and Substitution Violations

This section contains a discussion of generalized utility theory violations of the consequentialism, dynamic consistency, and substitution properties. The discussion is motivated by questions about the potential usefulness of generalized expected utility models. A special concern when substitution property violations for static (one-chance stage) lotteries are allowed, is whether *dynamic consistency* and/or *consequentialism* should hold in nonexpected utility models for use in economic theory as positive models that are descriptively accurate and can be used to make economic predictions.

Machina (1989) argues that models violating the substitution property for static lotteries should have the properties of dynamic consistency and nonconsequentialism to be useful in economic theory (see also Chew and Epstein (1989)). Nonconsequentialism means that the choice between A' and B' at time 1 in Figure 1–1 cannot be made without knowing that there was a previous 10 percent probability of arriving at the choice node at time 1, and a 90 percent probability of the outcome \$0 which might have happened had Option C been chosen at time 0. Such a dynamically consistent nonexpected utility model would not always obey the substitution property applied to static single stage lotteries and could thus descriptively model the simultaneous preference among single stage

Table 1–1.   Classification of Decision Makers Who Violate Substitution Principle for Static Lotteries ($A > B$ and $D \leqslant E$ Occurs)

	Dynamic Consistency	
	Inconsistent $CA' \lesssim CB'$ and $A' \gtrsim B'$ occurs	Consistent $CA' \gtrsim CB' \leftrightarrow A' \gtrsim B'$
Consequentialist $A \gtrsim B \leftrightarrow A' \gtrsim B'$	Beta	Delta
Not Consequentialist $A \lesssim B$ and $A' \gtrsim B'$ occurs	Epsilon	Gamma

Notes:
$\gtrsim$ and $\lesssim$ indicate preference order.
A, A', B, B', C, D, and E are options in figure 1–1.
Alpha-type (expected utility) preferences obey substitution priciple, consequentialism, and dynamic consistency.

lotteries of A over B but E over D in the figure. However, using a dynamically consistent nonexpected utility model, under option C the planned choice between A' and B' at time 0 in the decision tree in figure 1–1 would have to agree with the actual choice made at time 1. A decision maker with these preferences would be classified as a gamma-type according to Machina's (1989) categorization of decision makers into *alpha, beta, gamma*, and *delta* types, as shown in table 1-1. Alpha-types use expected utility and thus obey the substitution property, consequentialism, and dynamic consistency. Betas, gammas, deltas (and an added type: *epsilons*) sometimes violate the substitution property for static lotteries.

Machina is concerned that economic researchers will not accept a model that can potentially predict dynamically inconsistent choices. This behavior arises by being a consequentialist and isolating the focus at time 1 only on A' and B', perhaps choosing A' over B', having planned on CB' over CA' originally. The argument against dynamic inconsistency is normative. It hinges on the possibility that a person can be made to "make book" against his/her own choices, making the person into a perpetual money pump, cycling among options to eventual ruin. Adding to this normative argument the descriptive observation that such money pumps are not observed in economic markets, Machina (1989) rejects dynamic inconsistency. Thus, he rejects beta-type preferences (consequentialist, not dynamically consistent, substitution property violators) and, implicitly, epsilon-type preferences (which differ from betas only in not being consequentialists). So, Machina rejects the two types of preferences that may be descriptively most common. Upon reflection, I believe that I tend to be a beta-type in casual decision making. LaValle (1992) suspects most people are epsilon-types in casual decisions.

It seems that a better approach to economic modeling, due to the need for descriptive validity, would be to continue the search for mathematically tractable theories that are descriptively valid, both for individual judgment behavior and for the observed aggregate market behavior. I believe that nonexpected utility models were developed in response to both types of substitution property violations, those for static choices and those for dynamic (multiple-stage) choices. Since experimental evidence suggests that this is how people see the problem and make their choices, a descriptively valid model of decision making under risk should definitely allow the planned choice to differ from the actual choice, violating dynamic consistency. Since economic models rely on descriptively accurate models of unaided consumer decision making, dynamic inconsistency should be allowed in those models (Keller, 1989b).

Sarin (1989) presents the philosophical debate over whether dynamic consistency should hold in *normative* models and suggests that a decision maker may wish to violate dynamic consistency in some limited prescriptive settings. Sarin (1992) further argues that although recent generalizations of utility theory can descriptively model such dynamically inconsistent choices, they do not form a coherent normative theory for decision analysis. For example, the lottery dependent utility theory of Becker and Sarin (1987) will allow planned choices to differ from actual. Applying their model to option C in figure 1–1's decision tree problem, at time 0, a beta-type consequentialist who is not dynamically consistent might note that CB' is strategically equivalent to E and thoose the *planned choice CB'* over *CA'*, which is strategically equivalent to D. Then, whenever the decision node at time 1 arises, this consequentialist beta-type revises the tree and only compares A' and B', and may choose A' as the *actual choice*.

Whether a particular generalized model represents dynamically consistent choices may depend not on the model per se, but on the way it is applied to choice situations and how the decision maker frames and reframes choices over time. (LaValle (1992) addresses the problems encountered by nonseparable utility theories with respect to the framing of the decision horizon.) As an example of one way to apply a generalized utility model, Becker and Sarin (1989) show how to analyze the lottery dependent expected utility of alternatives using a modified approach for folding back a decision tree. Following this analysis procedure yields delta-type preferences that are dynamically consistent (since planned choice equals actual choice), because plans are always made by working backwards through the entire tree. This procedure is also consequentialist, since folding back the decision tree to determine choice is done by isolating focus on the current and future stages only. However, Machina (1989) presents three arguments against such delta-type preferences:

1. strategically equivalent lotteries will not be indifferent (LaValle (1989), LaValle and Wapman (1986));
2. delta-types can display aversion to costless information in decision trees (Wakker, 1988); and
3. folding "back is only appropriate when the objective function is separable across the various subdecisions of a problem."

Summary

This chapter contains an overview of properties required by expected utility theory and experiments investigating descriptive violations of these properties. The properties are known by a variety of terms and are not mutually exclusive. Their intertwining makes difficult the task of sorting out the implications and potential applications of different theories that relax certain properties. The remaining chapters in this volume take on this task.

The potential contributions of the new generalized utility theories have been obscured by some confusion over the purposes and possible uses of various theories (Keller (1989a,b)). Despite the muddied waters, the consensus remains that expected utility is a coherent normative theory for decisions under risk, but not all its properties are descriptively valid. Further, the new generalized utility theories' contributions will be primarily for descriptive or predictive purposes. However, in special cases, the generalized utility theories may be used for prescriptive guidance of choice under risk. Also, in economic theoretic modeling, positive models are needed that are descriptively accurate and mathematically tractable so economic predictions can be made. More investigation of generalized utility models and their properties is needed to find appropriate economic theoretic models.

Acknowledgments

Some of the discussion on utility theory properties in this chapter is a revision of portions of my paper, "The Role of Generalized Utility Theories in Descriptive, Prescriptive, and Normative Decision Analysis," in *Information and Decision Technologies* (Keller, 1989b) which was presented at the conference on "Utility: Theories, Measurements, and Applications," June 1989, in Santa Cruz, California. I thank the conference organizer, Ward Edwards; the conference participants (especially George Wu, Irving LaValle, R. Duncan Luce, and John Miyamoto); two referees; and Henry McMillan for helpful comments.

References

Allais, M. (1953). "Le Comportemente de L'homme Rationnel Devant le Risque: Critique des Postulats et Axiomes de L'ecole Americaine." *Econometrica*, 21, 503–546.

Becker, J.L. (1986). "A New Model of Decisions Under Risk Using the Concept of Lottery Dependent Utility Function. Unpublished doctoral dissertation. Graduate School of Management, University of California at Los Angeles.

Becker, J., and R. Sarin (1987). "Lottery Dependent Utility." *Management Science*, 33(11), 1367–1382.

Becker, J., and R. Sarin (1989). "Decision Analysis Using Lottery Dependent Utility. "*Journal of Risk and Uncertainty*, 2, 105–117.

Bell, D. (1982). "Regret in Decision Making Under Uncertainty." *Operations Research*, 30, 961–981.

Bostic, R., Herrnstein, R.J., and R.D. Luce (1990). "The Effect on the Preference-reversal Phenomenon of Using Choice Indifferences." *Journal of Economic Behavior and Organization*, 13, 193–212.

Bunn, D. (1984). *Applied Decision Analysis*. McGraw-Hill, New York.

Camerer, C. (1989). "An Experimental Test of Several Generalized Utility Theories." *Journal of Risk and Uncertainty*, 2, 61–104.

Camerer, C. (1992). "Recent tests of generalizations of expected utility theory." In W. Edwards (Ed.), *Utility Theories: Measurements and Applications*. Kluwer Academic Publishers, Boston, MA.

Chew, S.H. (1983). "A Generalization of the Quasilinear Mean with Applications to the Measurement of Income Inequality and Decision Theory Resolving the Allais Paradox. *Econometrica*, 51, 1065–1092.

Chew, S.H. (1985). "Implicit-weighted and Semi-weighted Utility Theories, M-estimators, and Nondemand Revelation of Second-price Auctions for an Uncertain Auctioned Object." Working paper #155. Department of Political Economy, The Johns Hopkins University, Baltimore, MD.

Chew, S.H. and L. Epstein (1989). "Non-expected Utility Preferences in a Temporal Framework with an Application to Consumption-savings Behavior." Working paper. Department of Political Economy, The Johns Hopkins University, Baltimore, MD.

Chew, S.H., Epstein, L., and U. Segal (1988). "Mixture Symmetric Utility Theory." Working paper. University of Toronto.

Chew, S.H., and K.R. MacCrimmon (1979a). "Alpha-nu Choice Theory: A Generalization of Expected Utility Theory." Working paper #669. Faculty of Commerce and Business Administration, University of British Columbia, Vancouver, BC.

Chew, S.H., and K.R. MacCrimmon (1979b). "Alpha Utility Theory, Lottery Composition and the Allais Paradox." Working paper #686. Faculty of Commerce and Business Administration, University of British Columbia, Vancouver, BC.

Chew, S.H., and W.S. Waller (1986). "Empirical Tests of Weighted Utility Theory." *Journal of Mathematical Psychology*, 30, 55–72.

Coombs, C. (1969). "Portfolio Theory: A Theory of Risky Decision Making." *La Decision*. Centre National de la Recherche Scientifique, Paris.

Coombs, C. (1975). "Portfolio Theory and the Measurement of Risk." In M. Kaplan and S. Schwartz (Eds.), *Human Judgment and Decision Processes* (pp. 63–85). Academic Press New York.

Coombs, C., and L. Huang (1970). "Tests of a Portfolio Theory of Risk Preference. "*Journal of Experimental Psychology*, 85(1), 23–29.

Currim, I.S., and R. Sarin (1989). "Prospect Versus Utility." *Management Science*, 35(1), 22–41.

Currim, I.S., and R. Sarin (in press). "Robustness of Expected Utility Model in Predicting Individual Choices." *Organizational Behavior and Human Decision Processes*.

Daniels, R., and L.R. Keller (1990). "An Experimental Evaluation of the Descriptive Validity of Lottery Dependent Utility Theory." *Journal of Risk and Uncertainty*, 3, 115–134.

Daniels, R., and L.R. Keller (forthcoming 1992). "Choice-based Assessment of Utility Functions." *Organizational Behavior and Human Decision Processes*. Academic Press.

Dekel, E. (1986). "An Axiomatic Characterization of Preferences Under Uncertainty: Weakening the Independence Axiom." *Journal of Economic Theory*, 40, 304–318.

Dyer, J.S., and R. Sarin (1982). "Relative Risk Aversion." *Management Science*, 28(8), 875–886.

Edwards, W. (1955). "The Prediction of Decisions Among Bets." *Journal of Experimental Psychology*, 50, 201–214.

Edwards, W. (1962). "Subjective Probabilities Inferred from Decisions." *Psychological Review*, 69, 109–135.

Ellsberg, D. (1961). "Risk, Ambiguity, and the Savage Axioms. *Quarterly Journal of Economics*, 75, 643–669.

Fishburn, P.C. (1983). "Transitive Measurable Utility." *Journal of Economic Theory*, 31, 293–317.

Fishburn, P.C. (1984). "SSB Utility Theory: An Economic Perspective." *Mathematical Social Science*, 8, 63–94.

Fishburn, P.C. (1988). *Nonlinear Preference and Utility Theory*. The Johns Hopkins University Press, Baltimore, MD.

Fishburn, P.C. (1989). "Foundations of Decision Analysis: Along the Way." *Management Science*, 35(4), 387–405.

Green, J. and B. Jullien (1988). "Ordinal Independence in Nonlinear Utility Theory. *Journal of Risk and Uncertainty*, 1(4), 355–387.

Grether, D.M. and C.R. Plott (1979). "Economic Theory of Choice and the Preferences Reversal Phenomenon." *American Economic Review*, 69(4), 623–638.

Hammond, P.J. (1988). "Consequentialist Foundations for Expected Utility." *Theory and Decision*, 25, 25–78.

Howard, R.A. (1992). "In Praise of the Old Time Religion." In W. Edwards (Ed.), *Utility Theories: Measurements and Applications*. Kluwer Academic Publishers, Boston, MA.

Kahneman, D. and A. Tversky (1979). "Prospect Theory: An Analysis of Decision Under Risk." *Econometrica*, 47(2), 263–291.

Keeney, R.L. (1992). "On the Foundations of Prescriptive Decision Analysis." In W. Edwards (Ed.) *Utility Theories: Measurements and Applications* Kluwer Academic Publishers. Boston, MA.

Keeney, R.L. and H. Raiffa (1976). *Decisions with Multiple Objectives: Preferences and Value Tradeoffs*. Wiley, New York.

Keller, L.R. (1985a). "The Effects of Problem Representation on the Sure-thing and Substitution Principles." *Management Science*, 31(6), 738–751.

Keller, L.R. (1985b). "Testing the 'Reduction of Compound Alternatives' Principle." *OMEGA, The International Journal of Management Science*, 13(4), 349–358.

Keller, L.R. (1985c). "An Empirical Investigation of Relative Risk Aversion. *IEEE Transactions on Systems, Man, and Cybernetics*, 15(4), 475–482.

Keller, L.R. (1989a). "Decision Research with Descriptive, Prescriptive, and Normative Purposes—Some Comments." In *Annals of Operations Research*, 19. Volume edited by LaValle, I. and Fishburn, P. on "Choice Under Uncertainty," pp. 485–487.

Keller, L.R. (1989b). "The Role of Generalized Utility Theories in Descriptive, Prescriptive, and Normative Decision Analysis." *Information and Decision Technologies*, 15, 259–271.

LaValle, I.H. (1989). "New Choice Models Raise New Difficulties: Comment on 'Analytical Issues in Decision Methodology'." In I. Horowitz (Ed.), *Organization and Decision Theory*. Kluwer-Nijhoff, Boston, pp. 63–81.

LaValle, I.H. (1992). "Small Worlds and Sure Things: Consequentialism by the Back Door. In W. Edwards (Ed.), *Utility Theories: Measurements and Applications*. Kluwer Academic Publishers. Boston MA.

LaValle, I.H. and K.R. Wapman (1986). "Rolling Back Decision Trees Requires the Independence Axiom!" *Management Science*, 32, 382–385.

Leland, J. (1988). "A Theory of 'Approximate' Expected Utility Maximization." Working paper. Social and Decision Sciences, Carnegie-Mellon University, Pittsburgh, PA.

Lichtenstein, S. and P. Slovic (1971). Reversals of Preference Between Bids and Choices in Gambling Decisions. *Journal of Experimental Psychology*, 89(1), 46–55.

Loomes, G. and R. Sugden (1982). "Regret Theory: An Alternative Theory of Rational Choice Under Uncertainty." *Economic Journal*, 92, 805–824.

Luce, R.D. (1992). "Rational Versus Plausible Accounting Equivalences in Preference Judgments." In W. Edwards (Ed.), *Utility Theories: Measurements and Applications*. Kluwer Academic Publishers, Boston, MA.

Luce, R.D. and L. Narens (1985). "Classification of Concatenation Structures According to Scale Type." *Journal of Mathematical Psychology*, 29, 1–72.

Machina, M. (1982). "'Expected Utility' Analysis Without the Independence Axiom." *Econometrica*, 50, 277–323.

Machina, M.J. (1987a). "Choice Under Uncertainty: Problems Solved and Unsolved." *Economic Perspectives*, 1(1), 121–154.

Machina, M.J. (1987b). "Decision-making in the Presence of Risk." *Science*, 236, 537–543.

Machina, M.J. (1989). "Dynamic Consistency and Non-expected Utility Models of Choice Under Uncertainty. *Journal of Economic Literature*, XXVII, December, 1622–1668.

MacCrimmon, K. (1965). "An Experimental Study of the Decision Making Behavior of Business Executives. Unpublished doctoral dissertation. Graduate School of Management, University of California, Los Angeles, CA.

MacCrimmon, K. and Larsson, S. (1979). "Utility Theory: Axioms Versus Paradoxes." In M. Allais and O. Hagen (Eds.), *Expected Utility Hypotheses and the Allais Paradox*. Reidel, Dordrecht.

Miyamoto, J. (1992). "Generic Analysis of Utility Models." In W. Edwards (Ed.), *Utility Theories: Measurements and Applications*. Kluwer Academic Publishers, Norwell, MA.

Quiggin, J. (1982). "A Theory of Anticipated Utility". *Journal of Economic Behavior and Organization*, 3, 323–343.

Sarin, R.K. (1989). "Analytical Issues in Decision Methodology." In I. Horowitz (Ed.), *Decision and Organization Theory*. Kluwer-Nijhoff, Boston, MA.

Sarin, R.K. (1992). "What Now for Generalized Utility Theory?" In W. Edwards (Ed.), *Utility Theories: Measurements and Applications*. Kluwer Academic Publishers, Boston MA.

Savage, L.J. (1954). *The Foundations of Statistics*. Wiley, New York.

Segal, U. (1984). "Nonlinear Decision Weights with the Independence Axiom." Working paper. Economics Department, University of California, Los Angeles.

Segal, U. (1992). "The Independence Axiom Versus the Reduction Axiom: Must we Have Both?" In W. Edwards (Ed.), *Utility Theories: Measurements and Applications*. Kluwer Academic Publishers, Boston, MA.

Shafir, E.B., Osherson, D.N., and E.E. Smith (1989). "An Advantage Model of Choice." *Journal of Behavioral Decision Making*, 2, 1–23.

Tversky, A., Sattath, S., and P. Slovic (1988). "Contingent Weighting in Judgment and Choice." *Psychological Review*, 95(3), 371–384.

von Neumann, J., and O. Morgenstern (1947). *Theory of Games and Linear Programming*. Second edition. Wiley, New York.

von Winterfeldt, D., and W. Edwards (1986). *Decision Analysis and Behavioral Research*. Cambridge University Press, New York.

Wakker, P.P. (1988). "Nonexpected Utility as Aversion of Information." *Journal of Behavioral Decision Making*, 1, 169–175.

Weber, M., and Camerer, C. (1987). "Recent Developments in Modelling Preferences Under Risk." *OR Spektrum*, 9, 129–151.

Yaari, M.E. (1987). "The Dual Theory of Choice Under Risk." *Econometrica*, 55, 95–115.

II THE OLD TIME RELIGION AND ITS IMPLEMENTATION

2 IN PRAISE OF THE OLD TIME RELIGION

Ronald A. Howard

Introduction

Let me begin by stating why I became an active participant in this discussion of the foundations of decision analysis. For many years, I had been blithely practicing in the field in the belief that all important questions about the underpinnings of the subject were now thoroughly understood and generally agreed upon. I knew that various theoreticians were developing alternate axiomatizations of decision theory, as they always had, but I did not believe that the resulting theories were being seriously proposed as bases for decision making. The onset of foreboding occurred when a prominent theorist made clear to me that he would reject a commonly accepted norm of decision analysis in making certain of his own decisions. I have previously described the conversation with the theorist that initiated my current militancy (Howard, 1988). However, I shall repeat it now for easy reference and because it so succinctly illustrates the issues at hand.

The choice situation offers two options, A and B, for receiving monetary payments depending on the role of a die. The die has six faces numbered 1 through 6, and you have no basis on which to assign other

W. Edwards (ed.), *UTILITY THEORIES: MEASUREMENTS AND APPLICATIONS.*
Copyright © 1992. Kluwer Academic Publishers, Boston. All rights reserved.

Table 2–1. The Theorist's Practical Choice

Die:	1	2	3	4	5	6
A	$600	700	800	900	1000	500
B	$500	600	700	800	900	1000

than equal probability to the six faces. The possible monetary amounts you can receive are $500, $600, $700, $800, $900, and $1,000, according to the face that is tossed. However, the monetary payment associated with each face depends on the option you play as shown in Table 1.

If you play with option A, then face 1 pays $600, face 2, $700, up to face 5 which pays $1,000 but then face 6 pays $500. If you play with option B then face 1 pays $500, face 2, $600, etc., up to face 6 which pays $1,000. The question is, given a choice, which option do you prefer. The theorist said that for the problem as stated he would prefer A over B because for five out of the six possible faces he would win more with A than B. However, if the payoff were in thousands of dollars rather than in dollars, then he would prefer B over A, because of the great regret he would experience should the die produce face 6.

When I recounted this conversation to my decision analytic colleagues, they thought they must have misunderstood what I was saying because they could see no difference between the two options. They simply said that each possible payment had a probability of one-sixth regardless of the option, so what difference would it make which option was selected. If the theorist had been any less distinguished, or if he had suggested that his choices were descriptive of certain people's behavior but not what he would do when playing for real dollars, then there would have been no reason to be concerned about the discrepancy between his opinion and my own. But under the circumstances, the difference of opinion was troubling. Upon further inquiry, I found that the theorist was not alone in proposing that people should depart from the norms that have for so long guided decision analysis. This finding required me to examine my position and either to change or to affirm my views. The examination has led me to affirm my belief in the fundamental rules of decision analysis and to resolve to argue cogently for them in an attempt to correct what I perceive as an unproductive heresy.

To this end, I shall first discuss some of the basic issues, terms, and concepts that must support any discussion of the rules for decision making. Then, I will present the rules that we currently use in a simplified form. Next, I will discuss the desiderata, both essential and desirable, for any formally defined decision-making system, and show the extent to which our current rules satisfy the desiderata. I shall then describe in general terms how other proposed rules fare when considered against the desiderata. In particular, I shall reconsider two well-known problems posed by Allais (1953) and Ellsberg (1961) that are said by some to require new rules for their proper treatment. Though these problems are sometimes called paradoxes I shall refer to them as phenomena, since in my view they reflect a need for education rather than a flaw in the theory. I shall show that these phenomena require only a careful application of our rules, and not a revision of them, and that rejection of the rules would led to a violation of some of the most fundamental desiderata for decision making. I end with a discussion of whether the rules apply when "equity" is a consideration and comment on their use in group decision making.

Background Considerations

Descriptive versus Normative Theories

A fundamental distinction we must agree on is that between descriptive and normative theories. A descriptive theory is one that purports to describe the world as it is. Its quality is measured by the extent to which it accurately characterizes and predicts the behavior of actual systems, and in the present context, the behavior of people. Thus, the inverse square model for the gravitational attraction of two bodies is an excellent descriptive model for the behavior of many planetary objects, although it may be difficult to apply to some problems, for example, the classical three-body problem.

A normative theory, on the other hand, establishes norms for how things should be. Therefore normative models have no place in the physical sciences because they deal with fact rather than with human will. However, for decision-making situations, where human will is very much an issue, then it is not only possible but often desirable to propose norms or standards for decision making so cogent that, once accepted, any departure from them will be regarded as a mistake.

We should note that normative theories are important primarily when our natural behavior is not satisfactory to us; that is, the behavior does not satisfy the norms that we have for the process in question. To illustrate, suppose that we developed a normative theory of breathing.

The theory would tell us to breath more rapidly when we run upstairs and to breath more slowly when we are lying at rest. But since this is the behavior that we would naturally exhibit, few of us other than specially trained athletes and singers are likely to enroll in a course on breathing.

The need for normative aid seems to arise particularly in questions of uncertainty and decision making. In the area of uncertainty the roll of people who have made mistakes in probabilistic judgments reads like the roll of the geniuses of science. It appears that most humans are condemned to second-rate thinking where uncertainty is concerned. For example, the relationship between cigarette smoking and lung cancer is often seen as an associative logic linkage: If you smoke you are likely to get lung cancer; if you get lung cancer you are likely to have been a smoker. The conditional probabilities of cigarette smoking given lung cancer and of lung cancer given cigarette smoking are actually quite different, but without the precise formulation afforded by the notion of conditional probability it is difficult even to have the discussion. Upon seeing an analysis showing that the chance of getting lung cancer, given that you are a smoker, is considerably less than the chance of having been a smoker, given that you get lung cancer, a postdoctoral M.D. remarked that these results were impossible because his lung cancer ward is full of cigarette smokers.

As many cognitive psychologists have observed, the situation does not improve when we consider performance in decision making, which involves not only uncertainty but issues of preferences. Classroom study in decision analysis is heavily involved in purging such cognitive errors as including sunk costs or failing to recognize dominance. The reason we call them cognitive errors is that they violate the normative paradigm.

We should not be surprised that education is required to align our thoughts with what is so. When I first encountered in high school science classes the notion that the pressure of a body of water depended only on its depth and not on the size of the body, I could not reconcile it with common sense. I said, "You mean that Boulder Dam would have to be just as thick even if Lake Mead extended only one foot behind it rather than for dozens of square miles?" I still remember walking home from class and thinking of a thin wax paper barrier situated exactly one foot behind Boulder Dam and realizing that the pressure would be the same on both sides, so that the existence of the rest of Lake Mead really did not make any difference. Then it became obvious that pressure depended only on depth whereas that morning it had been "obvious" that it did not.

Since we appear to be condemned to using instruments in matters of uncertainty, just as is a pilot when flying in bad weather, we should be grateful that we have had such an excellent set of instrument builders. In the area of probability I am grateful to many but particularly to Laplace, Jeffreys, and Jaynes for providing what I consider to be the most useful underpinnings of the study of uncertainty. In the area of preference, particularly for preference where risk is concerned, I am indebted to Daniel Bernoulli for the form of the result and to Von Neumann and Morgenstern for the mathematical justification of the form.

The theory of decision based on these foundations is normative: the theory says how you should act if you wish certain properties to be true of your behavior. The theory can be used as a descriptive theory, and then the test is whether it describes what people do. Decision analysis is the professional discipline based on the normative decision theory. A decision analysis might use a descriptive model of other decision makers if that model adequately characterized their behavior (not too likely, my psychologist friends tell me). There is no need for this descriptive model to have any relation to the normative theory on which decision analysis is based.

Characterization

To describe decision making we must first characterize the decision situation. We begin with the notion of an epoch, a point in time at which the thought about the decision is taking place. We characterize the future by creating different kinds of distinctions (Spencer-Brown, 1979) with two or more degrees of each kind. To determine whether a distinction is sufficiently defined we use the clarity test (Howard, 1988). A distinction meets the clarity test if a clairvoyant with the power to know any physically definable event or number in the future or the past could say which degree of the distinction occurred without any use of judgment.

With these kinds and degrees of distinction we create possibilities: the mutually exclusive and collectively exhaustive collections formed by choosing one degree of each kind of distinction. To each possibility that we have created we may associate one or more measures (numbers of interest that are connected with this possibility). We assess our degree of certainty on each possibility by dividing our certainty among successive distinctions, a process we call assigning a probability to each possibility.

Thus for each course of action or alternative we have a description of potential futures in terms of possibilities and their associated probabilities. Each possibility that we have created we think of as a prospect, that is, as a future life whose salient features are described by the possibility we have defined, but which is, in fact, imbued with many uncertainties and future choices. I use the word *prospect* rather than *possibility* when discussing preferences over futures rather than just their logical existence. "Prospect" connotes the "looking forward" to a future about which we have preferences. Note, too, that a prospect can include effects on other people, the environment, etc.

For each alternative we shall use the word *deal* to describe the range of prospects and their associated probabilities. Thus the essence of decision making in this characterization is to choose among alternatives, each described as a deal.

Choice

The question is what process to use for choice among deals. We seek decision quality, that is, quality thought about the decision that will lead to clarity of action. We must realize that the map is not the territory, that the abstraction we have made of the decision process is not an accurate and complete representation of the decision situation, but rather a means of achieving clarity of action.

Our task is to select rules for making the decision such that if these rules are followed we will be sure that no process errors have occurred. We can think of this as selecting rules for an agent who will make the decision on our behalf. We would clearly not want to indulge the idiosyncrasies of the agent by allowing him to use rules of which we did not approve.

A proper set of rules, or decision theory, is indispensable to decision analysis; however, it is only a part of decision analysis. The professional skills of the analyst are required to be sure that the decision is properly framed, or better, to frame the best decision (Matheson, 1990). Decisions do not occur naturally—they are acts of will: decision opportunities, or, more briefly, decisions are declared into existence by the decision maker. Helping the decision maker declare the right decision at the right time is the essence of effective aid in framing.

The analyst must also be skilled in eliciting creative alternatives, accurately eliciting and assessing information, and in representing appropriately the preferences of the decision maker. The result will be the formal description of the decision problem, the decision basis. However, our current concern is with the normative rules to be used in making the decision.

The Rules of Thought

I shall now discuss the rules of thought that I consider to constitute the foundation of decision analysis. These rules apply to thought about making a decision at a particular epoch; to the extent that future decisions are involved, the thought about them is thought that occurs at the present epoch.

The Probability Rule

The first rule is the *probability rule*. This rule states that deals will be described by possibilities and probabilities, or equivalently by prospects and associated probabilities, as outlined above.

The Order Rule

The second rule is the *order rule*, which states that all prospects of all deals under consideration can be ordered in terms of preference. We can visualize this as placing them in a list with the most preferred prospects at the top and the least preferred at the bottom. It is permissible for two prospects to be at the same level in the list, that is, to consider oneself indifferent between them. What is not allowed is that the same prospect appear at two different levels in the list.

The decision basis need not remain unchanged in this process. We can consider this rule as a commitment to introduce sufficient distinctions into the basis until the resulting prospects can be ordered according to the rule's requirements.

The Equivalence Rule

The third rule is the *equivalence rule*: If three prospects A, B, and C are at different positions in the list with A above B above C, then you can specify some probability that will make you indifferent between receiving prospect B for sure and receiving a deal that has probability p of yielding prospect A and one minus p of yielding prospect C. The probability p is called a preference probability because it does not correspond to the uncertainty of any event in the world that could be revealed by a clairvoyant. The prospect B is said to be the certain equivalent of the deal with probability p of A and 1-p of C.

Satisfying the equivalence rule may once again require introducing new distinctions into the basis. For example, I may be clear that I prefer a two week trip to Tahiti to receiving $100 to receiving nothing. However, when I am asked what chance of a two week trip to Tahiti versus nothing is just equivalent to $100, then I may have to inquire more about the trip. I may want to know about accommodations, meals, tours, etc. and thus create new distinctions and consequently new prospects before I am ready to assess preference probabilities.

The Substitution Rule

The fourth rule, the *substitution rule*, states that you are indifferent between receiving a prospect for sure and receiving any deal for which it is the certain equivalent. What this means is that you may use preference probabilities in all calculations as if they were probabilities of real events.

The Choice Rule

The fifth and last rule is the *choice rule*, the only rule that requires action. The rule states that if prospect A is above prospect B in your ordered list, and if you face two deals with these same two prospects, but the first deal gives you a higher probability of prospect A, then you must prefer the first deal to the second. In other words, you must prefer the deal with the higher probability of the prospect you consider more desirable.

Based on these rules and the general rules of logic, you can build an entire edifice of consequences that represent rational thought about decision making.

Axioms and Theorems: The Decision Composite

Let us stop to examine this process of construction. In developing a formal theory, certain properties are postulated as axioms, ideas so simple and transparent that there is no question about whether you would wish to follow these ideas in situations that were entirely described by them. The rules of thought we have discussed are the axioms of decision theory that we shall use. They correspond in the development of Euclidian geometry to such axioms as the idea that a straight line is the shortest distance between two points. Based on the axioms, we develop, in decision theory and geometry, a number of theorems that must be true, respectively, for decisions or figures in a plane; the axioms imply the theorems. We often have a choice in the development of a subject as to which set of axioms we should use, a choice usually based on esthetics and on the ease of proving the theorems from the axioms. If some theorems are taken as axioms, then some axioms may end up being theorems. We must look at the entire collection of axioms and theorems to judge the usefulness of the formal structure.

In the case of decision theory, I shall call this collection of axioms and their implied theorems the decision composite. Since the choice of what is an axiom and what is a theorem is, as we have said, somewhat arbitrary, we should really be concerned with the desirability of the decision composite. We shall now turn to this question.

Desiderata

I shall list the properties that I consider desirable for any decision composite. I shall proceed by first discussing the properties that are essential in any situation, then those that are essential in particular situations, and finally those that are, if not essential, then of great practical importance.

Essential Properties. The essential properties proposed for the decision composite are:

1. *The decision composite must allow me to form inferences about uncertain distinctions even in the absence of a decision problem.* This means that probability must stand on its own epistemologically.
2. *The decision composite must be applicable to any decision I face regardless of type or field.* Once a student remarked, "I can see that these rules would be useful for investments, but surely you are not proposing them for making important decisions about the health of your family." I replied, "These rules are the best way I know to make decisions. My family deserves the best. In matters of life and death, I do not want to make a mistake."
3. *The decision composite must require that I prefer a deal with a higher probability of the better prospect, in conformity with the choice rule we have discussed.* Note that even a masochist will desire to follow the choice rule in the pursuit of abuse and physical pain.

4. *The decision composite must require that I be indifferent between two deals that I consider to have the same probabilities of the same prospects.* In other words, I should be indifferent between two deals for which I have created the same descriptions.

5. *Reversing the order of contemplating uncertain distinctions should not change inference or decision.* This means, in particular, that changing the order of receiving a given body of information should not change any inference or decision. For example, if I received a set of data *A* and thereafter a set of data *B*, then I should assign the same probability on future distinctions and make the same decisions as if I had received first set of data *B* and then set of data *A*. This property is sometimes called *Invariance to Data Order*. It is so appealing that it might be taken as an axiom, a rule of thought.

6. *If I prefer alternative (deal) I over alternative II when the uncertain event* A *occurs and if I prefer I over II when* A *does not occur, then I must prefer alternative I over II when I am uncertain about the occurrence of* A. Furthermore, I want this to be true even if I am indifferent between I and II for one of the two possibilities for event *A*. To illustrate, if I would prefer to drive my car to work rather than to ride my motorcycle when it rains and if I am indifferent between the two means of transporation when it is fair then if there is any uncertainty about the weather my decision should be to drive the car.

7. *Once I have selected my best alternative, the non-informative removal of the opportunity to choose any other alternative must not affect my decision.* Non-informative means that the change does not provide information about the other dimensions. I sometimes illustrate this property by considering the case of someone who has entered an ice cream parlor and inquired about the flavors for sale. The server replies that vanilla, chocolate, and strawberry are available. The customer says, "I'll have chocolate." A moment later the server returns to announce, "I am sorry, we have no strawberry." The customer replies, "In that case I'll have vanilla." Such behavior would not be consistent with this property, which is sometimes called the *Independence of Immaterial Alternatives* property.

8. *The addition of a new alternative to the basis cannot make an existing alternative less desirable to me.* That is, while a new alternative may well improve the decision situation, it certainly cannot hurt it. In the extreme, I can simply ignore the new alternative and chose the one I previously considered best.

9. *The possibility of obtaining clairvoyance on any uncertainty cannot make the decision situation less attractive.* The emphasis here is on decision situation. I may well be engaged in doing a puzzle or waiting in line to see a mystery movie and decline to be told either the answer to the puzzle or the villain in the mystery without violating this property. In other words, in any situation in which suspense is not a part of the enjoyment and in which I face a choice, I should welcome new information, for it can never hurt and may well result in my obtaining a better deal.

10. *At this epoch my thoughts about how I will behave and choose in the future must be consistent.* For example, if I believe that I will prefer $10 over $5 tomorrow and I am making a decision today that may lead me to that choice, then I cannot say that I am uncertain about whan I will do when I face the decision. This does not mean that I will not be free to make any choice I like tomorrow or to change my tastes, but only that my present thoughts about what I will do must be consistent. This property is sometimes called *Sequential Consistency.*

11. *It should make no difference to my current decision when I face a series of actions whether I consider the sequential process of information revelation and what I will do in the face of each such revelation, or whether I consider all possible future actions I might take and all future possibilities I might learn, with their associated probabilities, and then find the best set of actions.* This property is called *Equivalence of Extensive Form and Normal Form Analysis.* It is closely related to property 5 discussed above.

Essential Properties With a Value Measure.   While not strictly necessary, most decision analysis problems are formulated in a way that allows a value measure to be placed on each prospect. This value measure is a fungible and alienable resource, usually money, in which the difference between two prospects can be interpreted as the willingness to pay to change from one prospect to the other.

A resource is fungible if you are indifferent to substituting one unit or fraction of a unit for another such quantity in any deal. In other words, all units of a fungible resource are indistinguishable and divisible. Furthermore, the resource must be such that more is always preferred to less, so that higher prospects in the preference list will correspond to more of the resource. In practice, it is difficult to think of a resource other than money that meets these requirements, although in some settings measures like "time saved" may be adequate.

The value measure must be alienable, capable of being transferred to the ownership of another, if the value of clairvoyance results are to be interpreted as guidance for selecting information-gathering processes that must be contracted for. For example, you cannot pay a laboratory to conduct a test by signing over some of your "time saved."

The introduction of a value measure is useful for two reasons. First, because it allows the preference comparison of prospects to be conducted against a familiar scale of value. The second reason is that it allows the possibility of computing a value of clairvoyance in terms of this measure on any uncertainty or collection of uncertainties in the problem.

When we use a value measure we can add the following essential properties for the decision composite:

1. *Since the value measure is chosen so that more will always be preferred to less, the higher the prospect in the prospect list the higher must be the value measure.* This ensures that there will be no possibility of making me a "money pump" if I follow my expressed preferences.
2. *For each deal I must be able to compute the amount of the value measure I would have to receive in exchange for the deal in order to be indifferent to selling it.* This threshold selling price of the deal I shall call the certain equivalent. This property requires that certain equivalents exist.
3. *I must be able to compute the value of adding any new specified alternative to the decision basis: the value must be nonnegative.*
4. *I must be able to compute the value of clairvoyance on any uncertain distinction or collection of uncertain distinctions; the value of clairvoyance cannot be negative.*
5. *Payments of value that cannot be changed must have no effect on future decisions.* For example, except for informational and tax effects, the price for which I am just willing to sell something must not depend on what I paid for it. More generally, when I am ranking prospects that I consider to be equivalent to changes in wealth, how I arrived at my present state of wealth must not matter. This is the "sunk cost" principle.
6. *There must be no willingness-to-pay to avoid regret.* My preferences must be on prospects—the futures I face. Regret is a bad thought that arises when I think about futures I might have received instead of the future I did receive.
7. *At least simple stochastic dominance must be satisfied.* This means that if for any x the probability of receiving a value measure of at least x with alternative I is at least as great as the probability of receiving a

value measure of at least x with alternative II, and if it is greater for some x, then I must prefer alternative I to alternative II.

You will notice that several of these properties are special cases or refinements of the essential properties when there is no value measure. For example, the requirement that the value of clairvoyance be nonnegative is just a precise statement of the requirement that the decision situation can never be made less desirable by the possibility of clairvoyance.

Practical Considerations. In addition to these essential properties, there are certain practical or methodological considerations that are highly desirable, if we are to have a discipline of decision analysis instead of only a theory of decision making. One practical consideration is that the individual evaluation of prospects must be possible. This means that in the language of the rules of thought we discussed earlier, the prospects can be placed in order individually rather than being considered in pairs or triplets, etc.; therefore, we can ask preference questions like, "Would you rather have $500 than $100?" rather than "Would you rather have $500 when you might have had $1,000, or $100 when you might have had $50?" Some proposed theories appear to require asking the latter type of question. A second practical consideration is that the methodology of tree roll back, or equivalently, influence diagram evaluation be available to solve the decision problem by determining the best deal. While in principle we could adopt methodologies that violated these practical considerations, the cost of decision analysis would become prohibitive for current uses.

Rating the Present Theory

As you might have guessed, the old time religion decision composite based on the five rules of thought we have discussed satisfies all the desiderata suggested, both conceptual and practical. Furthermore, and most importantly, I have heard of no other theory that satisfies the essential desiderata, much less the practical ones.

Why then is there a demand for new theory? The general reason is that some people think that it is reasonable to depart from the recommendations of the normative theory. They believe this because many people do depart from the recommendations of the normative theory in decision experiments and because in at least one case, that of *equity*, the recommendations seem conceptually inappropriate even to some thoughtful researchers. I personally believe that neither of these challenges constitutes an effective attack on the normative theory. I shall first discuss the experimental challenge and then the conceptual challenge.

The Experimental Challenge

Some researchers are uncomfortable because the normative theory is not a good descriptive theory of decision making. They would like to consider what is currently observed in some decision-making situations as "OK" rather than as mistakes in terms of the normative theory. I believe that just as for me in the case of hydrostatics, the answer lies in education rather than in changing the rules of the game. To illustrate I shall discuss two of the cases that are often offered to justify the development of a new normative theory.

The Allais Problem

Consider a version of a famous problem in decision theory, the Allais Problem. Suppose you are fortunate enough to have the chance to win a large sum of money as follows. According to the toss of a coin you will receive the opportunity for an attractive deal in either Room A or Room B. If you receive Room A, you will have to choose between two deals, Deal L1 and Deal L2. Deal L1 is easy to describe: if you choose Deal L1 you will receive a sure $1,000,000. Deal L2, however, is uncertain. With Deal L2 you have a 10 percent chance of winning $5,000,000, an 89 percent chance of winning $1,000,000, and a 1 percent chance of winning nothing. The chance mechanism is such that *you* assign these probabilities of winning each amount. Which do you prefer, Deal L1 or Deal L2? If you receive Room B, you will have to choose between Deal L3 and Deal L4, both of which are uncertain. Deal L3 has a 10 percent chance of paying you $5,000,000 and a 90 percent chance of paying you nothing. Deal L4 has an 11 percent chance of paying you $1,000,000 and an 89 percent chance of paying you nothing. Do you prefer Deal L3 or Deal L4?

Now let us suppose that you have to instruct an agent to make the choices for you in whichever room you receive. For example, you could instruct the agent to choose Deal L1 in Room A and Deal L3 in Room B. But other instructions are possible such as L2 and L4, or L1 and L4, or L2 and L3. You could even be indifferent between the deals offered in one room or the other or both. What instructions would you give to your agent? If it cost you $100 to have the agent follow your instructions rather than leave the choice to the agent's whim, would you pay? Empirically, a sizable fraction of any group will instruct the agent to choose L1 and L3. I find that people giving this instruction often say they would pay $100 or

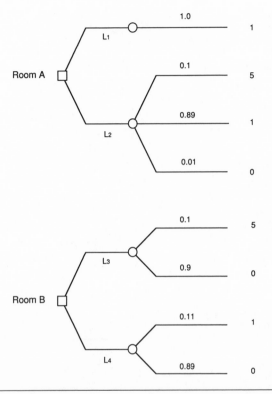

Figure 2–1. The choices in each room.

more to assure that those instructions would be followed rather than, for example, the alternate instructions L2 and L4. Let us examine this behavior in more detail.

Analysis. Figure 2–1 shows decision trees for the possibilities arising in Room *A* and in Room *B*. The payoffs are in millions of dollars. Recall that Room *A* or Room *B* is chosen by the toss of a coin, so that a more accurate representation of the entire situation appears in figure 2–2. Your task of delegation is to inform your agent which deal to select in each room that you might receive. Let us examine the probabilities of winning each amount of money if you give each of the four instructions L1, L3; L1, L4; L2, L3; and L2, L4.

Figure 2–3 shows the consequences of the instruction L1, L3. They are a 5 percent chance of $5,000,000, a 50 percent chance of $1,000,000, and

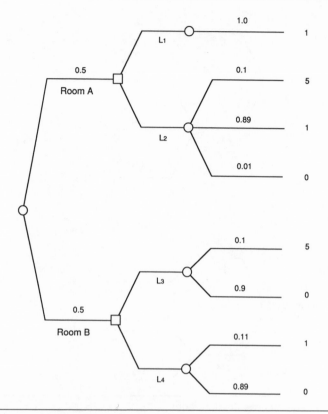

Figure 2–2. The decision situation.

a 45 percent chance of nothing. Figure 2–4 shows the corresponding consequences of the L1, L4 choice. We see that there is no chance of winning $5,000,000, a 55.5 percent chance of winning $1,000,000, and a 44.5 percent chance of winning nothing. Figure 2–5 shows the results of the L2, L3 choice, namely, a 10 percent chance of winning $5,000,000, a 44.5 percent chance of winning $1,000,000, and a 45.5 percent chance of winning nothing. Finally, figure 2–6 shows the results of the L2, L4 delegation. We see that there will be a 5 percent chance of winning $5,000,000, a 50 percent chance of winning $1,000,000, and a 45 percent chance of winning nothing. But we have seen these results before. They are the same probabilities of these payoffs we derived for the L1, L3 delegation in figure 2–3. This means that the L1, L3, and L2, L4 choices will lead to exactly the same probabilities of the same payoffs, and,

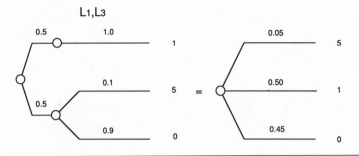

Figure 2–3. The instruction *L*1, *L*3.

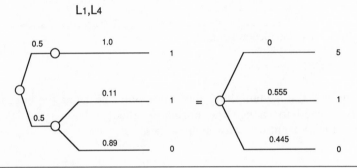

Figure 2–4. The instruction *L*1, *L*4.

therefore, that anyone who paid $100 to insure that the instructions would be L1, L3 rather than L2, L4 would have wasted his money. Recall that we said that an essential desideratum for a theory of decision making was that a person be indifferent between deals with the same probabilities of the same prospects.

The Allais Problem fools people because it encourages them to be fearful about the 1 percent chance of losing their $1,000,000 in Room *A*, while it induces them to be greedy and ignore this risk when they are confronted by Room *B*. In other words, Room A promotes focussing on uncertainty, whereas Room *B* encourages concentrating on payoffs. The version of the problem discussed here requires people to be consistent in their tradeoff between greed and fear, namely, their risk preference. I consider the Allais Problem to be a phenomenon and not a paradox. The fact that people will make choices that they will later see to be mistaken

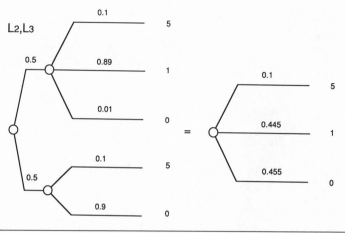

Figure 2–5. The instruction L2, L3.

(Tversky and Kahneman 1981) illustrates only the need for education, and not a need to change the normative theory. This is the lesson I learned in my adventures with hydrostatics.

The Ellsberg Problem

Another famous problem requires people to express preferences for payoffs that depend on the color of a ball drawn from an urn with uncertain composition; I present my own version. The urn is shown pictorially in figure 2–7; it contains 90 balls of which 30 are red and 60 are either blue or yellow. We know that the blue and yellow balls were selected from a large supply of both colors by a colorblind child. Again, you have the opportunity to receive an attractive deal based on the urn in one of two rooms according to the toss of a coin. In either room you will play a game exactly once, and must choose a payoff scheme for it.

If you receive Room A, then the payoff schemes are shown in figure 2–8. If you play with payoff scheme I, then if a red ball is drawn you will receive $100 and otherwise nothing. If you play with payoff scheme II, then only a blue ball will pay you $100. Which scheme do you prefer, or are you indifferent? If you receive Room B, your payoff schemes are as shown in figure 2–9. Payoff scheme III will pay you $100 for either a blue or yellow ball, otherwise nothing. Payoff scheme IV will pay you $100 for

L2,L4

Figure 2–6.   The instruction L2, L4.

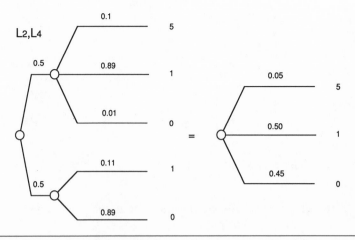

30 Red Balls
?   Blue Balls
?   Yellow Balls
----
90 Total Balls

URN

Figure 2–7.   The composition of the urn.

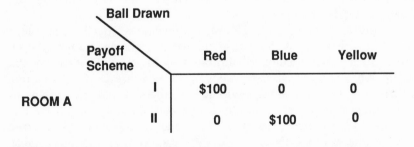

Ball Drawn

Payoff Scheme	Red	Blue	Yellow
I	$100	0	0
II	0	$100	0

ROOM A

Figure 2–8.   The payoff schemes in room A.

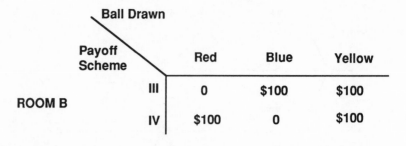

Figure 2–9. The payoff schemes in room B.

either a red or a yellow ball, again otherwise nothing. Which scheme do you prefer, or are you indifferent?

Now suppose once again that an agent will make your choices for you. What would your instructions be? Would they change if the potential prize was $100,000 rather than $100? Would you pay 1 percent of the prize amount to have your instructions followed rather than be subject to the whim of the agent? In my experience, many people prefer to play with payoff scheme I in Room A. In Room B, most people prefer to play with payoff scheme III. When both rooms are considered, many people in any group will make the choice I, III and be willing to pay a small sum for it.

Analysis.   Recall that the room is selected by tossing a coin. The problem is so constructed that if you make the choice I, III, you will receive a 50–50 chance of winning $100, regardless of the color of ball drawn. Furthermore, you will receive a 50–50 chance of winning $100, regardless of the color of the ball drawn, if you select II, IV. In other words, you have expressed a preference between two situations that have the same probabilities of the same prizes. Again, this is a violation of a fundamental desideratum.

Of course, the choice of II, IV over I, III would be equally inconsistent, as would be having a preference in one room but being indifferent in the other room. The situation is illustrated by showing the nine possible delegations for choice in each room shown in figure 2–10. Of the nine delegations, six are eliminated because of their inconsistency: they are inconsistent with any state of information you could have about the urn. Suppose, for example, that you knew that the 60 balls of uncertain composition were mostly blue. Then you can see from the payoff tables that you would prefer payoff scheme II in Room A and payoff scheme III

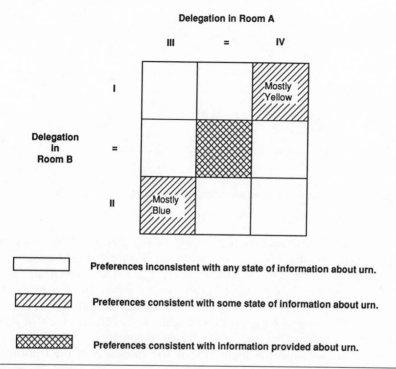

Figure 2–10. Consistency characteristics of the possible delegations.

in Room B. Conversely, if you knew that the balls were mostly yellow, then you would prefer schemes I and IV. If you could make neither statement about the composition of the urn, then your preference would have to be described by indifference between payoff schemes I and II, and between schemes III and IV, a situation described by the central box in the figure. The point is that only the three shaded diagonal boxes represent choices consistent with anything that you might know about the urn. We shall now show that only the choices in the central box are consistent with the information actually provided about the urn.

Let B be the event that a blue ball is drawn. Let n be the number of blue balls in the urn; n can take on the values $0, 1, 2, \ldots, 60$. Then we can write[1]

$$\begin{aligned} \{B\,|\,\&\} &= \Sigma\,\{B\,|\,n\&\}\{n\,|\,\&\} \\ &= \Sigma\,(n/90)\{n\,|\,\&\} \\ &= (1/90)\,\Sigma\,n\{n\,|\,\&\} \\ &= (1/90)\langle n\,|\,\&\rangle \end{aligned}$$

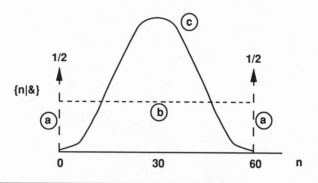

Figure 2–11.   Some possible assignments for $\{n \mid \&\}$.

We see that the probability that a blue ball is drawn is 1/90 times the mean of the distribution on n that we assign. Figure 2–11 shows some of the possible assignments we might make for $\{n \mid \&\}$. The assignment marked **a** corresponds to equal likelihood that either all or none of the balls are blue. Assignment **b** says that each number of blue balls from 0 to 60 is equally likely. Assignment **c** would be the binomial distribution resulting if you said that each of the balls was equally likely to be blue or yellow. The assessment **a** might arise if you thought that the colorblind child simply dipped the urn into a large vat of balls, either blue or yellow, depending upon which he came to first. The assignment **c** might be appropriate if he wandered through the warehouse picking up a ball every now and then.

But what do we really know about the composition of the urn? What we know is that, if every blue ball in the urn is replaced by a yellow one and vice versa, the problem is unchanged. We call this the invariance to relabeling of blue and yellow balls, a case of exchangeability. This means that whatever distribution we assign to n must be symmetric about $n = 30$. All the distributions in figure 2–11 meet this test as would many others—there is no justification in the problem for assigning any distribution to n lacking this property. Of course, this requires that the mean of any such distribution must be 30 and therefore that the probability of a blue ball must be equal to 30/90 or 1/3. And, of course, the probability of a red ball equals the probability of a blue ball equals the probability of a yellow ball equals 1/3—not approximately 1/3, but exactly 1/3. Thus we can say that in the problem as stated, there is no justification for delegating to your agent any other choice than indifference between the payoff schemes in both of the rooms.

It is important to note the qualification above, "In the problem as stated". On one occasion, I had a student, well-versed in the prevalence of different kinds of colorblindness in children, develop a model that led her to assign different probabilities to a blue and a yellow ball. The point is that there is no need to consider probabilistic "ambiguity." We need only recognize and characterize the information on which the probability assignment is based. Like the Allais Problem, the Ellsberg Problem affirms the need for education to guide choices that otherwise may later be seen as unwise.

The Conceptual Challenge: Equity

Some people feel that the rules of decision making that we have discussed are challenged by the notion of *equity*. To illustrate their concern, suppose that a mother is faced with giving a present either to her son John or her daughter Mary. She is indifferent between the prospect of John's getting the present and the prospect of Mary's getting the present. Those concerned with equity say that it is reasonable for the mother to prefer to flip a coin to determine which child gets the present rather than to give it to, say, Mary without such a coin toss. That is, she might prefer a 50/50 probabilistic mix of the prospects to either prospect. It should be clear that such a choice would violate the rules since all prospects are at the same level on the preference list.

There are several points that could be made in terms of this example. It is admittedly contrived because most parents could find some reason for preferring that one child or the other receive the present, perhaps by considering the recent history of presents received, special interests, current behavior, etc. However, if the problem is as posed then the rules would indicate that there should be no difference between the probabilistic mixture and giving the present to either child.

Let us ask whether it is important to the mother that she inform the children about the basis on which the choice was made. For example, does the mother say, "John and Mary, I have a present here, and I am going to flip a coin to see who gets it", or does she flip the coin in private and appear before the children with the simple statement, "Mary, I have a present for you" (in the case where Mary has won the coin toss *in absentia*)? In other words, are we really talking about the prospects "John gets present" and "Mary gets present", or the prospects of each child's getting the present with knowledge that the present was received as the result of a coin toss?

If the mother is trying to send a signal about impartiality by informing the children of the coin toss, then it appears that the prospects are not as originally described. In other words, the prospects are not only the original two of each child's getting the present, but two more where each child gets the present with the knowledge that the receipt of the present was the result of the toss of a coin and not of a conscious decision on the part of their mother. If the mother is truly indifferent regarding all four prospects, then it should not make any difference whether she gives the present to one of the children or flips a coin. If, however, she would prefer the prospects where the children know that the receipt was the result of a coin toss and not of her conscious decision, then both these prospects will be at a higher level than the other two and the preferred strategy will be the one of tossing the coin. Thus in this case, there is no reason to adopt any rules other than our standard ones to govern reasonable behavior.

As you might expect, the discussions of equity are not primarily concerned about giving a present to children, but about making decisions where some calamity or benefit may fall upon certain people. The notion is that having every person have an equal chance of receiving this distinction is somehow more "equitable" than giving it to any person, even though the decision maker is indifferent to who receives it. We could resolve this problem in the same way as we did the decision of the mother by considering the prospects as decidedly different. However, another issue arises. That is *equity*, not from the point of view of the giver, but from the point of view of the receiver.

Here we must distinguish two main cases, one in which all the participants in the process have agreed to the process and a second in which this is not so. In the case of voluntary agreement to the process, there is no notion of equity, equal probability, or fairness required since the action was entirely voluntary. Thus, in forming a new company various participants may receive different amounts of stock in the enterprise because their abilities are different. Once the deal has been voluntarily entered into, no one can claim that any particular person's share was inequitable—because he or she accepted the deal when they could have rejected it. We, therefore, hve no need of the notion of equity in voluntary arrangements.

In the case of involuntary arrangements, we distinguish between receiving a benefit and a harm. If what is to be given is a benefit owned by the giver that anyone would be happy to receive then the only decision that matters is that of the giver, and whatever he or she thinks is fair must be fair no matter how special the tastes and preferences of that giver are.

For example, a billionaire walking in the street might give $10 million to a passer-by because she reminds him of his mother. Is that fair? Who knows? She certainly would be very happy to get the $10 million. Another example is that of triage, where limited medical facilities are available following a disaster. The providers of charitable medical benefits may allocate them as they wish.

The challenging case is the one where calamity is being visited upon people without their consent. Here the notion that it is more equitable to have the harm fall on each person with equal probability has to be a perversion of the word equitable. Imagine a terrorist holding 100 hostages who drew the name of the one to be executed from an urn rather than by simply walking up to a person and shooting him or her. Would we praise this terrorist for being so equitable? There is no equitable way to coerce innocent people.

In summary, the issue of equity does not impugn the normative rules in any case of ethical individual decision making. The use of the concept of equity is potentially unconscionable in group decision making where some harm is to be delivered unto the innocent. The notion of equity challenges not the normative rules, but rather their ethical application.

The Role of the Normative Theory in Practice

Having just touched on the realm of practice, it is appropriate to comment on two issues that are often discussed. The first is whether the normative theory is "prescriptive;" the second is whether it is applicable to group decision making.

Normative/Prescriptive

It is clear from my use of the word *normative* that I am using it in the sense of rules that *should* govern decision making. Some authors have chosen to use the word normative in another sense, and to introduce a new word *prescriptive*. They use normative to mean an ideal description of individual decision making that should not necessarily be followed in actual practice. They use the word prescriptive to refer to the decision process to be recommended to a decision maker, even if the normative rules are violated by this process.

It seems to me that what these authors refer to as prescriptive rules, I would refer to as the approximations that are appropriate when applying the norms in practice. These approximations are not mistakes in the sense that they are violations of the norms of decision making, but are rather the interpretations required to apply the norms sensibly in the world.

To illustrate this distinction, consider a group of people deciding how to share the cost of a meal. The principle of "each should pay for what he has ordered" and the norms of arithmetic would constitute a decision process that could clearly be carried out by the diners. However, it is often the case that the diners regard the cost of going through the calculations as more onerous than any error that might arise by using the simpler process of dividing the bill by the number of diners, perhaps with minor adjustments made for people who ate lightly or heavily. Note that this procedure does not reject the norms of arithmetic, but rather accepts the higher decision rule that you should not spend more resources on a decision process than the results of that process are worth to you. Note, for example, that if the exact bills could be magically delivered to the individuals then there would be no need for the approximation.

When I coined the term *decision analysis*, I defined it as *applied decision theory*. Decision analysis is the engineering use of the norms of decision theory (the old time religion) in the practical world. The only time it would be worth taking a risk of violating the norms would be when the cost of assuring that they were satisfied was more than the cost of the potential violation, as in the meal example. In other words, if analysis were free and instantaneous, I can see no excuse for violating the norms in any decision, and therefore no reason to think of decision analysis or decision engineering as any different from any other engineering discipline that (by its nature) requires approximation. Consequently, I find no need to use the word *prescriptive* instead of *normative* to describe any aspect of practice.

Individual and Group Decision Making

Another source of confusion among many practitioners is whether the rules for decision making that we have discussed are applicable to group as well as individual decisions. A group could voluntarily accept these rules to govern group decision making. In this case, we would be using the decision rules as a metamodel or metaprocess for decision making by the group. Subgroups could be appointed to formulate the basis elements of alternatives, information, and preferences, and another subgroup could carry out the formal analysis to find the best decision. I once thought this would be an excellent way to carry out the process of decision making in society (Howard, 1975), but I changed my mind because of the inevitable coercive nature of government. For private organizations it might still make a useful model.

However, one would have to be, professionally, extremely humble in applying such a metamodel, even in a private organization. We know from the seminal work of Arrow that there is no group decision process except dictatorship that satisfies a few simple requirements that we would place on any sensible decision process. The problems of gaming, misrepresentation, agenda manipulation, may all make sense to certain individuals in the group. Some people may be motivated to be deceptive about their representations of the basis elements. (Note that for an individual decision maker acting in self-interest, there is no advantage to any of the gaming tactics that may appear advantageous in a group.)

Consequently, in a group decision process, I would be very reticent to offer a warranty on the quality of decision making that applied to more than the evaluation of the given basis. Note that this is very different from having a specified decision maker who has *personally* accepted all the basis elements as appropriate for the organization. Indeed, this is the type of situation in which I feel most comfortable when conducting a decision analysis, for I can use effective procedures to guide the analysis.

To analyze an important decision, I and my closest colleagues at Strategic Decisions Group advise that the decision maker appoint two major participants, a content certifier and a process certifier. The content certifier, usually a senior member of the client organization, is responsible to the decision maker for the content of the decision basis. The process certifier, a professional consultant, is responsible to the decision-maker for the elicitation of all basis elements, for the structure of the basis, and for the execution of the analysis.

To ensure the integrity of the decision process, we require that each assessment in the decision basis be accompanied by a "pedigree." In addition to the names of the content and process certifiers, the pedigree specifies the person responsible for the judgment represented in this particular assessment, the author, and the person responsible for conducting the elicitation process in which it was assessed—the analyst. In the case of a probability assessment, the pedigree contains a general description of the distinction being assessed and the clarity test definition of the distinction. The pedigree also records any notes regarding the general assumptions that are being made in the assessment and a list of the people who participate in the discussion. Then, if, at some later time, the decision maker asks, "Who said that the probability of technical success was 0.2?", we can without delay present the whole story for the decision maker's approval. A common comment is, "Well, I understand what was being assessed. Frank (the author) is our expert on this subject and as long as John and Mary (participants) were parties to the discussion, I see no reason to question it." When all assessments in the basis, whether of alternatives, information, or values, can be so scrutinized and evaluated, then I can give the strong warranty both that I have accurately represented the basis and that the course of action recommended is the one consistent with the basis.

When it comes to applying the individual decision-analysis paradigm, not only in a group situation, but in a government situation, then my position moves on from one of being professionally humble to one of being ethically repelled. To put the case as briefly as possible, a government action is inherently coercive, both in the way the funds for it will be raised and in the way the law will be used to govern the behavior of peaceful individuals. If the analysis is performed in terms of stakeholders who must be satisfied, I ask who appointed them to take and spend my money. I ask in any decision process how many votes does the taxpayer or other victim of the democratic process get in this assemblage of special interest groups. While I do not doubt the good faith of many who choose to participate in the process, to do so is to be an accomplice in coercion. In my view, the only ethically proper role in participating in government action would be in redressing the effects of previous government coercion. However, even in this role the analyst may find that he or she has become a party to further coercion.

Conclusion

Let me summarize my position on axiomatizations of decision theory that are at variance with the decision composite I have taken as fundamental in this chapter. If these alternate decision theories are to be used descriptively, then no one can object to them. Their test will be whether they describe human decision making. It might be very useful to have more powerful descriptive theories than we have at present. Such theories could provide a new foundation for results in fields from descriptive economics to consumer marketing.

What I take issue with is any suggestion that revisionist approaches should be used normatively to guide individual human decision making, and, in particular, decision analysis. I know of no scheme other than the one that I have presented that meets all the desiderata I have described in this chapter. I am personally unwilling to sacrifice any of these properties for any benefit that has yet been offered. My concern is that the advocacy of these revisionist approaches for normative decision making may do harm by appearing to make inferior thought acceptable. In summary, "the old time religion is good enough for me." We need more evangelists, not alternate bibles.

Acknowledgment

I wish to thank Ward Edwards, Irving LaValle, and David and James Matheson for many helpful comments that improved the clarity of the paper.

Note

1. Notation: $\{\cdot \mid \cdot\}$ = Prob$(\cdot \mid \cdot)$; $\langle \cdot \mid \cdot \rangle$ = Exp$(\cdot \mid \cdot)$; & is initial state of information (Howard, 1966).

References

Howard, R.A. (1966). "Information Value Theory." *IEEE Transactions on Systems, Science and Cybernetics*, SSC-2(1), 22–26.

Howard, R.A. (1975). "Social Decision Analysis." *Proceedings of the IEEE*, 63(3), 359–371.

Howard, R.A. (1988). "Decision Analysis: Practice and Promise." *Management Science*, 34(6), 679–695.

Matheson, D. (1990). "When Should you Reexamine Your Frame?" Dissertation. Department of Engineering-Economic Systems, Stanford University.

Spencer-Brown, G. (1979). *Laws of Form*. E.P. Dutton, New York.

Tversky, A., and D. Kahneman (1981). "The Framing of Decisions and the Psychology of Choice." *Science*, 211, 453–458.

3 ON THE FOUNDATIONS OF PRESCRIPTIVE DECISION ANALYSIS

Ralph L. Keeney

Introduction

In the recent past, there has been significant interest in the interactions among normative, descriptive, and prescriptive theories of decision making. The volumes by Bell, Raiffa, and Tversky (1988) and Fishburn and LaValle (1989) present numerous viewpoints on these theories. An important aspect of this work is research on sets of axioms for normative decision making. Increasingly, these axioms have tried to account for human characteristics of decision making that have been descriptively observed. Contributions to this work include Bell (1982), Machina (1982), Becker and Sarin (1987), Fishburn (1988), and Luce (1988). Sarin (1988) and Keller (1992) both summarize many key issues of this work. However, these works rarely address the axioms appropriate for prescriptive decision making. That is the main concern of this chapter.

Before proceeding, it is useful to briefly define my use of normative, descriptive, and prescriptive. *Normative* approaches to decision making focus on rational procedures for decision making and how decisions should be made in order to be logically consistent with these rational procedures. *Descriptive* decision making is concerned with explaining how

W. Edwards (ed.), UTILITY THEORIES: MEASUREMENTS AND APPLICATIONS. Copyright © 1992. Kluwer Academic Publishers, Boston. All rights reserved.

people make decisions and with predicting the decisions that they may make. *Prescriptive* decision making is concerned with helping people make informed, and hopefully better, decisions.

One main thesis of this chapter is that the choice of axioms to guide the analysis of prescriptive decision making is a decision problem. It is a decision problem facing the analyst who is attempting to help a decision maker or decision makers. The axioms provide a basis for any analysis and this is the means by which the analyst helps the decision maker. Part of this chapter addresses the objectives to be achieved by that analysis and the objectives to be achieved by the choice of axioms to support that analysis.

The Decision Problem of Selecting Axioms

Normative, descriptive, and prescriptive theories clearly address different questions. In addition, they are distinct in terms of the breadth of their problem focus, the criterion for appraising appropriate axioms, and the judges who apply those criteria. A useful framework to examine axioms is illustrated in table 3–1 where we have three rows representing the normative, descriptive, and prescriptive theories, and five columns. The first three columns are part of a matrix representing all decision problems, classes of decision problems, and specific decision problems. The next two columns indicate the criterion for evaluating axioms and the judges who apply the criteria.

With respect to normative theory, the focus is on all decision problems. The criterion for evaluating a set of axioms is whether or not they

Table 3–1. Features that Distinguish Normative, Descriptive, and Prescriptive Theories of Decision Making

| | Problem Focus | | | | |
| | | Classes of | Specific | | Judges of |
Theories	All Decisions	Decisions	Decisions	Criterion	Theories
Normative	×			Correctness	Theoretical Sages
Descriptive		×		Empirical Validity	Experimental Researchers
Prescriptive			×	Usefulness	Applied Analysts

× = focus of attention on theories

are logically correct, meaning that they are rational and lead to logically consistent decisions. The appraisal on logical correctness requires a conclusion reached by "wise sages," meaning those individuals concerned with the theoretical foundations of decision making.

Descriptively, the choice of axioms is not one of preference or professional belief. Rather, the issue is whether the axioms describe the manner in which people do make decisions. Since this question needs to be empirically tested by experimental researchers, the focus is typically on classes of decision problems, where a class is defined as any set of specific decision problems that are conveniently aggregated (for example, group decisions, investment decisions, decisions involving safety issues). In this regard a tremendous amount of evidence indicates that expected utility theory is not a good descriptive theory for all problems or even classes of problems. Perhaps, in some specific cases, such as when an individual has chosen to behave according to the axioms of expected utility theory, then the theory is an appropriate descriptive theory also.

Prescriptively, the cell of interest is the one addressing specific problems. A decision analyst focuses on one decision problem at a time and is not particularly concerned with whether the axioms utilized to support the analysis for that given problem are appropriate for classes of problems or all other problems. The main criterion is whether the axioms are useful for the problem being faced. However, there are insights for the selection of axioms for a specific decision problem that may come from addressing classes of decision problems. An example concerning equity is discussed later in this chapter.

Let us indicate where axiom systems, such as those for expected utility, fit into the overall set of assumptions necessary for prescriptive decision analysis. In this regard, the categorization in table 3–2 may be useful. Here we have theoretical assumptions, which are often referred

Table 3–2.   A Categorization of Assumptions Required for Prescriptive Decision Analysis

	Focus of Assumptions				
	Identifying Problem	Quantifying Objectives	Describing Impacts	Integrating Information	Communicating Insights
Theoretical Assumptions			FOCUS OF FORMAL AXIOM SYSTEMS		
Operational Assumptions					

to as axioms, and operational assumptions concerning practice. With regard to a specific decision problem, there are five aspects that need to be addressed by assumptions. These concern structuring the problem, quantifying objectives, describing possible impacts, integrating information to provide guidance for decision making, and communicating the insights of the analysis. The foundation for any specific analysis is structuring the problem, which means identifying the alternatives and qualitatively specifying objectives in a manner useful for quantitative analysis. The axioms of expected utility theory, and newly suggested competing systems of axioms, essentially address only theoretical issues concerning the quantification of objectives and impacts and their integration to imply preferences about alternatives. Invariably, these systems of axioms do not address structuring nor communicating insights from the analysis. Furthermore, none of the axiom systems address operational aspects of implementing a given methodology based on a set of axioms.

A set of operational assumptions to implement prescriptive decision analysis is outlined in Keeney (1980). To provide some notion of what is meant by operational assumptions, let me briefly outline these here. To identify alternatives, screening procedures are suggested to reduce large numbers of potential alternatives to a few feasible quality contenders for the best course of action. These should be the focus of the resulting decision analysis. The specification of objectives involves generating an objectives hierarchy and defining attributes to measure the degree to which those objectives are achieved. Then, a utility function is developed over the attributes using independence assumptions such as those discussed in Fishburn (1970) and Keeney and Raiffa (1976). The description of the possible consequences of the alternatives requires quantification of judgment. This may involve creating models, gathering and processing of data, and assessing probability distributions based on judgments. The decision-making task involves calculating expected utilities for the alternatives and sensitivity analysis to analyze the implications of different assumptions. Furthermore, some calculations focus on expected utilities of subsets of the attributes for each of the alternatives. However, expected utility is difficult to interpret, since it is unique only up to positive linear transformations. Hence, for communication purposes, expected utilities should be converted into equivalent amounts of a specific attribute with all other attributes fixed at common levels.

In summary, for a prescriptive analysis, a combination of theoretical and operational assumptions is necessary. The choice of appropriate theoretical axioms depends, among other things, on the implementation of these axioms in given situations. The specific nature of this relationship is

Table 3–3. The Objectives of The Analysis of Specific Decision Problems

---

Maximize the quality of the analysis
    Provide insight for the decision
        Create excellent alternatives
        Understand what and why various alternatives
          are best
        Communicate insights
    Maximize professional interest
        Derive enjoyment from the analysis
        Learn from the analysis
    Contribute to the field of decision analysis
    Minimize effort necessary
        Minimize time utilized
        Minimize cost

---

discussed in the next section, which outlines the objectives of specific decision analyses and the objectives of the axioms to support those analyses.

Objectives of Analysis and Objectives of Axioms

The objectives achieved by selecting a set of axioms are means to completing a quality analysis. Thus, let me list a set of objectives for a quality analysis to serve as a basis for selecting axioms. A hierarchy of objectives for analysis is presented in table 3–3. The overall objective is to maximize the quality of the analysis. There are four major objectives contributing to this overall objective. They are to provide insight for the decision being analyzed, to maximize professional interest, to maximize contribution to the field of decision analysis, and to minimize the effort necessary. Three of these major objectives are broken into components.

The insights desired from an analysis pertain to creating and developing the best possible alternatives, to understanding what alternatives are best under what conditions and why, and to communicating the insights to decision makers so they can make better decisions. These three component objectives relate to the structure in table 3–2 as follows: creating alternatives is a part of the first aspect of analysis; understanding what is best pertains to aspects two through four; and communicating pertains to aspect five. The axioms of expected utility theory directly relate to aspects

Table 3–4.   The Objectives of Selecting Axioms for a
Decision Analysis

Provide the foundation for a quality analysis
  Address problem complexities explicitly
  Provide a logically sound foundation for analysis
  Provide for a practical analysis
  Be open for evaluation and appraisal

---

two through four, and hence to the objective of understanding what is best and why. The professional objectives of concern are those of the analyst concerning the analysis. These are to enjoy the analysis and to learn from it as well as to contribute to the field of decision analysis. Regarding effort, it is desirable to minimize the cost and time required to provide the insight and professional contributions.

The selection of axioms should be based on objectives that are a means to achieve a better understanding of the alternatives that are best. However, since these axioms provide a basis for the analysis, they also influence all of the other objectives. The objectives of selecting axioms are listed in table 3-4. The overall objective is to provide a foundation for quality analysis. This is divided into four major objectives: to address the complexities of the decision problem explicitly, to provide for a logically sound and practical analysis, and to be open to evaluation and appraisal. Perhaps some elaboration is appropriate.

Numerous complexities can render a decision problem difficult. These include significant uncertainties, multiple objectives, intangible concerns, impacts over time, portfolio effects, multiple stakeholders, and more than one decision maker. In a specific decision problem, perhaps not all of these complexities are present. However, the analysis should be able to address all of those complexities that are present in an explicit and logically sound manner that does not oversimplify the issues. It is often precisely by addressing these complexities head-on that the analysis can be worth its effort.

The objective pertaining to logical soundness implies that you want a fundamental set of assumptions on which the analysis is based. These assumptions should be complete, meaning that they alone are sufficient to prescribe how to address all features of the decision problem to be analyzed. Furthermore, it is important that these assumptions be understandable to the individuals having an interest in the decision problem, meaning the stakeholders and the decision makers.

The axioms should be practical, meaning that it is feasible to conduct an analysis based on these axioms. This implies, on the one hand, that the resulting analysis should be as simple as possible while remaining consistent with the other objectives of axioms. On the other hand, practicality implies that the expertise is available to conduct the analysis consistent with the axioms and that the information required to implement the axioms, that is, regarding impacts and preferences, is attainable. If this information concerns possible impacts, the practicality objective implies that one can collect the necessary data or build models to estimate them. If the information pertains to value judgments, the practicality objective implies that one can assess the information in a logically sound and consistent manner.

The final objective of selecting a set of axioms is that they provide for an analysis that is open to evaluation and appraisal. This implies both that concerned individuals, including of course the decision makers, can understand the analysis and understand how the axioms guide the analysis if that is of concern. Directly related to this is that you want it perceived that the analysis based on the axioms is open to evaluation and appraisal. The important point is that interested individuals should be able to appraise the analysis; it is not sufficient that this appraisal is theoretically possible for an individual with an extremely analytical mind.

Prescriptive Appraisal of Expected Utility Theory

Expected utility theory, as developed over the years by Ramsey (1931), von Neumann and Morgenstern (1947), Savage (1954), and Pratt, Raiffa, and Schlaifer (1964), provides, from my perspective, an excellent foundation for prescriptive decision analysis. Let us consider it sequentially in relation to the objectives of axiom systems.

First, the expected utility axioms allow you to address the complexities of decision problems. They do not oversimplify the complexities away. For instance, they do not implicitly or explicitly assume that preferences are linear in monetary consequences nor that preferences of stakeholders cannot be accounted for in an analysis. The expected utility axioms are logically sound. This does not mean that they are the only set of logically sound axioms or that they are logically sound for every single decision problem. In fact, one advantage to the clarity of the assumptions is that they provide a foundation to examine their appropriateness in any given situation. When it is found that they are inappropriate, as for the class of problems concerning equity discussed in section five, then, of course, the expected utility theory axioms do not apply.

There have been numerous examples to illustrate the practicality of expected utility theory. It is sometimes difficult, because of the complexities of the problem, to obtain the necessary information, but the balance of the effort expended versus the insights gained from the analysis seems appropriate. Indeed, the analyst can choose the level of effort providing for analyses of different depth. This choice of effort increases the likelihood of valuable insights worth that effort, which is an advantage to the expected utility axioms.

Regarding openness to evaluation, individuals can certainly appraise and understand the axioms and they can also understand the manner in which these axioms relate to a specific analysis. For most decision problems, the assumptions are perceived by individuals to be a sound foundation for the analysis.

It is important to recognize that any decision analysis is essentially a model of a specific decision situation. No model is perfect, in that it addresses all aspects of the real problem. Indeed, the intent of models are to simplify from reality in a manner that addresses significant aspects of the problem and lends insights about those aspects. In terms of table 3–2, discrepancies between the real world and the model can be introduced in analysis by discrepancies between the theory in the model and the real world situation and discrepancies between the application of the operational assumptions for the model and the real world. When the expected utility axioms are utilized, it is likely that the discrepancies between the model and the real world result much more from the differences between implementing the operational assumptions and the real world than between the theory and its appropriateness for the real world. It does not seem reasonable to have the equivalent of third place accuracy using a more complicated set of theoretical assumptions when the second place

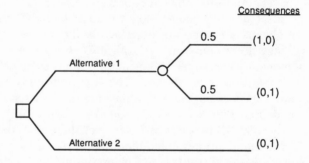

Figure 3–1. A Decision problem where consequences are equally preferable, but because of equity, alternatives are not equally preferable.

accuracy of the expected utility assumptions is much more accurate than the first place accuracy of applying the operational assumptions. Consequently, even in the case where a more complex axiomatic system may seem theoretically more appropriate, which I do not believe is often the case prescriptively, only a "big" violation of expected utility theory would be prescriptively relevant. For example, even if one were prescriptively intransitive in a given content, expected utility theory is still likely a good axiomatic base for the analysis unless one prefers A to B by a large amount, B to C by a large amount, and C to A by a large amount. If such a case occurred, then I would not suggest the use of expected utility theory for that problem.

A Class of Problems for which Expected Utility is a Poor Prescriptive Foundation

Let us consider a decision problem with consequences described by two attributes indicating respectively the utility of the outcome to individual 1 and the utility of the outcome to individual 2. In selecting an alternative, there are three objectives: to maximize satisfaction of individual 1, to maximize satisfaction of individual 2, and to select equitably an alternative. We will presume that a "decision maker" made interpersonal utility comparisons between the two individuals and scaled their utility functions each on a zero to one scale. We will further assume these scales were defined such that to the decision maker a utility of zero to each individual is equivalent and a utility of one to each individual is equivalent. The equity of concern addresses the equity of the decision process or what is sometimes referred to as ex ante equity.

Consider figure 3–1 which shows two alternatives. Alternative 1 yields a 0.5 probability at consequence $(1, 0)$ and a 0.5 chance at consequence $(0, 1)$, where $(1, 0)$ means a utility of 1 to individual 1 and a utility of 0 to individual 2. Alternative 2 yields for sure the consequence $(0, 1)$. Diamond (1967) noted that although the consequences $(1, 0)$ and $(0, 1)$ are indifferent to the decision maker, alternative 1 is preferred to alternative 2. The reason is, of course, that alternative 1 is more equitable since each individual has a 0.5 chance of receiving the preferred consequence, whereas alternative 2 is inequitable and gives the preferred consequence for sure to individual 2. This preference is in violation of the sure-thing axiom, or alternatively, the substitutability axiom, of expected utility theory. Recognizing such a violation in a given problem context is sometimes an insight for the decision makers.

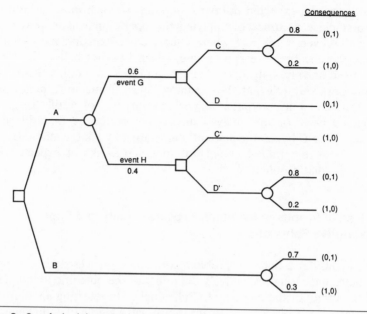

Figure 3–2. A decision problem involving equity.

Given the violation mentioned above, I would not utilize the axioms of expected utility theory, as commonly applied, to prescriptively analyze a decision problem involving ex ante equity. Rather, I would evaluate strategies to appropriately address the equity concern, since equity is a function of the complete decision strategy. Such an analysis would allow one to evaluate strategies in terms of three numbers: the expected utility to individual 1, the expected utility to individual 2, and an index measuring ex ante equity. A simple example directly adapted from a related problem addressing risk equity in Keeney and Winkler (1985) is illustrative.

Figure 3–2 illustrates a decision problem that begins with alternatives A and B. With alternative B, the uncertainty yields consequence (0, 1) with probability 0.7 or consequence (1, 0) with probability 0.3. With alternative A, events G or H occur with probability 0.6 and 0.4, respectively. If event G occurs, a decision must be made between alternatives C and D, and so forth. We will assume that the preference for equity implies that a better balance of the chances of getting consequences (1, 0) and (0, 1) is preferable when all other implications are equal.

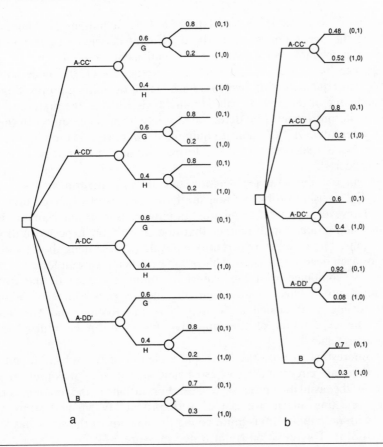

Figure 3–3a,b.   A strategic analysis of the decision problem involving equity. (a) normal form analysis. (b) reduced compound lotteries.

Suppose extensive form analysis were used to fold back the decision tree. Since all the consequences are indifferent in terms of the expected utilities to the two individuals, alternative C is preferred to alternative D and alternative D' is preferred to alternative C' because of equity. Thus, alternative A is equivalent to a 0.8 chance at consequence $(0, 1)$ and a 0.2 chance at consequence $(1, 0)$. It follows, using extensive form analysis, that alternative B should be preferred to alternative A.

In normal form analysis the decision strategies for this problem are shown in figure 3–3(a). Here, the strategy A-CC' means that alternative A will be chosen followed by alternative C, if event G occurs, and alternative C' if event H occurs. Other strategy definitions are similar. Reducing the uncertainties yields the equivalent decision tree in figure 3-3(b). For example, strategy A-CC' is equivalent to a 0.48 chance at consequence (0, 1) and a 0.52 chance at consequence (1, 0). Since both possible consequences of all five strategies are all-or-nothing propositions for exactly one of the equally valued individuals 1 and 2, the preferences between alternatives must be determined solely by ex ante equity. In this regard, alternative A-CC' is most equitable ex ante, so it is the preferred strategy. Note that with extensive form analysis, this strategy is not even considered.

One can use the strategic decision tree in normal form analysis to analyze the decision problem using the basic notions of expected utility theory. However, the index to measure equity needs to be determined for each decision strategy in a manner that does not follow expected utility assumptions. The result is a "certainty equivalent" describing the ex ante equity of each decision strategy. This number, which is certain for a given strategy, is combined with the expected utilities for each of the two individuals into a function for evaluating the decision strategies. With proper scaling as discussed in Sarin (1985) and Keeney and Winkler (1985), the expectation of this objective function can be utilized to evaluate strategies.

It is interesting to note that with the violation of the substitutability axiom, there are circumstances where a randomized strategy is preferred to any of the available pure strategies. For instance, the randomized strategy selecting alternative A-CC' with probability 5/6 and strategy A-DC^1 with probability 1/6 is more equitable than any of the strategies in Figure 3-3(b). This situation is illustrated in figure 3-4.

Misconceptions About the Expected Utility Axiom

There are three crucial misrepresentations about the prescriptive use of the expected utility axioms. These are briefly discussed in this section.

The first misconception is that the expected utility axioms are not appropriate for decision problems involving more than one decision maker. This is simply not true. The axioms themselves never mention the need for or role of a decision maker. They simply say that one can obtain preference judgments necessary to construct the probabilities and utilities for the decision problem. If you had a group decision, skipping for the moment whatever that might mean, and this group was willing to somehow specify the necessary preference judgments to utilize in the

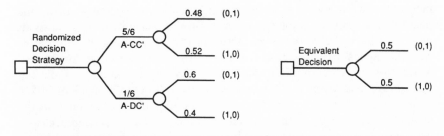

Figure 3–4. A randomized strategy is preferrable to any pure strategy in the decision problem involving equity.

analysis, then the analysis might be very helpful. More on this point relates to the next misconception.

With expected utility axioms, there is no need to even have an identifiable decision maker or decision makers. Again, the axioms require that a utility function and probabilities are obtained from preference judgments. The analyst may identify a knowledgeable interested party to construct appropriate utility functions or may even complete the analysis with various utility functions that are provided directly from the analyst's understanding of the problem. If the resulting analysis provides insights that reach the decision makers and influence decisions, this could be very important and certainly qualifies as decision analysis. This point is important, so let me outline an example. Suppose I alone did an analysis of disarmament options for the superpowers. Furthermore, suppose I alone, based on research, suggested reasonable utility functions for both sides and reasonable probabilities. A complete sensitivity analysis regarding these was part of the analysis. If the insights of the analysis were published and somehow influenced the decision makers involved in disarmament negotiations, this might be one of the most important decision analyses in history. Indeed, for such a problem, which will likely continue for several years, there is no way that we can now forecast who all the decision makers will be in the future. This is just one additional complexity of extremely difficult problems, and the axioms of decision analysis do allow us to address this complexity responsibly.

From a prescriptive viewpoint, it does not follow that the alternative strategy with the highest expected utility should necessarily be chosen. Furthermore, this in itself is not in violation of the expected utility assumptions. It follows from the expected utility assumptions that the alternative with the highest expected utility is the best of those alternatives considered, given all of the assumptions that went into the decision model. Since the model is always a simplification of the real world, one needs to interpret the implications of the model along with considerations not explicitly in the model. These latter factors may render the alternative with the highest expected utility not being the best alternative for the real world choice. As a simple example, if a very complex analysis indicated that alternative A was preferred to alternative B by an equivalent of $20 million and if legal considerations were intentionally not included in the analysis, then if decision makers felt that the legal considerations clearly were in favor of alternative B by an amount much greater than an equivalent of $20 million, alternative B should be chosen. In such a situation, I would claim that the decision analysis was used and that it was properly used. Again, the bottom line here is that prescriptive analysis is to provide insights to decision makers in making informed decisions, it is not to provide answers or indicate "correct" decisions.

Summary

In summary, let me repeat that prescriptively, an analyst has a choice of axioms to use to provide a foundation for analyzing a decision. The decision problem facing the analyst should be guided by the objectives to be achieved by the analysis and by the selection of axioms for that analysis. Indeed, the axioms of expected utility, or a competing set of axioms, provide only part of the overall set of assumptions necessary for prescriptive decision analysis. Specifically, they do not address the operational assumptions that are necessary for decision analysis.

For most decision problems, the expected utility axioms provide an excellent basis for decision analysis, a conclusion supported by Howard (1992) and LaValle (1992). They allow one to address the problem complexities explicitly without oversimplifying these complexities away, and they are logically sound and practical to implement, although it is somewhat difficult in practice to obtain all the necessary information. This difficulty is due to the nature of the decision problems and not the axioms themselves. Finally, the axioms of expected utility provide for an analysis that is open to evaluation and appraisal. There are cases where such appraisal would suggest that the axioms of expected utility are not appropriate for a given problem. An example concerning equity is illustrated in this chapter. In these situations, part of the analysis can be based on expected utility theory and done in a manner consistent with appropriate analysis for other aspects of the decision problem such as equity concerns.

The essence of quality decision analysis is to focus on the decision problem and to focus mostly on what is complex about the decision problem. It is here that one can likely gather the maximum insight for the least effort. Tackling the complex and unique is also more professionally rewarding and contributes much more toward moving decision analysis forward.

Acknowledgments

This work was partially supported by the National Science Foundation with Grant PRA-8520692 and the Risk Sciences Institute of the International Life Sciences Institute with a grant to the University of Southern California.

References

Becker, J.L., and R.K. Sarin (1987). "Lottery Dependent Utility." *Management Science*, 33, 1367–1382.

Bell, D.E. (1982). "Regret in Decision Making Under Uncertainty." *Operations Research*, 30, 961–981.

Bell, D.E., Raiffa, H., and A. Tversky (Eds.), (1988). *Decision Making: Descriptive, Normative, and Prescriptive Interactions*. Cambridge University Press. Cambridge.

Diamond, P.A. (1967). "Cardinal Welfare, Individual Ethics, and Interpersonal Comparisons of Utility: Comment." *Journal of Political Economy*, 75, 765–766.

Fishburn, P.C. (1970). *Utility Theory for Decision Making*. Wiley, New York.

Fishburn, P.C. (1988). "Expected Utility: An Anniversary and a New Era." *Journal of Risk and Uncertainty*, 1, 267–283.

Fishburn, P.C. (1988). *Nonlinear Preference and Utility Theory*. The Johns Hopkins University Press, Baltimore, MD.

Fishburn, P.C., and I.H. LaValle (Eds.), (1989). *Choice Under Uncertainty*. Baltzer Scientific Publishing Company, Basel, Switzerland.

Howard, R.A. (1992). "In Praise of the Old Time Religion." In W. Edwards (Ed.), *Utility Theories: Measurements and Applications*. Kluwer Academic Publishers, Boston, MA.

Keeney, R.L. (1980). *Siting Energy Facilities*. Academic Press, New York.

Keeney, R.L., and H. Raiffa (1976). *Decisions with Multiple Objectives*. Wiley, New York.

Keeney, R.L., and R.L. Winkler (1985). "Evaluating Decision Stretegies for Equity of Public Risks." *Operations Research*, 33, 955–970.

Keller, L.R. (1989). (1992). "Properties of Utility Theories and Related Empirical Phenomena." In W. Edwards (Ed.), *Utility Theories: Measurements and Applications*. Kluwer Academic Publishers, Boston, MA.

LaValle, I.H. (1992). "Small Worlds and Sure Things: Consequentialism by the Back Door." In W. Edwards (Ed.), *Utility Theories: Measurements and Applications*. Kluwer Academic Publishers, Boston, MA.

Luce, R.D. (1988). "Rank-dependent, Subjective Expected-utility Representations." *Journal of Risk and Uncertainty*, 1, 305–332.

Machina, M.J. (1982). "Expected Utility Analysis Without the Independence Axiom." *Econometrica*, 50, 277–323.

Pratt, J.W., Raiffa, H., and R. Schlaifer (1964). "The Foundations of Decision Under Uncertainty: An Elementary Exposition." *Journal of American Statistical Association*, 59, 353–375.

Ramsey, F.P. (1931). "Truth and Probability." In R.B. Braithwaite (Ed.), *The Foundations of Mathematics and Other Logical Essays*. Harcourt Brace, New York. Reprinted in H.E. Kyburg and H.E. Smokler (Eds.), (1964), *Studies in Subjective Probability*. Wiley, New York.

Sarin, R.P. (1985). "Measuring Equity in Public Risk." *Operations Research*, 33, 210–217.

Sarin, R.P. (1988). "Analytical Issues in Decision Methodology." In I. Horowitz (Ed.), *Decision and Organizational Theory*. Kluwer-Nijhoff, Dordrecht.

Savage, L.J. (1954). *The Foundations of Statistics*. Wiley, New York.

von Neumann, J., and O. Morgenstern (1947). *Theory of Games and Economic Behavior*. (2nd ed.) Princeton University Press, Princeton, NJ.

4 GENERIC ANALYSIS OF UTILITY MODELS

John M. Miyamoto

Introduction

It is now firmly established that expected utility (EU) theory and sub-jective expected utility (SEU) theory are descriptively invalid (Kahneman and Tversky, 1979; Luce, 1988b; MacCrimmon and Larsson, 1979; Slovic and Lichtenstein, 1983; Weber and Camerer, 1987). Descriptive utility theory is undergoing extensive revision, stimulated by empirical find-ings that challenge existing theories, and by new theories that more adequately account for the cognitive processes that underly preference behavior (Becker and Sarin, 1987; Bell, 1982; Kahneman and Tversky, 1979; Loomes and Sugden, 1982; Luce, 1988a, 1990; Luce and Narens, 1985; Quiggin, 1982). Although these developments are undoubtedly salutory for the theory and practice of decision making, it might appear that in the short term they undermine the usefulness of multiattribute utility theory (MAUT), or at least that part of MAUT that is built upon EU or SEU assumptions. (Henceforth, I will refer only to SEU theory, noting that EU theory can be construed as a special case of SEU theory.) A substantial part of MAUT methodology is based on preference assumptions that characterize classes of utility models under the assump-

W. Edwards (ed.), UTILITY THEORIES: MEASUREMENTS AND APPLICATIONS.
Copyright © 1992. Kluwer Academic Publishers, Boston. All rights reserved.

tion that SEU theory is valid (Keeney and Raiffa, 1976; von Winterfeldt and Edwards, 1986). The strong evidence against the descriptive validity of SEU theory might appear to undermine or even invalidate those parts of MAUT methodology that assume SEU theory in deriving implications from patterns of preference. A major goal of this chapter is to show that this is in fact not the case.

Of course, not all methods of MAUT analysis are based on SEU theory. For example, formalizations of MAUT models in terms of preferences under certainty or strengths of preference do not require SEU assumptions (Dyer and Sarin, 1979; Keeney and Raiffa, 1976; Krantz, Luce, Suppes, and Tversky, 1971; von Winterfeldt and Edwards, 1986). The present critique is only relevant to that part of MAUT methodology that is based on the assumptions of EU or SEU theory. I will refer to this as the risk-based part of MAUT. The essential feature of risk-based MAUT is that in this framework specific utility models are formalized in terms of preferences among hypothetical lotteries, rather than in terms of strengths of preference, or riskless preferences. For example, in the risk-based methodology, additive, multiplicative, and multilinear utility models are formalized by utility independence assumptions that describe how preference among gambles for particular attributes are affected by the levels of other attributes (Keeney and Raiffa, 1976). Similarly, Pratt (1964) described measures of risk aversion, defined in terms of choices between lotteries and certain outcomes, that describe the shape of utility functions. Tests of utility independence assumptions and of Pratt's characterizations of risk aversion are important in risk-based MAUT because they are used to diagnose the form of utility functions in specific domains. Such assumptions constitute necessary and sufficient conditions for specific utility models under the assumption that SEU theory is valid. Comprehensive descriptions of risk-based MAUT methodology are available in Keeney and Raiffa (1976) and von Winterfeldt and Edwards (1986); these monographs also describe methods of utility modeling that are not risk-based, that is, methods of utility modeling that do not require the assumption that SEU theory is valid.

The question addressed in this chapter is whether empirical violations of SEU theory undermine risk-based MAUT methodology. Should we cease to regard tests of utility independence and Pratt's (1964) risk characterizations as meaningful in descriptive research because they carry their implications within the framework of SEU theory? Alternatively, we might continue to incorporate risk-based MAUT into descriptive and prescriptive analyses with pious remarks concerning the approximate validity of SEU theory, while harboring a bad conscience over the unknown consequences of the divergence between SEU theory and empirical reality. What I want to show in this chapter is that there is a third alternative that is clearly preferable to either of the first two. I will propose a new theoretical framework within which risk-based MAUT methods can be justified, which does not commit one to the descriptively invalid claims of SEU theory. In other words, I will show how methods of utility modeling that were heretofore justified within the SEU framework can be reinterpreted and justified within a new utility theory that is more consistent with what we presently know about preference behavior.

The theory that I will propose is called *generic utility theory* (Miyamoto, 1988). In formalizing generic utility theory, an attempt was made to construct an axiomatic preference theory that would satisfy three desiderata:

1. The assumptions of the framework should be consistent with existing empirical studies of preference;
2. The framework should provide a basis for methods of MAUT modeling that were previously based on SEU theory; and
3. Utility analyses developed within the framework should be interpretable from a wide variety of theoretical standpoints.

The first desideratum is the obvious requirement that the theory should not be refuted by existing findings. The second reflects the desire not to lose risk-based MAUT methods as we shift from a SEU to a non-SEU framework. The third reflects the desire for a truly generic theory, that is to say, one that is consistent with many theories and has few distinctive features of its own. Because the assumptions of generic utility theory are weak, they are implied by a number of other utility theories including EU and SEU theory (Luce and Raiffa, 1957): prospect theory (Kahneman and Tversky, 1979); the dual bilinear model (Luce and Narens, 1985); Karmarkar's (1978) subjectively weighted utility (SWU) model; rank dependent utility theory (Luce, 1988a, 1990), (Quiggin, 1982), (Yaari, 1987); and Edwards' (1962) additive subjective expected utility (ASEU) and nonadditive subjective expected utility (NASEU) models[1]. Although the assumptions of generic utility theory are weak, they are sufficiently strong to constitute a logically sufficient basis from which to derive the implications of utility independence assumptions and Pratt's risk characterizations. Thus, with minor modifications to be described below, we can continue to use risk-based methods for analyzing utility models while basing the analyses on weak assumptions that are empirically more plausible than SEU theory. Generic utility theory is generic in the true sense of the word because it possesses this mixture of weakness and strength: Standard risk-based methods for analyzing utility models can be formalized under the assumptions of generic utility theory, and utility analyses that are carried out under these assumptions are interpretable from the standpoint of stronger theories that imply it.

It must be emphasized that generic utility theory is not proposed as a general theory of preference under risk, and hence, it is not a competitor of stronger theories like prospect theory, the dual bilinear model, and rank dependent utility theory. Rather, the purpose of generic utility theory is to provide a framework for utility modeling. Utility modeling, as I understand the term, is the enterprise of investigating the form of utility functions in specific domains, like the domains of health outcomes or environmental outcomes. When engaged in utility modeling, one's primary goal is to construct a mathematical model that characterizes someone's values in the given domain, rather than to test general assumptions of preference theory. A foundation for utility modeling may remain noncommittal on important issues in preference theory if empirical criteria for utility models can be formulated without resolving these issues. Working within the generic utility framework, researchers can reach agreement in the utility analysis of particular outcome domains, even while continuing to debate fundamental issues of preference theory. Thus, generic utility theory complements stronger theories, such as SEU theory, prospect theory, rank dependent utility theory, and the dual bilinear model, by providing a framework for utility modeling that is meaningful from the standpiont of these theories, without committing one to assumptions that are idiosyncratic to one strong theory and not to others. These remarks assume that in the near future no descriptive theory will predominate to the exclusion of all competitiors, for if such a dominating theory were established, one would naturally axiomatize and test utility models within the framework of this dominant theory, and the interpretability of analyses from alternative standpoints would be irrelevant.

The remainder of this chapter consists of four sections. First, I will present generic utility theory, and discuss its axiomatic foundation. Second, I will define more carefully the class of utility theories that are consistent with generic utility theory. Prospect theory is the most complex of these cases, and I will discuss it first. It will then be clear what types of theories are consistent with generic utility theory. Third, an empirical investigation of a multiplicative utility model will be presented within the generic utility framework. This empirical study exemplifies the use of generic utility theory in utility modeling. Finally, the role of generic analyses will be discussed with respect to general issues in theory construction and utility modeling.

The Generic Utility Representation

Let C denote a set of consequences; let p denote any fixed probability such that $p \neq 0, 1$; let (x, p, y) denote a gamble with a p chance of winning x and a $1 - p$ chance of winning y; let $G(p)$ denote the set of all (x, p, y) with $x, y \in C$. $G(p)$ will be referred to as the set of p-gambles. I will not distinguish notationally between the preference ordering over outcomes and gambles. Thus, I write $x \geqslant_p y$ if outcome x is at least as preferred as outcome y, and $(w, p, x) \geqslant_p (y, p, z)$ if the gamble (w, p, x) is at least as preferred as the gamble (y, p, z). Many theories of preference under risk postulate the existence of a real-valued function, U, and positive weights, s and t, that depend on p such that $s + t = 1$ and

$$(w, p, x) \geqslant_p (y, p, z) \quad \text{iff} \quad sU(w) + tU(x) \geq sU(y) + tU(z), \quad (1)$$

for every (w, p, x) and (y, p, z) in $G(p)$. The utility representation defined by condition (1) will be called *the standard model for p-gambles*. This model is implied by EU theory with the constraint that $s = p$ and $t = 1 - p$. It is also implied by SEU theory and Karmarkar's (1978) SWU theory, with somewhat different constraints on the coefficients, s and t. These utility theories are described more fully below. An axiomatization of (1) is stated in Krantz et al. (1971, chapter 6).

The generic utility representation is a generalization of the standard model for p-gambles. Let $S(p)$ be the set of all (a, p, x) such that $a, x \in C$ and $x \geqslant_p a$, and let $T(p)$ be the set of all (b, p, y) such that $b, y \in C$ and $b \geqslant_p y$. I will call $S(p)$ an *upper triangular set of p-gambles*, and $T(p)$ a *lower triangular set of p-gambles*. The terminology is motivated by the fact that if C were a set of money rewards and each (a, p, x) were assigned the coordinates (a, x) in the $C \times C$ plane, then the upper triangular set would be the set of all gambles that are on or above the main diagonal, and the lower triangular set would be the set of all gambles that are on or below the main diagonal (see figure 4–1). A set of gambles will be said to be triangular if it is either an upper of lower triangular set.

Suppose that $R(p)$ is a triangular set of p-gambles. The structure $(C, p, R(p), \geqslant_p)$ will be said to have a generic utility representation iff there exists a real-valued function, U, and real coefficients, α and β, such that $\alpha > 0, \beta > 0$, and

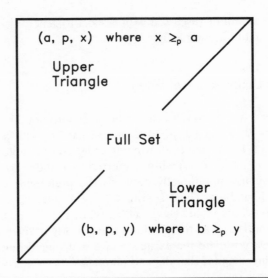

Figure 4–1.   A gamble of the form, (a, p, x), is assigned the coordinates, (a, x). Gambles above the diagonal are in the upper triangular set, and gambles below the diagonal are in the lower triangular set.

$$(a, p, x) \geqslant_p (b, p, y) \quad \text{iff} \quad \alpha U(a) + \beta U(x) \geqslant \alpha U(b) + \beta U(y) \quad (2)$$

for every (a, p, x), $(b, p, y) \in R(p)$. The coefficients, α and β, depend on the value of p, but since p is held constant in the present analysis, α and β can be treated as constants. The generic utility representation differs from the standard model for p-gambles only in that the domain of the representation is restricted to the preference order over gambles in a triangular set. To see why this is more general than the standard model, suppose that $S(p)$ is an upper triangular set of p-gambles, and $T(p)$ is a lower triangular set of p-gambles. It could be the case that $(C, p, S(p), \geqslant_p)$ satisfies the generic utility representation with respect to one pair of coefficients, α' and β', and $(C, p, T(p), \geqslant_p)$ satisfies the generic utility representation with respect to a second pair of coefficients, α'' and β'', while $\alpha' \neq \alpha''$ and $\beta' \neq \beta''$. The standard model requires that $\alpha' = \alpha'' = s$, and $\beta' = \beta'' = t$. The generic utility representation also differs from the standard model in that condition (2) places no restriction on the coefficients, α and β, other than that they are positive. Although condition (2) is consistent with theories that require that the coefficients satisfy $\alpha + \beta = 1$, it does not require that this constraint be satisfied.

An axiomatization of the generic utility representation is presented in Appendix 1 of this chapter. Ironically, the most interesting feature of the axiomatization is that it differs so little from axiomatizations of the standard utility model for p-gambles. Essentially, one takes an axiomatization of the standard model and modifies the axioms to apply only to p-gambles in a triangular set. Aside from the restriction to a triangular set of p-gambles, the main differences between the axiomatizations of the generic utility representation and the standard model is that first-order stochastic dominance is assumed (Axiom 4 of Appendix 1), which is slightly stronger than the independence assumption in the axiomatization of the standard model (Krantz et al., 1971), and an existential assumption (Axiom 10 of Appendix 1) is added to ensure that the preference order does not contain empty gaps (if $x >_p y$, then there exists z such that $x >_p z >_p y$). The representation and uniqueness theorem for the generic utility representation is stated in Appendix 1, and the proof of the theorem is sketched. Although the axiomatization of the generic utility representation is a straightforward generalization of previous work on additive models, the method used in proving the existence of the representation is new. Because the preference order in the generic theory is only defined over a triangular set of p-gambles, special techniques are required to prove the existence and interval-scale uniqueness of the utility scale (Miyamoto, 1988). From the standpoint of axiomatic measurement theory, the proof is a nontrivial extension of additive conjoint measurement. Wakker (1989a, 1989b) independently proved a utility representation theorem that includes the generic utility representation as a special case.

Next, I will show that prospect theory implies that the generic utility representation is satisfied by particular classes of gambles. This relationship is important because it establishes that studies of utility models within the generic utility framework can be interpreted from the standpoint of prospect theory. Furthermore, it implies that axiomatizations of MAUT models that were previously formalized under SEU assumptions can be incorporated into prospect theory. The discussion of prospect theory will clarify the point that any theory that implies that the generic utility representation is capable of axiomatizing MAUT models.

Prospect Theory

Here, I will only develop those aspects theory that are needed to show the relation between it and generic utility theory. The discussion will focus on the prospect theory analysis of preferences for p-gambles. Many important features of prospect theory, such as the editing or framing of gambles, the shapes of the value and probability weighting functions, and its generalization to gambles with three or more outcomes, will be omitted (see Kahneman and Tversky, 1979, 1984; Tversky and Kahneman, 1981).

Prospect theory postulates that the subjective value of an outcome is evaluated in terms of a comparison to a reference level. An outcome is categorized as a gain if it exceeds the reference level, and as a loss if it is below the reference level. For present purposes, the main reason for distinguishing gains from losses is that different rules determine the subjective value of a gamble, depending on whether the outcomes of the gamble are gains or losses. To describe these rules, suppose that $V(a, p, x)$ denotes the subjective value of (a, p, x). V is a real-valued function that preserves the preference order over p-gambles (and other gambles not discussed here). According to prospect theory, there exists a real-valued function, v, that maps outcomes to subjective values, and a function, π, that maps probabilities to subjective weights in the unit interval. For example, $v(x)$ is the subjective value of the outcome x, and $\pi(p)$ is the subjective weight of the probability p. Let r denote the reference level in the outcome domain. Prospect theory requires that v and π satisfy the constraints $v(r) = 0$, $\pi(0) = 0$, and $\pi(1) = 1$.

Figure 4–2 presents a graphical representation of the classification of p-gambles in prospect theory. Suppose that a gamble (a, p, x) is assigned the coordinates (a, x) in figure 4–2, where the horizontal axis represents an ordering of the first outcome, a, in terms of increasing subjective value, and the vertical axis represents an ordering of the second outcome, x, in terms of increasing subjective vlaue. Gambles of the form (a, p, r) lie on the horizontal axis, and gambles of the form (r, p, x) lie on the vertical axis; the axes cross at the point (r, r). A p-gamble (a, p, x) is *regular* if $a >_p r >_p x$, or $x >_p r >_p a$. The regular p-gambles are located in the upper left and lower right quadrants of figure 4–2. If (a, p, x) is regular, the value of (a, p, x) is given by the equation,

$$V(a, p, x) = \pi(p)v(a) + \pi(1 - p)v(x). \qquad (3)$$

A gamble (a, p, x) is said to be *irregular* if $a \geqslant_p r$ and $x \geqslant_p r$, or $a \leqslant_p r$ and $x \leqslant_p r$. The irregular p-gambles are located in the upper right and lower left quadrants of figure 4–2. To specify the value of an irregular gamble, there are two cases to consider. If $a \geqslant_p x \geqslant_p r$, or $a \leqslant_p x \leqslant_p r$, then the value of (a, p, x) is given by the equation,

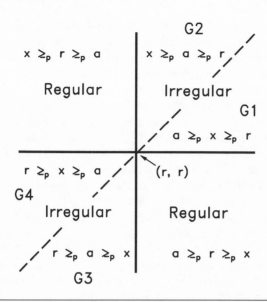

Figure 4–2. A gamble of the form, (a, p, x), is assigned the coordinates, (a, x). Quadrants are labeled according to whether the gambles are regular or irregular. G1, G2, G3, and G4 denote subsets of irregular gambles (see text).

$$V(a, p, x) = \pi(p)v(a) + [1 - \pi(p)]v(x). \qquad (4)$$

This rule, equation (4), applies to gambles in subquadrants G1 and G4 of figure 4–2. If $x \geqslant_p a \geqslant_p r$ or $x \leqslant_p a \leqslant_p r$, then the value of (a, p, x) is given by the equation,[2]

$$V(a, p, x) = [1 - \pi(1 - p)]v(a) + \pi(1 - p)v(x). \qquad (5)$$

This rule, equation (5), applies to gambles in subquadrants G2 and G3 of figure 4–2. It is not possible to review here the arguments for applying different rules in the evaluation of these gambles (Kahneman and Tversky, 1979, 1984; Miyamoto, 1987). For present purposes, what is important is that prospect theory postulates one rule for regular prospects, a second rule for the irregular gambles in G1 ∪ G4, and a third rule for the irregular gambles in G2 ∪ G3.

I should point out that the definition of regular and irregular p-gambles adopted here is slightly different from Kahneman and Tversky's (1979) definition. If a or x equals r, then Kahneman and Tversky classify (a, p, x) as a regular gamble and use equation (3) to determine $V(a, p, x)$, but the present definitions classify (a, p, x) as an irregular gamble and use equations (4) or (5) to calculate $V(a, p, x)$. This difference has no effect on substantive theory, because if a or x equal r, the value of $V(a, p, x)$ is the same regardless of whether (a, p, x) is classified as a regular or irregular gamble. In other words, if (a, p, x) lies on the vertical or horizontal axis of figure 4–2, the value of $V(a, p, x)$ remains the same if the value is computed by the rule for either adjacent quadrant. The advantage of altering Kahneman and Tversky's classification of gambles is that it simplifies the discussion of MAUT analyses without altering any of the empirical claims of prospect theory (see note 6).

It should be obvious that prospect theory implies that generic utility theory is satisfied by the gambles *within* the sets G1, G2, G3, and G4, for these are triangular sets of p-gambles, and equations (4) and (5) imply that the preference orderings within these sets satisfy the generic utility representation, condition (2), with possibly different coefficients for different subsets. Prospect theory also implies that the standard model for p-gambles is violated, at least for some values of p. The full argument for this cannot be given here, but it rests on the fact that the prospect theoretic analysis of the Allais paradox implies that $\pi(p) \neq 1 - \pi(1 - p)$ for at least some p. For any such p, the standard model for p-gambles is violated, because there is no single pair of coefficients that satisfies the standard model with respect to every gamble in G1 $\cup$ G2. To see this, note that if (a, p, x) is in G1, then $V(a, p, x)$ is given by equation (4), whereas if (a, p, x) is in G2, then $V(a, p, x)$ is given by equation (5). The coefficient for $v(a)$ is either $\pi(p)$ or $1 - \pi(1 - p)$, depending on whether (a, p, x) is in G1 or G2, thus violating the standard model for p-gambles which requires that these coefficients be identical for a given choice of p. A similar argument shows that there is no single pair of coefficients that satisfies the standard model with respect to every gamble in G3 $\cup$ G4. Thus, prospect theory implies that the generic utility representation is satisfied by the preference ordering within subsets of the form G1, G2, G3 or G4, but it denies that the standard model for p-gambles is satisfied by the preference order over G1 $\cup$ G2, or G3 $\cup$ G4, at least for some values of p. The example of prospect theory shows why it is desirable to generalize the standard model for p-gambles to the generic utility representation.

Before leaving the discussion of prospect theory, I should mention a final technical point. Prospect theory implies that the preference orderings on G1, G2, G3, and G4 satisfy the generic utility representation, condition (2), but it does not imply that the preference orderings on these subsets satisfy all of the axioms for generic utility theory. The reason is that some of the axioms are not logically necessary, that is, they are not implied by the generic utility representation. The three nonnecessary axioms for the generic utility representation are all existential axioms, that is, axioms that assert the existence of gambles of specified forms (see Axioms 8 to 10 of Appendix 1). Axiom 8 is a restricted solvability assumption similar to solvability assumptions in additive conjoint measurement (Krantz et al., 1971, chapter 6). Axiom 9 makes the innocuous claim that there exist x and y such that $x >_p y$, and Axiom 10 asserts that if $x >_p y$ then there exists z such that $x >_p z >_p y$. The existential assumptions are technical assumptions that are usually not tested empirically. They are usually accepted or rejected on theoretical grounds, depending on whether the topological conditions that they formalize are reasonable in the intended interpretation. The main empirical axioms of generic utility theory are necessary assumptions in the sense that they are implied by condition (2). As prospect theory implies condition (2), it implies the main empirical axioms of generic utility theory, but it does not imply the existential axioms of the theory.[3]

Compatibility of Utility Theories with Generic Utility Theory

The example of prospect theory illustrates what is at issue when asking whether a utility theory is compatible with generic utility theory. A theory is compatible with generic utility theory if it implies that condition (2) is satisfied with respect to a triangular set of p-gambles. If a theory implies (2), it implies the main empirical axioms of generic utility theory. Although it need not imply the existential axioms of generic utility theory, these axioms are very plausible whenever the outcome domain includes attributes like money or survival duration that vary continuously in value. Table 4–1 lists theories that are compatible or incompatible with generic utility theory in this sense. All of these theories describe preferences for more general classes of gambles than the p-gambles mentioned in table 4–1, but only the representation of p-gambles is relevant to the present discussion.

Obviously, any utility theory that implies the standard model for p-gambles, condition (1), is compatible with generic utility theory. Therefore EU and SEU theory and Karmarkar's (1978) SWU theory are combatible with generic utility theory. Edwards' (1962) ASEU and NASEU models postulate that a single pair of coefficients weight the

Table 4–1. Compatability Between Other Theories and Generic Utility Theory.

Compatible Theories	Functional Form for $U(a, p, x)$, where $1 > p > 0$, and $a \leq_p x$.	Comments
Expected utility (EU)	$pU(a) + (1 - p)U(x)$	1, 2
Additive subjective expected utility (ASEU)	$w(p)U(a) + [c - w(p)]U(x)$	1, 3
Non-additive subjective expected utility (NASEU)	$w_1(p)U(a) + w_2(1 - p)U(x)$	1, 4
Subjectively weighted utility model (SWU)	$w(p)]U(a) + [1 - w(p)]U(x)$	1, 5
Prospect theory	$\pi(p)U(a) + [1 - \pi(p)]U(x)$ if $x \leq_p r$, $[1 - \pi(1 - p)]U(a) + \pi(1 - p)U(x)$ if $r \leq_p a$.	6, 7
Dual bilinear model	$S^-(p)U(a) + [1 - S^-(p)]U(x)$	6, 8
Rank dependent utility	$g(p)U(a) + [1 - g(p)]U(x)$	6, 9

Incompatible Theories		
Weighted utility	$\dfrac{pW(a)U(a) + (1 - p)W(x)U(x)}{pW(a) + (1 - p)W(x)}$	1, 10
Lottery dependent expected utility	$pU(a, c_F) + (1 - p)U(x, c_F)$	1, 11

Comments:
1. The functional form is identical when $a \geq_p x$.
2. Luce and Raiffa (1957), von Neumann and Morgenstern (1944).
3. c is a positive constant, and $c > w(p) > 0$ (Edwards, 1962).
4. $w_1(p) > 0$, $w_2(p) > 0$ (Edwards, 1962).
5. $w(p) = p^\alpha/[p^\alpha + (1 - p)^\alpha]$, for some α (Karmarkar, 1978).
6. The functional form for $U(a, p, x)$ is analogous, but not identical, in the case where where $a \geq_p x$.
7. $1 > \pi(p) > 0$ if $1 > p > 0$ (Kahneman and Tversky, 1979).
8. $1 > S^-(p) > 0$ if $1 > p > 0$ (Luce and Narens 1985; Luce, 1990; Narens and Luce, 1986).
9. $1 > g(p) > 0$ if $1 > p > 0$ (Chew, 1984; Luce, 1988a; Segal, 1984).
10. $W(a)$, $W(x) > 0$ (Chew and MacCrimmon, 1979; Chew, 1983; Fishburn, 1983).
11. $c_F = H(a, p, x)$, for some real-valued function H (Becker and Sarin, 1987; Sarin, to appear).

utilities of outcomes over the full set of p-gambles, but they do not require that the coefficients sum to one. Because the generic utility representation does not require that the coefficients sum to one, these models are also compatible with generic utility theory. As noted above, prospect theory implies that the generic utility representation (2) is satisfied by any triangular set of p-gambles for nongains or for nonlosses. The dual bilinear model (Luce and Narens, 1985; Luce, 1990) and rank dependent utility theory (Chew, 1984; Luce, 1988a; Quiggin, 1982; Segal, 1984; Yaari, 1987) imply that the generic utility representation is satisfied on any triangular set of p-gambles. Unlike prospect theory, these theories do not postulate that the utility representations differ depending on whether gamble outcomes are more or less preferred than a reference level. Recently, Luce (1990, 1992) has formulated a rank and sign dependent utility theory that integrates the distinction between gains and losses into the structure of rank dependent utility theory. Although this theory cannot be discussed here, its relation to generic utility theory is much like that of prospect theory. Rank and sign dependent utility theory implies the generic utility representation (2) with respect to any triangular set of p-gambles with nongain or nonloss outcomes.

Weighted utility theory (Chew and MacCrimmon, 1979; Chew, 1983; Fishburn, 1983) and lottery dependent utility theory (Becker and Sarin, 1987; Sarin, 1992) are two theories that do not imply the generic utility representation (2) except in special cases where these theories reduce to EU theory. I will not demonstrate the incompatibility of weighted utility theory and lottery dependent utility theory with generic utility theory, but the incompatibility is proved by finding utility and weighting functions that satisfy the axioms of these theories, while nevertheless implying violations of the axioms for generic utility theory. Intuitively, the reason these theories are incompatible with generic utility theory is that these theories do not satisfy what Machina (1989) calls replacement separability. A utility theory satisfies replacement separability (with respect to two-outcome gambles) if there exist functions F_1 and F_2 such that $U(a, p, x) = F_1(a, p) + F_2(x, 1 - p)$. Generic utility theory requires replacement separability within a triangular set of p-gambles, whereas weighted utility and lottery dependent utility theories do not.

In summary, a utility theory is compatible with generic utility theory if it implies condition (2) with respect to a triangular set of p-gambles. Empirical or theoretical analyses that are conducted within generic utility theory will be interpretable from the standpoint of any theory that is compatible with generic utility theory. This does not exclude the possibility that analyses in the generic utility framework will be informative from the standpoint of theories that are incompatible with it, but the interpretation from these standpoints will be less straightforward.

Empirical Application of Generic Utility Theory

Next, a generic utility analysis of a MAUT model will be presented to show concretely why such analyses are interpretable from diverse theoretical standpoints. The topic of this analysis, the utility of survival duration and health quality, is of importance and independent interest in the decision analysis of medical therapy selection (Loomes and McKenzie, 1989; McNeil and Pauker, 1982; Miyamoto and Eraker, 1985; Weinstein et al., 1980). Suppose that (Y, Q) denotes a health outcome consisting of Y years of survival in health state Q, followed by death at the end of the Y-th year. The health state, Q, is assumed to be approximately constant during the Y years of survival. The problem investigated here is that of determining the form of the joint utility function $U(Y, Q)$. This is a special case of the problem of determining the utility of time streams of health states. A time stream of health states is a sequence, $(Q_1, Q_2, Q_3. \ldots)$, where each Q_i represents the health quality during the i-th time period. The problem of time streams will not be discussed here (compare Stevenson, 1986; Pliskin, Shepard, and Weinstein, 1980; Mehrez and Gafni, 1989).

Pliskin et al. (1980) formalized various health utility models, including multiplicative and additive models for the combination of duration and quality.[4] The utility of Y and Q is multiplicative if there exist utility scales for duration and quality, denoted F and G, respectively, such that

$$U(Y, Q) = F(Y) \cdot G(Q), \tag{6}$$

for every Y and Q. The utility of Y and Q is additive if there exist utility scales for duration and quality, denoted F' and G', respectively, such that

$$U(Y, Q) = F'(Y) + G'(Q), \tag{7}$$

for every Y and Q. It is well known that if EU theory is satisfied and the attributes Y and Q are mutually utility independent, then the bivariate utility function $U(Y, Q)$ must be multiplicative or additive (Keeney and Raiffa, 1976). Assuming EU theory, the additive model can be distinguished from the multiplicative model by the fact that the additive model implies the marginality property: It implies that gambles with identical marginal probability distributions over attributes are equal in preference (Fishburn, 1965). Thus, gambles A and B should be equally preferred if the utility model is additive and EU theory is valid.

Gamble A   *Gamble B*
50% chance, 25 years, pain   50% chance, 25 years, no pain
50% chance, 3 years, no pain   50% chance, 3 years, pain

Pliskin et al. pointed out that Gamble B is usually preferred to Gamble A and concluded that the additive utility model must be rejected. The multiplicative model is consistent with violations of marginality. Therefore, Pliskin et al. proposed that the utility of duration and quality is described by a multiplicative model, basing their hypothesis on the assumptions that EU theory is valid, that duration and quality are mutually utility independent, and that marginality is violated. They did not test empirically whether mutual utility independence was satisfied.

Working within the generic utility framework, Miyamoto and Eraker (1988) proposed an alternative formalization of the multiplicative model. They noted that survival duration and quality appear to be sign dependent attributes in the sense of Krantz et al. (1971). The concept of sign dependence is illustrated by the following examples. One generally prefers longer survival to shorter survival, but if the health state is exceptionally bad, one prefers shorter survival to longer survival. Exceptionally bad quality inverts the normal preference order over survival duration as if $G(Q) < 0$ for some Q, and $U(Y, Q) = F(Y) \cdot G(Q)$. Another significant fact is that one normally prefers good health to poor health, for example, 2 years in good health is preferred to 2 years in poor health, but one has no preference between 0 years in good health and 0 years in poor health. Thus, immediate death nullifies the preference order over health quality, as if $F(0) = 0$, and $U(0, Q) = F(0) \cdot G(Q) = 0$ for any choice of Q. The sign dependence of survival duration and health quality is diagnostic of a multiplicative utility model, but it is not sufficient for it. Miyamoto (1985) and Miyamoto and Eraker (1988) formulated an axiomatization of the multiplicative health utility model within the generic utility framework. The discussion of the axiomatization will be more straightforward if we only consider health states that are better than death. The utility analysis of worse-than-death health states involves complications that are irrelevant to our present purpose, which is to exemplify the generic approach to utility modeling. In presenting a generic utility formalization, we must choose whether to state axioms in terms of an upper or lower triangular set of p-gambles. As either choice is equally useful, I will arbitrarily choose to develop the axiomatization in terms of an upper triangular set.

Assuming, then, that the health states under investigation are all better than death and that the axioms for the generic utility representation are valid, one first postulates that survival duration is utility independent from health quality in the sense that preferences among gambles for survival duration are the same for any fixed choice of health quality. The following definition states the utility independence property within the generic utility framework:

DEFINITION 1. Suppose that the set of consequences, C, is the Cartesian product of a set of survival durations, D, and a set of health states, S, in other words, $C = D \times S$. Then, *survival duration is utility independent from health quality* iff the following equivalence holds: For every Y_1, Y_2, Y_3, $Y_4 \in D$ and Q_1, $Q_2 \in S$,

$$[(Y_1, Q_1), p, (Y_2, Q_1)] \geq_p [(Y_3, Q_1), p, (Y_4, Q_1)]$$
$$\text{iff}$$
$$[(Y_1, Q_2), p, (Y_2, Q_2)] \geq_p [(Y_3, Q_2), p, (Y_4, Q_2)]. \qquad (8)$$

whenever $(Y_2, Q_1) \geq_p (Y_1, Q_1)$, $(Y_4, Q_1) \geq_p (Y_3, Q_1)$, $(Y_2, Q_2) \geq_p (Y_1, Q_2)$, and $(Y_4, Q_2) \geq_p (Y_3, Q_2)$.

Definition 1 differs from the standard EU formulation of utility independence (Keeney and Raiffa, 1976) only insofar as it stipulates that all of the gambles in the independence relation must be members of an upper triangular set. Definition 1 is strictly weaker than the standard EU formulation of utility independence because the latter claims that the property is satisfied by all p-gambles, or by all gambles generally, depending on the formulation. The utility independence of health quality from survival duration is defined analogously to Definition 1 with the role of survival duration and health quality interchanged.

Just as in EU theory, generic utility theory implies that if survival duration and health quality are each utility independent from the other, then the joint utility function $U(Y, Q)$ is either multiplicative or additive (Miyamoto, 1988). In the present case, however, we do not need to postulate the utility independence of health quality from survival duration because the sign dependence relations between duration and quality are sufficient (in combination with the utility independence of duration from quality) to establish the validity of the multiplicative model. In particular, I adopt the assumption that immediate death nullifies the preference ordering over health quality; stated formally,

$$(0, Q_1) \sim_p (0, Q_2) \qquad (9)$$

for every Q_1, $Q_2 \in S$. Miyamoto (1985) proved the following theorem:

THEOREM 1. Suppose that the set of consequences, C, is the Cartesian product of a set of survival durations, D, and a set of health states, S; suppose that $R(p)$ is a triangular set of p-gambles with outcomes in C; suppose that $\geq_p$ is a relation on $R(p)$; and suppose that the structure $(C, p, R(p), \geq_p)$ satisfies the axioms for the generic utility representation (Appendix 1). If survival duration is utility independent from health quality (Definition 1), and if immediate death nullifies the preference order over health quality (equation (9)), then there exist scales U, F and G such that U preserves the preference order in the sense of equation (2), and

$$U(Y, Q) = F(Y) \cdot G(Q)$$

for every $Y \in D$ and $Q \in S$.

Theorem 1 is proved in Appendix 2. An interesting technical point regarding the assumptions of Theorem 1 is that the set of health states is allowed to be finite. The theorem applies even if there are only two health states in the set S. The assumptions of generic utility theory require that the set of consequences $C = D \times S$ be infinite, but this is satisfied because the set of possible survival durations is infinite.[5] From a practical standpoint, it is easier to test an axiomatization if the test does not require large numbers of different health qualities because it is time consuming to explain a large variety of health qualities to subjects. The present axiomatization allows us to restrict attention to a small set, S, of health states. Of course, even if the aximoatization is empirically supported with respect to the health states in S, it may be violated by preferences for health states that are not in S. In this case, the multiplicative model would have valid for the health states in S, but not for states outside of S.

Miyamoto and Eraker (1988) assumed that condition (9) was introspectively obvious and undertook to test the utility independence of survival duration from health quality in a sample of medical patients. Subjects were inpatients at the Ann Arbor VA Medical Center and the University of Michigan Hospital. Subjects included patients with cancer, heart disease, diabetes, arthritis, and other serious ailments. Each subject was asked to compare two health states, referred to as *survival with current symptoms* and *survival free from current symptoms*. "Current symptoms" was defined to be health symptoms at the severity and frequency experienced by the subject during the month preceding the interview. "Freedom from current symptoms" was simply survival without the health problems that comprised current symptoms. To be a subject in the experiment, a patient had to satisfy two criteria. First, it was required that subjects preferred twenty-four years of survival without current symptoms to twenty-five years of survival with current symptoms. Subjects who preferred twenty-five years of survival with current symptoms to twenty-four years without the symptoms were not included in the sample. Willingness to give up at least one year out of twenty-five in order to be free from their symptoms constituted an operational criterion for the claim that subjects regarded their health symptoms as severe. Second, it was required that every subject always preferred additional survival, up to twenty-five years, even if current symptoms prevailed. Thus, subjects were chosen who satisfied the assumption that the health states under investigation were better than death. Although utility modeling in the domain of health must ultimately analyze the impact of worse-than-death health states, this issue was avoided in the present study.

The main issue in the experiment was whether the certainty equivalents of gambles for survival duration would differ for survival with or without current symptoms. All gambles used as stimuli were even-chance gambles between a shorter and longer duration of survival. Hence, the stimulus gambles were drawn from an upper triangular set. In order to interpret data from the standpoint of prospect theory, each subject was asked to state his or her own reference level for survival duration. The concept of a reference level was explained to the subject as follow:

> I'm going to ask you about something called the aspiration level for survival. Since this concept is fairly complicated, I'll explain it in several steps. The aspiration level for survival is defined to be the length of survival that marks the boundary between those survivals that you regard as a loss and those survivals that you regard as a gain.
>
> For example, my own aspiration level for survival is about the age of sixty. This means that if I found out that I were going to live to the age of fifty or fifty-five (but no more), I would regard this as something of a loss. If I found out that I were going to live to sixty-five or seventy, I would regard this as something of a gain. The aspiration level for survival is not the same as my life expectancy, since my life expectancy is greater than sixty. It's also not the length of time I would want to live, since if I were in good health, I would want to live at least to eighty. The age of sixty is simply a target that marks the boundary between survivals that I would regard to some degree as a loss and survivals that I would regard to some degree as a gain.

I should mention that there's nothing special about the age of sixty. Some individuals place their aspiration level at a very large number, like ninety. For such a person, any survival less than the age of ninety would be regarded to some degree as a loss. I've also encountered individuals who set their aspiration level for survival at their present age. This does not mean that they no longer want to live. It means that they regard every year of survival as a gain. If such an individual learned that he had two years to live, he would regard this as gaining two years of survival, rather than to emphasize some longer survival of which he's being deprived.

Does this concept of an aspiration level of survival make sense to you? Can you tell me what your own aspiration level for survival is?

Subjects generally found these instructions meaningful, and would state a reference level without appearing to be confused.

The stimulus gambles in the experiment were even-chance gambles (p-gambles with $p = 0.5$) for which the second outcome was always greater than the first. Thus, the stimulus gambles were drawn from an upper triangular set of 0.5-gambles. The outcomes in the stimulus gambles ranged from zero years (immediate death) to a maximum of twenty-four years. A complete description of the stimulus gambles is given in Miyamoto and Eraker (1988). Each subject judged the certainty equivalents of six gambles for survival duration. The judgments were elicited in a block under the assumption that survival was accompanied by current symptoms, and in a second block under the assumption that survival was free from current symptoms. The relative order of the two blocks was counterbalanced across subjects. The two blocks of judgments were replicated on a second day with the health qualities associated with the blocks in the same order on the second day as on the first day. Thus, the experimental design within each subject was a 6×2 ANOVA in which the factors were gamble (6 levels) and health state (2 levels); there were two replications per cell in the ANOVA.

Earlier, I pointed out that prospect theory implies that the generic utility representation is satisfied by a triangular set of gambles, if every outcome is at least as preferred as the reference level, or if every outcome is equal or less preferred than the reference level. Assuming that self-reported reference levels were valid, we can determine whether a subject's reference level satisfied this requirement relative to the stimulus gambles of the experiment. The shortest duration in any stimulus gamble was zero years, and the longest duration was twenty-four years. For any subject whose reference level was his present age, the stimulus gambles were drawn from an upper triangular set of nonloss gambles, like the set

G2 in figure 4–2. For any subject whose reference level was equal or greater than present age plus twenty-four years, the stimulus gambles were drawn from an upper triangular set of nongain gambles, like the set G4 of figure 4–2. Subjects who fell into these two classes will be called *purely irregular subjects* because every stimulus gamble was irregular relative to their reference levels.[6] Prospect theory predicts that the preferences of purely irregular subjects satisfy generic utility theory. Hence, if the utility independence of survival duration from health quality is tested in the preferences of purely irregular subjects, the results of the test are interpretable from the standpoint of prospect theory, as well as from other theoretical standpoints.

There were twenty-seven subjects, seventeen of whom were purely irregular. From the standpoint of prospect theory, the analysis of the response of subjects who were not purely irregular is extremely complicated. For these subjects different, stimulus gambles were regular or irregular, depending on the value of the subject's reference level, and different analyses would be required for the regular and irregular gambles; furthermore, the division of gambles into regular and irregular gambles differed from subject to subject because subjects differed in their reference levels. Because of these complications, results will be presented only for the seventeen purely irregular subjects. A more comprehensive analysis of the data for all twenty-seven subjects is presented in Miyamoto and Eraker (1988). Among the seventeen purely irregular subjects, three subjects set the reference level at their present ages; these subjects will be referred to as low reference level subjects. Fourteen subjects set the reference level at a point equal or beyond present age plus twenty-four years; these subjects will be referred to as high reference level subjects. Descriptive statistics are presented in Table 2 for low and high reference level subjects, and for the two groups combined.

For simplicity, the condition where survivals were assumed to be accompanied by current symptoms will be called the "poor health" condition, and the condition where survivals were assumed to be free from current symptoms will be called the "good health" condition. The expressions "good health" and "poor health" were not used to designate these conditions when discussing them with subjects. The dependent measure, the certainty equivalents of gambles, was transformed prior to statistical analysis. To define the transformation, let CE denote the judged certainty equivalent of a gamble between a shorter duration (LOW) and a longer duration (HIGH). The assumed health state could be either poor health or good health. The transformed response, denoted PE, was computed by the rule,

Table 4–2. Descriptive Statistics for the Purely Irregular Subjects.

	Low Ref. Level n = 3		High Ref. Level n = 14		All Subjects n = 17	
	Mean	SD	Mean	SD	Mean	SD
Age	29.7	5.0	32.4	6.1	31.9	5.9
Ref. Level	29.7	5.0	66.9	6.7	60.3	15.9
Proportional Equivalents						
Good Health	0.53	0.02	0.55	0.20	0.54	0.18
Poor Health	0.63	0.18	0.56	0.21	0.57	0.21

$$PE = \frac{CE - LOW}{HIGH - LOW}. \tag{10}$$

Note that HIGH—LOW represents the range of the stimulus gamble. Therefore the transformed response represents the proportion of the range of the gamble that was exceeded by the certainty equivalent. The transformed response will be referred to as a proportional equivalent. There are two main advantages to using proportional equivalents in the analysis. First, the variance of a certainty equivalence judgment generally increases as the range of the stimulus gamble increases. Transformation of certainty equivalents to proportional equivalents tends to equalize the variance within different cells of the ANOVA. Second, mean proportional equivalents are more easily interpreted than mean certainty equivalents. For example, if the mean proportional equivalent were found to be 0.55, one may infer that the average certainty equivalent was slightly greater than the expected value of the gamble, but if the mean certainty equivalent were found to be 12.3 years, the result could not be interpreted without examining the specific durations that were used in the stimulus gambles. Table 4–2 contains the mean proportional equivalents in the good health and poor health conditions. On the average, subjects were close to being risk neutral, with a slight (nonsignificant) tendency to be risk seeking.

The utility independence of survival duration from health quality predicts that mean certainty equivalents in the good health condition should equal mean certainty equivalents in the poor health condition. Furthermore, there should be no interaction between the good health/ poor health distinction and the specific gamble being tested because equality in certainty equivalents is predicted to hold for each gamble individually. Since proportional equivalents are linearly related to certainty equivalents, utility independence implies the same predictions for proportional equivalents. In other words, if utility independence is satisfied, the ANOVA performed on proportional equivalents should have no main effect of health quality and no interaction between survival duration and health quality. Of course, some significant effects should be observed even if utility independence is satisfied because false rejections of null hypotheses (Type I errors) are a necessary consequence of random variation in judgments. Nevertheless, such rejections should not occur more frequently than the significance level of the test, nor should there be a qualitative pattern to such rejections.

A two-factor ANOVA was computed within the data of each subject. Five of the seventeen subjects had significant ($p < 0.05$) main effects for health state. If the null hypothesis for the main effect were true in all seventeen tests, the chance of five or more rejections would be less than 0.005 (computed as 1 minus the cumulative binomial probability of 4 or fewer rejections given 17 independent chances for rejecting at the 0.05 level). Therefore the observed number of significant main effects was inconsistent with utility independence. One subject had a significant ($p < 0.01$) interaction between health quality and gamble. If the true chance of rejecting the null hypothesis for interaction were 0.01, the chance of 1 or more rejections would be greater than 0.15. Therefore the observed number of significant rejections of the interaction hypothesis was compatible with utility independence. Figure 4–3 shows a scatter plot of mean proportional equivalents in the good health versus poor health conditions. Plus signs indicate subjects whose mean proportional equivalents were significantly different in the good health and poor health conditions. Asterisks indicate subjects whose mean proportional equivalents were not significantly different. The scatter plot indicates that the mean proportional equivalents of most subjects were close to equality in the two conditions. Even among subjects who significantly violated utility independence, the change in certainty equivalents as a function of assumed health state was generally smaller than 20 percent of the range in the gambles. Miyamoto and Eraker (1988) carried out an extensive power analysis of the test of utility independence. They found that the tests of the main effect of health quality were sufficiently strong to detect true effects that were greater than ± 0.10, but true effects smaller than ± 0.05 would have been difficult to detect in this experiment.

We may conclude from this analysis that at least some subjects violated utility independence of survival duration from health quality, but the departures were generally small; the majority of subjects were close

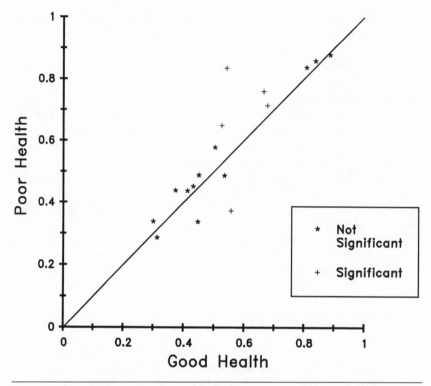

Figure 4-3. Scatter plot of mean proportional equivalents in the good health and poor health conditions.

to the predicted equality between good and poor health conditions. Assuming that generic utility theory is valid, and that immediate death nullifies the preference order over health quality, we may conclude that the preferences of most subjects satisfy a multiplicative utility model with respect to survival with and without current symptoms. Furthermore, the multiplicative utility model appears to be a good approximation even where it was violated.

The key issue in this discussion is not the validity of the multiplicative utility model per se, rather the purpose of this exercise is to illustrate the methodology of utility modeling within the generic utility framework. The stimulus gambles were selected from a triangular set of even-chance gambles. In addition, a subset of subjects was identified for whom every stimulus gamble was an irregular gamble relative to their reference levels.

Given these design characteristics, prospect theory predicts that the generic utility representation must be satisfied with respect to the stimulus gambles of the experiment. Therefore, the preceding interpretation of experimental results remains the same if generic utility theory is replaced by prospect theory as the theoretical framework of the analysis. The interpretation also remains the same in the framework of other theories that imply generic utility theory, for example, from the standpoint of EU and SEU theory, the dual bilinear model, rank-dependent utility theory, Karmarkar's SWU theory, and Edwards' ASEU and NASEU theories. Because these theories are compatible with generic utility theory, the preference assumptions stated in Theorem 1 continue to imply the multiplicative utility model, if generic utility theory is replaced by one of these stronger theories, and hence, the experimental test of utility independence has the same implications for health utility structure in the framework of these stronger theories. In this sense, the experimental analysis presented here is a generic analysis of a utility model, for its interpretation remains the same from diverse theoretical perspectives.

MAUT in a Generic Framework

It is not hard to show that additive, multiplicative, and multilinear utility models of arbitrarily many attributes can be axiomatized within the generic utility framework. Miyamoto (1988) axiomatized the additive and multiplicative utility models in the two-attribute case, and the generalizations to arbitrarily many attributes is straightforward. Log/power utility functions and linear/exponential utility functions can also be axiomatized within the generic utility framework, and experimental tests of these axiomatizations are also straightforward (Miyamoto, 1988; Miyamoto and Eraker, 1989). For the sake of brevity, these axiomatizations will not be stated here, but they follow the pattern displayed in Definition 1— standard MAUT assumptions are restricted to the preference order over a triangular set of p-gambles, and the implications of these assumptions are found to be the same in the generic utility framework as in the EU framework. The only exception to this claim is the axiomatization of the additive utility model. The marginality assumption that is used to axiomatize the additive model in the EU framework cannot be translated into the generic utility framework because its implications are derived under the assumption that the utilities of outcomes are weighted by the stated probabilities in a gamble, and generic utility theory allows this assumption to be violated. Miyamoto (1988) discovered a simple, testable axiomatization of the additive model in the generic utility framework, but this axiomatization will not be presented here.

The methodology for testing axiomatizations of utility models in the generic utility framework is generally like the experimental example presented here (Miyamoto, 1988; Miyamoto and Eraker, 1988, 1989). One formulates the appropriate independence assumptions in terms of a triangular set of p-gambles, and tests of these assumptions can be interpreted from the standpoint of any theory that implies the generic utility representation. If one intends to interpret results from the standpoint of prospect theory, one must employ some procedure for identifying reference levels. The results for purely irregular subjects are interpretable within prospect theory as well as within other theories that imply generic utility theory.

Although *testing* utility models is no more difficult in the generic utility framework than in the framework of EU theory, it should be pointed out that *scaling* utility functions for the given outcome domain is actually more complicated in the generic utility framework. Whereas EU theory postulates that $U(a, p, x) = pU(a) + (1 - p)U(x)$, where p and $1 - p$ are known because they are simply the stated probabilities of the outcomes, generic utility theory postulates that $U(a, p, x) = \alpha U(a) + \beta U(x)$, where α and β are unknown positive weights. Empirical scaling of utility functions is simpler in the EU framework because p and $1 - p$ are assumed to weight the utility of outcomes. Scaling utility functions in the generic utility framework will require the estimation of α and β for each individual.

Conclusions

At the outset of this chapter, it was stated that a major goal was to show that risk-based methods of MAUT modeling are not seriously undermined by the discovery of strong evidence against the descriptive validity of EU and SEU theory. It should now be clear why this is the case. Risk-based methods of MAUT modeling can be logically justified on much weaker assumptions than those of EU and SEU theory, and in particular, they can be justified under the assumptions of generic utility theory. In other words, axioms that imply specific utility models under EU or SEU assumptions imply these same classes of models under the assumptions of generic utility theory (Miyamoto, 1988). The only exception to this claim is Fishburn's (1965) characterization of the additive utility model in terms of marginal probability distributions, but the additive utility model has an alternative, easily tested axiomatization within the generic utility framework (Miyamoto, 1988). Therefore risk-based MAUT methods, which use axioms as diagnostic criteria for utility models in specific domains, can continue to be applied to descriptive modeling with only minor modifications in the implementation of these methods.

Generic utility theory is a useful framework for utility modeling because it is compatible with important non-EU theories that have been proposed as revisions or replacements of EU and SEU theory. Formalizations and empirical tests of utility models within generic utility theory are interpretable from the standpoint of stronger theories, which may not even be consistent with each other. Clearly, this is an advantage when one's primary interest is to determine the structure of utility within a specific domain, rather than to discover which fundamental theory is valid. As I have tried to stress, generic utility theory is a framework for utility modeling; it is not intended as a general foundation for preference under risk. Indeed, the very limitations that make it a useful tool for utility modeling also render it utterly inadequate as a general foundation. It is hoped that generic utility theory will stimulate useful investigations of empirical utility structures even while fundamental theoretical issues continue to be debated.

The formalization of MAUT models within the generic utility framework demonstrates that risk-based approaches to utility modeling can be imported into prospect theory, the dual bilinear model, and rank dependent utility theories (Miyamoto, 1988). This result is of independent importance, for it has not previously been shown how to develop MAUT axiomatizations in these theoretical frameworks. Especially in view of the current interest in non-EU theory development, it is reassuring to know that risk-based MAUT methods can be incorporated into such theories without extensive revision. We see here a third advantage of generic utility theory—any axiomatization that is developed within the generic utility framework automatically transfers to stronger theories that imply it. Thus, if one wants to determine whether a descriptive theory allows the risk-based formalization of standard MAUT models, one can check whether it implies the generic utility representation on a triangular set of p-gambles. An affirmative determination establishes that risk-based MAUT formalizations can be developed within the theory. A negative determination does not exclude the possibility that risk-based MAUT formalizations can be developed within the theory, but the methodology described here will not apply.

Acknowledgments

I would like to thank Ward Edwards, Earl Hunt, Irving LaValle, and Leigh Thompson for helpful comments on an earlier draft of this chapter. Conversations with Colin Camerer and Peter Wakker improved my understanding of current work in utility theory. Of course, I am solely responsible for inadequacies of the present investigations.

Appendix 1: Axiomatization of Generic Utility Theory and the Representation and Uniqueness Theorem

Let C be a nonempty set of consequences; let $R(p)$ denote a set of p-gambles with outcomes in C. Let $\geq_p$ denote the preference relation, defined on outcomes in C and also on gambles in $R(p)$. The axiomatization of generic utility theory will be stated in terms of an upper triangular set. The axiomatization presented here is similar to an axiomatization developed in Miyamoto (1988), but the present treatment is more explicit and transparent. Both the present axiomatization and Miyamoto (1988) are heavily influenced by Krantz et al. (1971, Chapter 6). Wakker (1989) independently proved a utility representation theorem that includes the generic utility representation as a special case.

Axiom 1 asserts that $\geq_p$ is a connected, transitive ordering of C. Axiom 2 asserts that $\geq_p$ is also a connected, transitive ordering of $R(p)$. (Remember that I am not distinguishing notationally between the preference order on C and the preference order on $R(p)$). Axiom 3 asserts that $R(p)$ is an upper triangular set.

AXIOM 1. For every $a, x \in C$, $a \geq_p x$ or $x \geq_p a$. For every $x, y, z \in C$, if $x \geq_p y$ and $y \geq_p z$, then $x \geq_p z$.

AXIOM 2. For every $(a, p, x), (b, p, y) \in R(p)$, either $(a, p, x) \geq_p (b, p, y)$ or $(b, p, y) \geq_p (a, p, x)$. For every $(a, p, x), (b, p, y), (c, p, z) \in R(p)$, if $(a, p, x) \geq_p (b, p, y)$ and $(b, p, y) \geq_p (c, p, z)$, then $(a, p, x) \geq_p (c, p, z)$.

AXIOM 3. For every $a, x \in C$, $(a, p, x) \in R(p)$ iff $x \geq_p a$.

The next axiom asserts that preferences for p-gambles satisfy first-order stochastic dominance with respect to the riskless preference order over C.

AXIOM 4. For any $a, b, c, d \in C$,

$$b \geq_p c \geq_p a \quad \text{iff} \quad (a, p, b) \geq_p (a, p, c), \tag{11}$$

and

$$d \geq_p b \geq_p c \quad \text{iff} \quad (b, p, d) \geq_p (c, p, d). \tag{12}$$

Axiom 4 implies that the orderings over the first and second components are mutually independent, and monotonically increasing with respect to each other. It should be noted that Axiom 4 is a strictly weaker condition than the independence axiom of expected utility theory which asserts that conditions (11) and (12) hold when a, b, c, and d can be either *lotteries* or consequences (Machina, 1989).

The next axiom is the Thomsen condition of additive conjoint measurement.

AXIOM 5. Let a, b, c, x, y, $z \in C$ be any elements satisfying $a \leqslant_p x$, $b \leqslant_p y$, $b \leqslant_p z$, $c \leqslant_p x$, $a \leqslant_p z$, and $c \leqslant_p y$. If $(a, p, x) \sim_p (b, p, y)$, and $(b, p, z) \sim_p (c, p, x)$, then $(a, p, z) \sim_p (c, p, y)$.

Next I will formulate an Archimedean axiom (Krantz et al., 1971).

DEFINITION 2. Let N be any set of consecutive integers (positive or negative, finite or infinite). A set $\{a_i \in C : i \in N\}$ is said to be *a standard sequence on the first component* if there exist x, $y \in C$ such that $x \not\sim_p y$, for every $i \in N$, we have $a_i \leqslant_p x$ and $a_i \leqslant_p y$, and for every i, $i + 1 \in N$, $(a_i, p, x) \sim_p (a_{i+1}, p, y)$. A standard sequence on the first component is said to be bounded if there exist u, v, $z \in C$ such that $u \leqslant_p z$, $v \leqslant_p z$, $a_i \leqslant_p z$, and $(u, p, z) \geqslant_p (a_i, p, z) \geqslant_p (v, p, z)$ for every $i \in N$. The definitions of *a standard sequence on the second component* and *a bounded standard sequence on the second component* are perfectly analogous. A standard sequence is said to be finite if N contains finitely many integers.

AXIOM 6. Every bounded standard sequence on their component is finite.

The next axiom is a qualitative condition that guarantees that the utility scales for the first and second components are linear with respect to each other. An analogous assumption is required in the axiomatization of the standard model for p-gambles (see Krantz et al., 1971, Chapter 6, Theorem 15).

AXIOM 7. Suppose that a, b, c, x, $y \in C$ and $a \leqslant_p w$, $b \leqslant_p x$, $b \leqslant_p w$, $c \leqslant_p x$, $y \leqslant_p a$, $z \leqslant_p b$, $y \leqslant_p b$, $z \leqslant_p c$. If $(a, p, w) \sim_p (b, p, x)$, $(b, p, w) \sim_p (c, p, x)$, and $(y, p, a) \sim_p (z, p, b)$, then $(y, p, b) \sim_p (z, p, c)$. If $(y, p, a) \sim_p (z, p, b)$, $(y, p, b) \sim_p (z, p, c)$, and $(a, p, w) \sim_p (b, p, x)$, then $(b, p, w) \sim_p (c, p, x)$.

Finally, we will require some existential assumptions. Axiom 8 is the restricted solvability assumption of additive conjoint measurement (Krantz et al., 1971, ch. 6) stated in terms of the gambles in $R(p)$. Axiom

9 asserts that the riskless preference order is not trivial. Axiom 10 asserts that there are no empty gaps in the preference ordering over outcomes.

AXIOM 8. For any a, b, c, x, $y \in C$, if $a \leqslant_p x$, $b \leqslant_p y$, and $c \leqslant_p x$ and $(a, p, x) \geqslant_p (b, p, y) \geqslant_p (c, p, x)$, then there exists $d \in C$ such that $d \leqslant_p x$ and $(d, p, x) \sim_p (b, p, y)$. For any a, b, x, y, $z \in C$, if $a \leqslant_p x$, $b \leqslant_p y$, and $a \leqslant_p z$ and $(a, p, x) \leqslant_p (b, p, y) \leqslant_p (a, p, z)$, then there exists $w \in C$ such that $a \leqslant_p w$ and $(a, p, w) \sim_p (b, p, y)$.

AXIOM 9. There exist x, $y \in C$ such that $x >_p y$.

AXIOM 10. If x, $y \in C$ and $x >_p y$, then there exists z such that $x >_p z >_p y$.

The following theorem asserts the existence of the generic utility representation and the interval-scale uniqueness of the utility scale.

THEOREM 2. (*Representation and Uniqueness Theorem for the Generic Utility Representation*): Let C be a nonempty set of consequences; let $R(\mathrm{p})$ denote a set of p-gambles with outcomes in C; let $\geqslant_p$ denote a relation on C and $R(p)$. If Axioms 1 to 10 are satisfied, then there exists a function $U: C \to$ Reals, and positive constants, α and β, such that

$$(a, p, x) \geqslant_p (b, p, y) \text{ iff } \alpha U(a) + \beta U(x) \geqslant \alpha U(b) + \beta U(y) \quad (13)$$

for every (a, p, x), $(b, p, y) \in R(p)$. Moreover if U', α' and β' are any other function and constants that satisfy (13), then there exist λ, τ, $\gamma \in Re$ such that λ, $\gamma > 0$, $U' = \lambda U + \tau$, $\alpha' = \gamma \alpha$, and $\beta' = \gamma \beta$. In other words, U is an interval scale.

PROOF. The proof consists in showing that Axioms 1 to 10 imply the axioms for a lower triangular additive structure defined in Miyamoto (1988). I will only sketch the proof. The following presentation assumes that the reader is familiar with Definition 7 and Theorem 1 of Miyamoto (1988).

Let juxtaposed symbols denote ordered pairs of elements in $C \times C$, that is, $ax \in C \times C$ is a typical element. Define an ordering, $\geqslant_g$, of $C \times C$ by

$$ax \geqslant_g by \text{ iff } (x, p, a), (y, p, b) \in R(p) \text{ and } (x, p, a) \geqslant_p (y, p, b). \quad (14)$$

The reason that the ordering of elements is inverted in the correspondence of ax to (x, p, a) is that the present axiomatization is formulated in terms of an upper triangular set of p-gambles, and the axiomatization in Miyamoto (1988) was formulated in terms of a lower triangular set. Obviously this difference is substantively unimportant because either formalization can be transformed into the other by a change of notation.

Axiom 4 and (14) imply that

$$a \geq_p x \text{ iff } (a, p, a) \geq_p (x, p, x) \text{ iff } aa \geq_g xx \tag{15}$$

Define $P \subseteq C \times C$ by $ax \in P$ iff $(x, p, a) \in R(p)$. By Axioms 3 and 4 and condition (15), $ax \in P$ iff $aa \geq_g xx$, which is the defining characteristic of the set P in Definition 7 of Miyamoto (1988); therefore, we may identify the set P defined here with the set P defined in Definition 7 of Miyamoto (1988). Let $M1 - M10$ denote the 10 axioms stated in Definition 7 of Miyamoto (1988). I claim that $(C, \geq_g)$ satisfies $M1 - M10$.

The following implications are obvious, given that conditions (14) and (15) are satisfied. Axiom $M1$ is implied by Axiom 1. Axiom $M2$ is implied by Axioms 2 and 3. Axiom $M3$ is implied by Axiom 2. Axiom $M4$ is implied by Axiom 4. Axiom $M5$ is implied by Axiom 5. Axiom $M6$ is implied by Axiom 7. Axiom $M7$ is implied by Axiom 6. Axiom $M8$ is implied by Axioms 4, 8 and 9. Axiom $M9$ is implied by Axioms 4 and 9. Axiom $M10$ is implied by Axiom 7; therefore, $(C, \geq_g)$ satisfies the axioms of Definition 7 in Miyamoto (1988). By Theorem 1 of Miyamoto (1988) there exists a function $\phi : C \to \text{Reals}$ and a constant $\lambda > 0$ such that

$$xa \geq_g yb \text{ iff } \phi(x) + \lambda\phi(a) \geq \phi(y) + \lambda\phi(b) \tag{16}$$

for every $a, b, x, y \in C$ such that $xa, yb \in P$. Define $U = \phi$ and $\alpha = \beta\lambda$ for some $\beta > 0$. Then, for any $(a, p, x), (b, p, y) \in R(p)$,

$$
\begin{aligned}
(a, p, x) \geq_p (b, p, y) \quad &\text{iff} \quad xa \geq_g yb && \text{by (14)} \\
&\text{iff} \quad \phi(x) + \lambda\phi(a) \geq \phi(y) + \lambda\phi(b) && \text{by (16)} \\
&\text{iff} \quad \alpha U(a) + \beta U(x) \geq \alpha U(b) + \beta U(y).
\end{aligned}
$$

Therefore the generic utility representation, condition (13), is satisfied. The uniqueness of U, α and β follows from the uniqueness result in Theorem 1 of Miyamoto (1988). **Q.E.D.**

Appendix 2: Proof of Theorem 1

The following proof of Theorem 1 is due to Miyamoto (1985). Conditions (8) and (9) are the hypotheses of Theorem 1. I must show that the multiplicative model, equation (6), is satisfied. Choose an arbitrary $Q_0 \in S$, and define a function $J : D \to \text{Reals}$ by $J(Y) = U(Y, Q_0)$. Because duration is utility independent of quality, J is linearly related to utility at any other fixed quality, that is,

$$U(Y, Q) = G(Q) \cdot J(Y) + H(Q) \tag{17}$$

for some real valued functions, G and H. Therefore

$$
\begin{aligned}
J(0) &= U(0, Q_0) = U(0, Q) && \text{by (9)}\\
&= G(Q) \cdot J(0) + H(Q). && \text{by (17)}
\end{aligned}
$$

Therefore $H(Q) = J(0) - G(Q) \cdot J(0)$. Substituting for $H(Q)$ in (17) yields

$$
\begin{aligned}
U(Y, Q) &= G(Q) \cdot J(Y) + J(0) - G(Q) \cdot J(0)\\
&= F(Y) \cdot G(Q) + J(0),
\end{aligned}
$$

where $F(Y) = J(Y) - J(0)$. Rescaling U by subtracting $J(0)$ yields the multiplicative model, equation (6). **Q.E.D.**

Notes

1. More precisely, the necessary assumptions of generic utility theory are implied by the stronger theories listed in the text. The (nonnecessary) existential assumptions are not implied by these theories, but they are very plausible in the context of these stronger theories. See the remarks on prospect theory for further discussion of this point.

2. Kahneman and Tversky's (1979) statement of prospect theory did not specify what rule governed the case described in equation (5), but equation (5) is implied by the 1979 theory, if one also assumes that (x, p, y) and $(y, 1 - p, x)$ are equally preferred (compare, Miyamoto, 1987). As this assumption is consistent with the spirit of Kahneman and Tversky's analysis, I treat it here as part of prospect theory.

3. This statement may concede too much. Depending on how one axiomatizes prospect theory, the existential axioms of prospect theory would imply Axioms 8 and 9 of generic utility theory. Only Axiom 10 is not ordinarily assumed in prospect theory, although it is quite plausible from that standpoint.

4. The notation used by Pliskin et al. (1980) for the multiplicative model was more complicated than the notation adopted here.

5. There are infinitely many possible survival durations; they are not claimed to be infinitely long or arbitrarily long.

6. Note that the definition of purely irregular subjects motivates the terminological alteration of prospect theory according to which (x, p, y) is classified as irregular if $x = r$ or $y = r$. The key idea is that prospect theory claims that a purely irregular subject evaluates every stimulus gamble by a single rule. If we had not altered the classification of irregular gambles in prospect theory, we would be forced to define "purely irregular" subjects in terms of both regular and irregular gambles, and the present discussion would appear more complicated.

References

Becker, J.L., and R.K. Sarin (1987). "Lottery Dependent Utility." *Management Science*, 33, 1367–1382.

104 UTILITY THEORIES: MEASUREMENTS AND APPLICATIONS

Bell, D.E. (1982). "Regret in Decision Making Under Uncertainty." *Operations Research*, 30, 961–981.

Chew, S., and K. MacCrimmon (1979). "Alpha-nu Choice Theory: A Generalization of Expected Utility Theory." Manuscript faculty of Commerce. University of British Columbia.

Chew, S. (1983). "A Generalization of the Quasilinear Mean with Applications to the Measurement of Income Inequality and Decision Theory Resolving the Allais Paradox." *Econometrica*, 51, 1065–1092.

Chew, S. (1984). "An Axiomatization of the Rank Dependent Quasilinear Mean Generalizing the Gini Mean and the Quasilinear Mean." Preprint. Department of Political Economy. The Johns Hopkins University, Baltimore, MD.

Dyer, J.S., and R.K. Sarin (1979). "Measurable Multiattribute Value Functions." *Operations Research*, 27, 810–822.

Edwards, W. (1962). "Subjective Probabilities Inferred from Decisions." *Psychological Review*, 69, 109–135.

Fishburn, P.C. (1965). "Independence in Utility Theory with Whole Product Sets." *Operation Research*, 13, 28–45.

Fishburn, P.C. (1983). "Transitive Measurable Utility." *Journal of Economic Theory*, 31, 293–317.

Kahneman, D., and A. Tversky (1979). "Prospect Theory: An Analysis of Decision Under Risk." *Econometrica*, 47, 276–287.

Kahneman, D., and A. Tversky (1984). "Choices, Values, and Frames." *American Psychologist*, 39, 341–350.

Karmarkar, U.S. (1978). "Subjectively Weighted Utility: A Descriptive Extension of the Expected Utility Model." *Organizational Behavior and Human Performance*, 21, 61–72.

Keeney, R.L., and H. Raiffa (1976). *Decisions with Multiple Objectives*. Wiley, New York.

Krantz, D.H., Luce, R.D., Suppes, P., and A. Tversky (1971). *Foundations of Measurement*, (Vol. 1). Academic Press, New York.

Loomes, G., and L. McKenzie (1989). "The Use of QALYs in Health Care Decision Making." *Social Science & Medicine*, 28, 299–308.

Loomes, G., and R. Sugden (1982). "Regret Theory: An Alternative Theory of Rational Choice Under Uncertainty." *The Economic Journal*, 92, 805–824.

Luce, R.D. (1988). "Rank-dependent, Subjective Expected-utility Representations." *Journal of Risk and Uncertainty*, 1, 305–332.

Luce, R.D. (1992). "Where Does Subjective Expected Utility Fail Descriptively?" *Journal of Risk and Uncertainty*, 5, 5–27.

Luce, R.D. (1990). "Rational Versus Plausible Accounting Equivalences in Preference Judgments." *Psychological science*, 1, 225–234.

Luce, R.D., and P.C. Fishburn (1991). Rank- and Sign-dependent Linear Utility Models for Finite First-order Gambles." *Journal of Risk and Uncertainty*, 4, 29–59.

Luce, R.D., and L. Narens (1985). "Classification of Concatenation Measurement Structures According to Scale Type." *Journal of Mathematical Psychology*, 29, 1–72.

Luce, R.D., and H. Raiffa (1957). *Games and Decisions: Introduction and Critical Survey*. Wiley, New York.

MacCrimmon, K.R., and S. Larsson (1979). "Utility Theory: Axioms or 'Paradoxes.'" In M. Allais & O. Hagen (Eds.), *Expected Utility and the Allais Paradox*. Reidel, Dordrecht, The Netherlands.

Machina, M.J. (1989). "Dynamic Consistency and Non-expected Utility Models of Choice Under Uncertainty." *Journal of Economic Literature*, XXVII, 1622–1668.

McNeil, B.J., and S.G. Pauker (1982). "Optimizing Patient and Societal Decision Making by the Incorporation of Individual Values." In R.L. Kane and R.A. Kane, (Eds.), *Values and Long-term Care* (215–230). D.C. Heath, Lexington, MA.

Mehrez, A., and A. Gafni (1989). "Quality-adjusted Life Years, Utility Theory, and Healthy-years Equivalents." *Medical Decision Making*, 9, 142–149.

Miyamoto, J.M. (1985). *The Utility of Survival Duration and Health Quality: A Conjoint Measurement Analysis* Publication No. 8512473. University Microfilms, Ann Arbor, MI.

Miyamoto, J.M. (1987). "Constraints on the Representation of Gambles in Prospect Theory." *Journal of Mathematical Psychology*, 31, 410–418.

Miyamoto, J.M. (1988). "Generic Utility Theory: Measurement Foundations and Applications in Multiattribute Utility Theory." *Journal of Mathematical Psychology*, 32, 357–404.

Miyamoto, J.M., and S.A. Eraker (1985). "Parameter Estimates for a QALY Utility Model." *Medical Decision Making*, 5, 191–213.

Miyamoto, J.M., and S.A. Eraker (1988). "A Multiplicative Model of the Utility of Survival Duration and Health Quality." *Journal of Experimental Psychology: General*, 117, 3–20.

Miyamoto, J.M., and S.A. Eraker (1989). "Parametric Models of the Utility of Survival Duration: Tests of Axioms in a Generic Utility Framework." *Organizational Behavior and Human Decision Processes*, 44, 166–202.

Narens, L., and R.D. Luce (1986). "Measurement: The Theory of Numerical Assignments." *Psychological Bulletin*, 99, 166–180.

Pliskin, J.S., Shepard, D.S., and M.C. Weinstein (1980). "Utility Functions for Life Years and Health Status." *Operations Research*, 28, 206–224.

Quiggin, J. (1982). "A Theory of Anticipated Utility." *Journal of Economic Behavior and Organization*, 3, 324–343.

Sarin, R.K. (1989). "Analytical Issues in Decision Methodology." I. Horowitz (Ed.), *Decision and Organization Theory*. Kluwer-Nijhoff Academic Publishers, Boston, Mass.

Segal, U. (1984). "Nonlinear Decision Weights with the Independence Axiom." Working Paper 353. Department of Economics. University of California, Los Angeles.

Slovic, P., and S. Lichtenstein (1983). "Preference Reversals: A Broader Perspective." *American Economic Review*, 73, 596–605.

Stevenson, M.K. (1986). "A Discounting Model for Decisions with Delayed Positive or Negative Outcomes." *Journal of Experimental Psychology: General*, 11, 131–154.

Tversky, A., and D. Kahneman (1981). "The Framing of Decisions and the Psychology of Choice." *Science*, 211, 453–458.

Von Neumann, J., and O. Morgenstern (1944). *Theory of Games and Economic Behavior*. Princeton University Press, Princeton, NJ.

Von Winterfeldt, D., and W. Edwards (1986). *Decision Analysis and Behavioral Research*. Cambridge University Press, New York.

Wakker, P. (1989a). *Additive Representations of Preferences: A New Foundation of Decision Analysis*. Kluwer, Dordrecht, The Netherlands.

Wakker, P. (1989b). "Continuous Subjective Expected Utility with Non-additive Probabilities." *Journal of Mathematical Economics*, 18, 1–27.

Weber, M., and C. Camerer (1987). "Recent Developments in Modelling Preferences Under Risk." *OR Spektrum*, 9, 129–151.

Weinstein, M.C., Fineberg, H.V., Elstein, A.S., Frazier, H.S., Neuhauser, D., Neutra, R.R., and B.J. McNeil (1980). *Clinical decision analysis* W.B. Saunders, Philadelphia, PA.

Yaari, M.E. (1987). "The Dual Theory of Choice Under Risk." *Econometrica*, 55, 95–115.

III GENERALIZED UTILITY IS NOT NORMATIVE

5 SMALL WORLDS AND SURE THINGS: CONSEQUENTIALISM BY THE BACK DOOR

Irving H. LaValle

Introduction

Over roughly the past decade, a large number of generalizations of the von Neumann-Morgenstern (1944) expected-utility (EU) theory of choice under risk and the Savage (1954) subjective-expected-utility (SEU) theory of choice under uncertainty have appeared; see Machina (1987) and Fishburn (1988, 1989) for recent surveys. These generalized models constitute a boon for empiricists since they collectively accommodate persistently observed and thoughtful choice behaviors, such as those identified by Allais (1953) and Ellsberg (1961), that are paradoxical within the EU or SEU framework. Indeed, a currently active topic within behavioral decision theory is to discriminate amongst the generalizations (see Camerer, 1992).

Is there also a useful *normative* or *prescriptive* role for these non-separable, or nonexpected utility (Machina, 1989) models? Should an individual confronted with a decision problem under uncertainty espouse a weighted utility (Chew, 1983), lottery-dependent utility (Becker and Sarin, 1989), states-additive SSB (LaValle and Fishburn, 1987a), or other generalized model, and then make the preference assessments required by that model, in order to clarify the choice(s) at hand? Sarin (1992), Harsanyi (1987), Hammond (1988), Burks (1977), and I caution against such a policy; these others take as fixed an ultimate set of consequences; whereas I do not. Moreover, I do not impose continuity assumptions or the machinery necessary for characterizing subjective probabilities, as does Hammond, and so I do not get all the way to SEU.

This work was motivated by two considerations. First, my collection over the past several years of a rogue's gallery of implementational difficulties encountered with one or another of the putatively normative nonseparable choice theories, largely reported in (LaValle, 1989), still left questions about why these rogues seemed hard to tame. Second, one of the rogues (namely, horizon choice in the Becker and Sarin model) came to mind when Ward Edwards (1988) issued a provocative challenge:

> Peter [Fishburn] and others are proposing that we look at less demanding sets of axioms, that give more room for the kinds of behavior that we do in fact observe . . . *But can we develop a technology from around those axioms*? [So doing] is, on the whole, not the goal of the people who are doing this, but if those of us who like technologies and who believe they are important want to take this kind of thing seriously, *we have to worry about whether technologies of this kind can be developed or not* . . . We are going to face challenges from the behavioral-decision-theory work. That story is by no means over; I agree with Peter on that. And I think it is going to be important, if we don't want to become an atheoretical practical discipline, that we continue to worry about these issues and see if we can get on with them in some manner that preserves the technology we have.

Edwards did not define *applicable technology*; my considered conclusion is that there are, at least, two necessary features of an applicable technology for helping real people make complex decisions: 1. the horizon of ramifications of the initial choices should be flexible and dependent upon the comfort of the decision maker in specifying relative preferences; 2. the way in which he or she draws the tree should not affect the indicated optimal choice, provided that all ways under consideration furnish the same real options and make the same use of information. For short, these are *horizon flexibility* and *invariance*. As will be shown in section two, they appear to entail cancellation/independence properties which usually fail to be observed in intuitive but thoughtful practice—to the glee of colleagues such as R.A. Howard (1992), who see therein an even more urgent need for decision—analytic consulting services.

This work will make them even more gleeful because its messages are that you can apply nonseparable choice theories only at the cost of using some technology that severely restricts horizon flexibility and/or invariance, and that, regardless of model-separability issues, you can allow your preferences to depend upon psychological factors that compare consequences only at the cost of a significantly inflated background informational burden.

I stress that very little in this work is novel. Indeed, my use of "Small Worlds" in the title is an acknowledgment that Savage (1954) considered the issue of horizons and their ideal irrelevance at several points and in some depth. The analysis in section two is implicit in Burks' (1977, chaps. 4, 5) elegant development, once one observes that a consequence in a short horizon tree amounts to a subtree in a longer-horizon model; see also Wakker (1989, p. 40). The kinship with Hammond (1988) is signalled in the subtitle and noted in section two, while the careful argumentation of Machina (1989) was invaluable in clarifying distinctions such as that between dynamic consistency and consequentialism; see also Keller (1992).

Section two defines four necessary conditions for an applicable technology; applies them to the example that concludes this section; states the main result—in the presence of the other three conditions, Horizon Flexibility entails the controversial Cancellation part of the Sure-Thing Principle—as well as other implications; and concludes by showing that imposing Horizon Flexibility along with the weakened Savage axioms of Machina and Schmeidler (1990) implies SEU.

Section three consists of cautionary remarks against such outcome-linking considerations as regret, elation, and disappointment and of observations concerning other important problem-formulation issues, such as time-extensive horizons and distributive equity. Section four concludes the paper.[1]

The remainder of this introduction concerns decision trees and tables, together with remarks about where to start and where to stop the model. Readers well versed in these matters may skip ahead to section two at this point.

Regarding where to *start* one's description of a choice problem, there is little practical alternative to starting with "Now", the point at which one is wrestling with the choice, rather than at some "Back Then" point in, perhaps, early childhood, when one made choices that might later have been regrettable. Considerations arising from potentially non-separable preferences make this issue nontrivial; however, it is of concern to Savage (1954, p. 83), Machina (1989), and others. But if you perceive that you have a choice problem, then you are conceding that you really did not perfectly envision all your possible futures at some "Back Then" point, and therefore you should revise your previous, incomplete plans. Moreover, whatever psychological or material effects that foregone decisions and surmounted risks, that is, paths not travelled, have had upon you can and should be taken as part of your description of "Now". They can also be incorporated into your description of each decision consequence (but see the cautions in section three about regret et al. in time-extended problems).

Where to *stop* elaborating the description of one's choice problem is a question that rarely arises in introductory courses because the very act of writing the problem or case description imposes a decision as to horizon, as well as what to include in some largest-possible analysis. Real decision analyses are usually iterative exercises (see Howard and Matheson (1983), Brown, Kahr and Peterson (1974), Raiffa (1968), Schlaifer (1969), Behn and Vaupel (1982), and von Winterfeldt and Edwards (1986)) with iterations often reflecting a rethinking of horizon choices. Other causes include rethinking the fineness of description of acts and events (LaValle, 1978, chap. 2), von Winterfeldt and Edwards (1986, p. 72)) and rethinking what other decisions and background uncertainties to include, and how to include them, so that one does not end up suboptimizing in the context of one's entire environment—the "temporal risk" problem (Markowitz (1959), Mossin (1969), Spence and Zeckhauser (1972), Kreps and Porteus (1978, 1979), Epstein (1980), Machina (1984), Pratt and Zeckhauser (1987), Pratt (1988)). Section three contains further comment.

Given that the horizon selected for analyzing a choice situation is somewhat arbitrary, it must be emphasized that the terms *consequence* and *outcome* have too great a connotation of finality. Consequence descriptions are subjective, at least to the extent that they incorporate perceived linkages to the background environment and the unmodeled future. On this point von Winterfeldt and Edwards (1986, pp. 65–66) observe:

> The most important outcome of a decision, in almost every case, is the opportunity to make more decisions. Most decisions therefore have instrumental outcomes . . . money is purely instrumental . . . [T]he idea of an outcome is also arbitrary. Outcome is simply a name applied to the endpoint at which you [cease elaborating a path] of the tree. Outcomes are essentially fictions, though indispensible ones; the truth is that life goes on after the outcome occurs.

Although a more appropriate term for them is *positions*, I shall concede to convention by continuing to use the term *consequences* in what follows.

I assume that the reader is familiar with the structuring of decisions as trees, consisting of act nodes, event nodes, and act and event branches (see, Raiffa (1968), von Winterfeldt and Edwards (1986)), as depicted in figure 5–1, in which c_1–c_6 denote consequences (positions) described

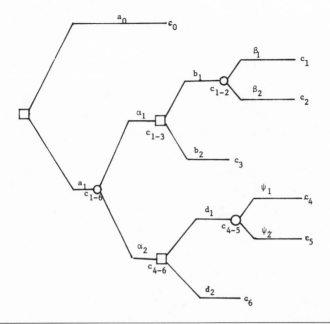

Figure 5–1.   Larger-world decision tree.

at the longest horizon under consideration, and the more elaborately subscripted c corresponds to stopping the elaboration of paths at some preliminary positions. Each such position labelled with a c, including "the consequences themselves," should be regarded as the position label for the infinitely elaborated future subtree commencing at that point, as well as a description of the preference-relevant aspects (including regret et al., if the decision maker so insists) of having arrived there rather than at some other point.

The smaller-world, shorter-horizon models of this same decision that result from stopping at preliminary position(s) are related to each other in the lattice diagram in figure 5–2. Strictly in between the full tree and the smallest nontrivial worldview with termination at c_{1-6} following a_1, there are exactly eight intermediate trees, each denoted by a dot in figure 5–2; going up from one dot to another represents expanding horizon(s) by making explicit the act or event node(s) on the line(s) connecting the two dots in question.

I also assume that the reader knows that any decision tree can be reexpressed in normal form as a decision table by applying a backwards

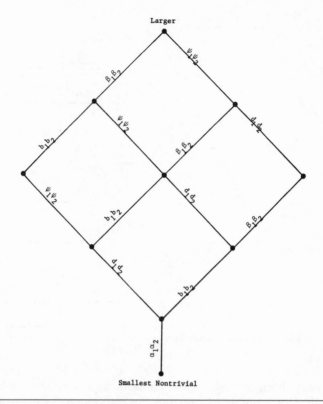

Figure 5–2.   Lattice of shrinkings from larger to smallest nontrivial world.

elaboration (but not rollback!) process (LaValle (1978), LaValle and Fishburn (1978b), von Neumann and Morgenstern (1944) in order to obtain economically specified strategies for the decision maker, and then applying it again on behalf of "Chance" in order to obtain the strategies—called *states*—for Chance. Savage (1954) and many others use the term *act* in place of strategy for the decision maker. As compared with the selection of an act branch emanating from an act node in the tree, strategies might be termed *grand acts* more appropriately, but I omit this adjective or else use the term *strategy* when confusion would result otherwise.

The result of applying this procedure to the full tree in figure 5–1 is table 5-1. Note first that the decision maker's strategies are parsimoniously defined, in that choosing a_0 precludes having to choose from $\{b_1, b_2\}$ and $\{d_1, d_2\}$, and so no such choices are specified or implied. Second, note

Table 5–1. Larger-World Normal Form

states→	$\alpha_1\beta_1$	$\alpha_1\beta_2$	$\alpha_2\psi_1$	$\alpha_2\psi_2$
strategies ↓				
a_0	c_0	c_0	c_0	c_0
$a_1b_1d_1$	c_1	c_2	c_4	c_5
$a_1b_1d_2$	c_1	c_2	c_6	c_6
$a_1b_2d_1$	c_3	c_3	c_4	c_5
$a_1b_2d_2$	c_3	c_3	c_6	c_6

Table 5–2. First Smaller-World Normal Form

states→	$\alpha_1\beta_1$	$\alpha_1\beta_2$	$\alpha_2{}^*$
strategies ↓			
a_0	c_0	c_0	c_0
$a_1b_1d_1$	c_1	c_2	c_{4-5}
$a_1b_1d_2$	c_1	c_2	c_6
$a_1b_2d_1$	c_3	c_3	c_{4-5}
$a_1b_2d_2$	c_3	c_3	c_6

Table 5–3. Second Smaller-World Normal Form

states→	$\alpha_1\beta_1$	$\alpha_1\beta_2$	$\alpha_2{}^*$
strategies ↓			
a_0	c_0	c_0	c_0
$a_1b_1{}^*$	c_1	c_2	c_{4-6}
$a_1b_2{}^*$	c_3	c_3	c_{4-6}

that the states are exclusive, exhaustive, and specify event selections by Chance that are functionally independent of, and provide for, every contingency that can arise given the strategy choice of the decision maker.

Suppose, however, that we had terminated our tree at position c_{4-5} so that its endpoints were c_0, c_1, c_2, c_3, c_{4-5} and c_6. The corresponding normal form is given by table 5–2. Here, an asterisk after α_2 means that we no longer have to (or indeed, can) distinguish between $\alpha_2\psi_1$ and $\alpha_2\psi_2$.

Finally, let us complete going down the northeast slope of the figure 5–2 lattice and suppose that we had terminated our horizon at c_{4-6}. Then we obtain the normal form in table 5–3, where the asterisks in the strategies mean that we can no longer make distinctions based upon explicit contingent choices between d_1 and d_2.

This is as far as we need to go for subsequent developments. It is instructive, however, to note at this point that table 5–3 corresponds to a partitioned version of table 5–1 in which table 5–1's final two columns, its second and third rows, and its fourth and fifth rows are in each case lumped together (due to horizon myopia). Sketch the appropriate dotted lines. It should be obvious, upon a little reflection, that any two horizon specifications of the same decision, which are compatible in the sense that one represents continuation(s) of the other, have normal-form tables in which the smaller corresponds to a partitioning (perhaps after rearrangements) of the strategies and a partitioning of the states of the other.

Not just any two horizon choices are compatible in this sense, as figure 5–2 indirectly indicates; our second smaller-world tree which stops at c_{4-6}, but goes all the way out to c_1-c_3, is not compatible with the tree that stops at c_{1-3}, but goes all the way out to c_4-c_6. Trees on the same level of the lattice are incompatible, but any two such trees have a crudest mutually-larger worldview: take one of them and just elaborate on it everything that was more elaborated on the other, but nothing else.

Extending horizons is not the only sort of alteration that can lead to normal forms related by partitioning. Finer description of act and event branches (=taking less of a bird's eye view), formulation of creative new decision alternatives, and realizing that the background environment will yield some free and materially useful information, all lead to different trees with larger and partitionable normal-form tables, whereas "pruning" some anticipatedly poor contingent choices leads to a smaller table. These operations suggest genuine improvements relative to your original tree, and so the modified tree with the bigger table should lead to a better decision.

Our interest, however, will remain on trees related solely by alternative horizon settings where one can hope that, in principle, a sufficiently introspective person could arrive at the same early choices in a smaller world as would be implied in any world made larger simply by horizon extension.

Back-Door Consequentialism

Necessary Conditions for an Applicable Technology

Four assumptions about the decision maker's preferences seem warranted for any conveniently applicable decision technology. With brief discussion, they are as follows:

ASSUMPTION E. *Existence of preferences.* Given any pair x_1, x_2 of consequences or strategies, the decision maker can in principle judge that exactly one of $x_1 > x_2$, $x_1 \sim x_2$, or $x_2 > x_1$ obtains; that is, that x_1 is better than, equally as good as, or worse than x_2, respectively. Then preference or indifference, $x_1 \geq x_2$, is complete (with $x \sim x$ for all x).

ASSUMPTION I. *Invariance.* Two representations of the same decision problem that are *strategically equivalent* (LaValle and Fishburn, 1987b) in the sense of containing the same real alternatives at the same levels of description, making the same use of information, and leading to the same real consequences (positions), should have the same preference ranking of strategies.

Despite its *descriptive* failure, even when only the consequences are redefined in logically equivalent ways, as in the dramatic lives-saved *versus* lives-lost frames in the McNeil, Pauker, Sox and Tversky (1982) experiment, Tversky and Kahneman (1986) regard invariance as *normatively* essential: "different representations of the same choice problem should yield the same preferences."

I shall use invariance to justify studying the example from the standpoint of its normal forms, found in tables 5–1 to 5–3, and read back onto the tree the appropriate conclusions for dynamically consistent contingent choices, thereby taking to heart Machina's (1989) painstaking demonstration that one, in effect, does not really need McClennen's (1986) concept of resoluteness in order to obtain his dynamically consistent choices once one recognizes that, in the absence of separability across paths, one's local preferences at a noninitial position should reflect paths not taken and, therefore, cannot be expected to coincide with local optimization using one's original, at-"Now" preferences.

This issue is confusing and warrants further comment. Keller's (1992) example and "Greek table" summarize matters well. With reference to this taxonomy of behavior, Machina (1989) shows that individuals with nonseparable-across-paths preferences simply cannot "have it all" by being both dynamically consistent and consequentialist (only looking at the future from any position). These are the "delta people," and Machina shows that their fate is to violate invariance. In his response to LaValle and Wapman (1986), Hazen (1987) takes the delta approach, as do Becker and Sarin (1989), the latter noting that trees cannot be simplified by certainty-equivalent substitutions without having potentially non-neutral effects upon preferences for initial acts. (LaValle (1989) had noted that such a certainty-equivalent substitution did affect preferences for initial acts.)

Our intended position, therefore, types us as "gamma people" and thus, as Machina showed, dynamically consistent satisfiers of invariance who are immune to manipulation, negative information value, and the like. It will follow that we are forced to move almost to alpha status. *Descriptively*, of course, we are probably most often "Epsilon people" (Keller, 1992) in our casual choices.

ASSUMPTION D. *Sure-thing Dominance.* In a normal form decision with a finite set S of states s, if the consequence profiles of strategies f and g are such that $f(s) \geq g(s)$ for every state s, then $f \geq g$; and if also $f(s) > g(s)$ for some state s, then $f > g$.

There are two parts to this assumption, corresponding to stopping at the semicolon and to going on to the end. The first part is the less demanding and is usually stated without the assumption that S is finite. It says that if under every state the consequence of f is at least as good as that of g, then one does not have to worry about which state obtains in order to conclude that f is at least as good a strategy as is g. By noting that $f \sim g$ if and only if $f \geq g$ and $g \geq f$, and similarly for their consequences, it is clear that this part implies the *sure-thing equivalence* property: if $f(s) \sim g(s)$ for every state s, then $f \sim g$. In words, if f and g are sure to result in equally good consequences in all states, then f and g are equally good strategies.

The second part is somewhat justified by the restriction that the table being considered was obtained from a tree with a finite number of branches. It says that if f is better than g given some state s and at least as good as g given every other state, then f is a better strategy than g. It entails an assumption that each state is judged to be sufficiently possible to make consequences in that state *matter* in the forming of preference judgments between strategies. In formal developments, states that cannot affect strategic preferences in this manner, no matter what consequences obtain therein, are called "null states". Since only finite decision trees are being considered, it is natural to suppose that the decision maker would not include an event branch anywhere that would be regarded as impossible and thus result in a null state. Hammond (1988) excludes null states too.

Without the second part of sure-thing dominance, the following could happen: $f(s') > g(s')$ for some s', $f(s) \sim g(s)$ for all other states s, and yet s' is regarded as a "virtual impossibility", so that $f \sim g$. A strict preference in a null state can fade off into holistic indifference.

For subsequent purposes, often only a weakened version of the second part is needed, namely, $f > g$ if $f(s') > g(s')$ for some state s' and $f(s) = g(s)$ for all other states s. Note the difference from the preceding paragraph: $\sim$ there becomes $=$ here.

Sure-thing dominance is not the same property as *cancellation* (Tversky and Kahneman, 1986), since cancellation does assert the non-dependence of preferences upon the common complementary profile. Savage's (1954) original formulation combines sure-thing dominance and cancellation (through his definition of event-conditional preferences) in a way that is suitable for his objectives but difficult to disentangle. Fishburn (1987) clearly separates the various aspects of "sure things," one of which is cancellation, which he calls the *sure-thing substitution principle*: if f and g have a common profile of consequences across a given, proper subset S^* of S (that is, $f(s) = g(s)$ for every s in S^*), then preference between f and g does not depend upon the nature of that common profile; in effect, the subset S^* of states and the common profile are cancellable and may be ignored in the preferential comparison of f and g. With given state probabilities and reduction (Fishburn, 1987) to lotteries, cancellation yields the linearity-in-probabilities property of von Neumann-Morgenstern (1944) utility.

The *descriptive* prevalence of violations of cancellation in the presence of invariance is now common knowledge, the Allais (1953) and Ellsberg (1961) "paradoxes" being the best known. I do not wish to assume cancellation in view of the fact that much of the past decade's work in normative choice theory has striven to rationalize one or the other of these sorts of behavior by developing nonseparable models which do not satisfy this property.

Assumptions E, I, and D, with invariance interpreted and applied as has been indicated, seem fundamental. *But are they consistent with the tree-horizon flexibility which an applicable technology would appear to mandate?*

ASSUMPTION F. *Horizon Flexibility*. Preferences at act nodes common to smaller-and larger-world representations of the same decision situation should not depend upon the representation. That is, one should be able "in principle" to specify consistent preferences on end positions in the two models so as to yield the same behavior.

Unfortunately, the four assumptions are too strong to coexist with nonseparable preferences.

Scrutiny of the Example

By Invariance and to police dynamic consistency, I shall argue primarily in terms of normal-form representations.

The excessive strength of the four assumptions, in their full generality, is shown by observing that they immediately yield consequentialist behavior (Hammond, 1988). To see this, consider the smallest nontrivial horizon a_0 leading to c_0 and a_{1**} leading to c_{1-6}, with a one-column normal-form table. (Given the asterisking procedure, the sure-thing state is called***!) By Assumption E, one of $c_0 > c_{1-6}$, $c_0 \sim c_{1-6}$, and $c_{1-6} > c_0$ holds, and with only one state, it follows from Assumption D that these preferences imply $a_0 > a_{1**}$, $a_0 \sim a_{1**}$, and $a_{1**} > a_0$ respectively. By Assumption H, realizing that $a_{1**} = $ "all strategies starting with a_1 at 'Now'" means that the analysis is over if $a_0 > a_{1**}$ and can be terminated if $a_0 \sim a_{1**}$. So one must (resp: can) "prune" the tree leaving only a_0 if $a_0 > $ (resp: $\sim$) a_{1**}, and one must prune a_0 off if a_0 is inferior. *But Assumption F says that these small-world preferences must stay put in any larger-world model.* So assume that $a_{1**} > a_0$ and recognize that Chance will determine whether the decision maker jumps to position c_{1-3} or to c_{4-6} by "it's" choice of a_1 or a_2. In either event, the preceding argument repeats as a_{1**} gets subdivided by horizon extension, and full consequentialism enters by the back door when the four Assumptions hold at all horizon settings. As Hammond (1988) shows, this entails cancellation.

Instead of working forward from the base of the lattice in figure 5–2, let us try to work back from table 5–1 to table 5–3 *via* table 5–2, to examine the force of the assumptions in the context of a problem that is already horizon extended.

In order to discuss tables 5–1 and 5–2 simultaneously, note, that as a bedrock minimum one must be able to assume existence of preferences on $\{c_0, c_1, \ldots, c_6, c_{4-5}\}$. First, notice that strategies a_0, $a_1 b_1 d_2$, and $a_1 b_2 d_2$, which do not involve any substituted smaller-world consequence, have similar representations between the two tables, except for duplication of c_0 (for a_0) and c_6 (for the other two). To require that preferences among these three strategies do not depend upon "splitting" the state a_{2*} into $a_2 \psi_1$ and $a_2 \psi_2$ is a very mild restriction that LaValle and Fishburn (1987a) call *irrelevance of immaterial uncertainty*: duplication of columns in normal-form tables by including as state variables outcomes of non-informative and consequence-preference-neutral randomizations has no effect upon preferences between strategies. It follows as an easy theorem for states-additive Skew-Symmetric Bilinear (SSB) preferences in that paper, and its authors have subsequently used it as a tool for conjecturing how normal-form models of a given sort relate to each other when the number of states varies (Fishburn and LaValle, 1988a), and also as a mild reasonableness check on a number of normatively proffered nonseparable models (almost all pass with flying colors). It is close in spirit to Milnor's (1954) column-linearity axiom and is also related to Marschak's (1963) concept of sufficient fineness of state descriptions.

I should note that I have in effect already used this property in obtaining the normal-form representations by the economical procedure in LaValle and Fishburn (1987b), especially in defining the states for table 5–1. If the one-branch-from-each-event-node procedure of von Neumann Morgenstern (1944) had been used instead, the result would have been eight columns: $\alpha_1\beta_1\psi_1$, $\alpha_1\beta_1\psi_2$, $\alpha_1\beta_2\psi_1$, $\alpha_1\beta_2\psi_2$, $\alpha_2\beta_1\psi_1$, $\alpha_2\beta_2\psi_1$, $\alpha_2\beta_1\psi_2$, and $\alpha_2\beta_2\psi_2$; each successive pair of these states yields the obvious column of table 5–1, and the column in table 5–1 just gets duplicated when one writes down this wider table. The LaValle-Fishburn procedure also implements the corresponding assumption for strategies: that cloning a strategy by making it specify contingent choices at act-nodes-unreachable, given earlier choices, doesn't improve the decision maker's prospects; this is related to Marschak's (1963) concept of sufficient fineness of *act* descriptions.

Nonetheless, suspicious nonseparabilists might take issue with this principle. Their objection might be, for example: "Wait a minute! When I was comparing a_0, $a_1b_1d_2$, and $a_2b_2d_2$, I did so in the *small* world while trying to keep in mind my other two alternatives, which resulted in an aggregated description c_{4-5} given state α_{2*}. Then you ask me to move to the larger world, and now I have distinct descriptions c_4 given $\alpha_2\psi_1$ and c_5 given $\alpha_2\psi_2$ for these other two strategies, and I don't see why my holistic preferences—even when confined to just the three strategies in question—can't under nonseparability depend upon the level of description of the other stuff. What you are saying is that my preferences over strategies with unelaborated endpoints, and thus necessarily over their consequences, can't depend upon the degree of elaboration of other endpoints!"

This objection touches upon one of the key elements of the difficulty: the evidently holistic and quite possibly nonbinary nature of the preferences being elicited in the nonseparable environment. This topic is addressed in section three.

But more bad news is in store. We will now see how preferences violating sure-thing substitution, or cancellation, can result in a contradiction. As a preliminary, keep firmly in mind that preferences are assumed to exist between any two elements of $\{c_0, \ldots, c_6, c_{4-5}\}$. Now suppose, in the larger world of table 5–1, that the consequences are such that $a_1b_2d_1 \sim a_1b_2d_2$; that is, in the presence of c_3, given α_{1*}, c_6 is as good, given α_{2*} as the conditional lottery yielding c_4, given $\alpha_2\psi_1$ and c_5, given $\alpha_2\psi_2$. But also suppose that separability fails by virtue of some c_1 and c_2 for which $a_1b_1d_1 \not\sim a_1b_1d_2$; that is, the Allais- or Ellsberg-type phenomenon in which preferences given α_{2*} may depend upon what obtains given

a_{1^*}. Now, go to the smaller-world table 5–2: to preserve $a_1b_2d_1 \sim a_1b_2d_2$ from table 5–1, it is necessary that $c_{4-5} \sim c_6$ by existence of preferences and sure-thing equivalence. But then, by sure-thing equivalence in table 5–2, we must have $a_1b_1d_1 \sim a_1b_1d_2$. This is a contradiction. *So Cancellation must hold after all!* It holds because the coalescence in table 5–2 of c_4 and c_5 into c_{4-5}, a "consequence" with crisp preferences vis-à-vis other consequences, forces the *conditional lottery* yielding c_4 and c_5 to itself have crisp preferences vis-à-vis other consequences and, by extension, profiles.

Our final necessary condition for "conformity far out" with assumptions E, I, D, and F follows from comparing tables 5–2 and 5–3, the latter being obtained from the former by not anticipating having to choose between d_1 and d_2, if tree event a_2 obtains. What horizon flexibility dictates is that "early choice behavior" be the same for both tables. This means, for example, that if $a_1b_{1^*}$ is optimal for table 5–3, then one or both of $a_1b_1d_1$ and $a_1b_1d_2$ is optimal for table 5–2. More generally, allowing for genuinely randomized (or "mixed") optimal strategies, if an optimal strategy for table 5–3 puts probability 0.40 on selecting $a_1b_{1^*}$, then an optimal strategy for table 5–2 would have to put probabilities on $a_1b_1d_1$ and $a_1b_1d_2$ which sum to 0.40.

Considering randomized strategies, as well as deterministic choices, is not a digression, since nontransitive preferences, (Fishburn (1982a, 1988), Bell (1982), Loomes and Sugden (1982, 1987)) give rise to genuinely randomized optima, (for purposes of breaking preference cycles); and in the Schmeidler (1989)/Gilboa (1987) nonadditive expected utility theory, preferences over strategies are transitive, but potentially "quasiconcave," in the sense that a randomization between two choices may be strictly preferable to the willful selection of either one of them; in this context, the role of randomization is to reduce ambiguity due to variation in preferences for the consequences across each of two rows in a normal-form table by probabilistically averaging the rows themselves.

What is needed for consistency of deterministic or probabilistic choice in the context of tables 5–2 and 5–3 is a path-independence condition akin to that introduced by Plott (1973) (see also Sen (1977) for a lucid and painstaking exposition of this and other related choice properties). If preferences are transitive and known *not* to be quasiconcave, then the path-independence condition is obvious: row i in table 5–3 is optimal if and only if some row in table 5–2 belonging to the block corresponding to row i is optimal in the context of table 5–2. (This is the normal-form equivalent of Burks' (1977) tree-marking procedure.)

When optimal choice may need to be *randomized due to nontransitivity*, no such path-independence property can hold. Simple examples in Fishburn and LaValle (1988b) show, even in the absence of uncertainty, that differently sequenced choices among three acts with sure consequences over which preferences cycle yield radically different final "optimal" solutions. What you end up with depends on whether you treat the three as a one-stage, three-branched act node, or whether you string out the choice "Hamlet fashion": "to b or not to b, and if not to b, then to a or to d". In the latter case, which of a, b, and d you sequence first, as well as how you go about evaluating the two-stage situation, determines the "optimal" outcome! It is clear from such strategically equivalent sequencings that *the four assumptions imply Transitivity*.

When preferences are transitive but potentially strictly quasiconcave, I do not know at present whether the appropriate "joint-versus marginal/conditional randomizing probabilities" property necessarily or even frequently holds. Contributions in a slightly simpler context (no coalescence of c_{4-5} and c_6 into c_{4-6}) by Kalai and Megiddo (1980), Machina and Parks (1981), and Machina (1985) suggest a negative conclusion.

These complexities, in examining world views made smaller by not rendering explicit some contingent act choices, serve to underscore Savage's wise qualification that his treatment represented only a "first attack"! (1954, p. 86.)

There is another sense in which choice consistency between tables 5–2 and 5–3 invokes cancellation again. Note in table 5–2 that, with c_{4-5} and c_6 being consequences, existence of preferences between c_{4-5} and c_6 implies, by sure-thing dominance, that $a_1b_1d_1 \geqslant a_1b_1d_2$ if and only if $a_1b_2d_1 \geqslant a_1b_2d_2$, so that contingent choice between d_1 and d_2 is independent of the contingent choice between b_1 and b_2. But, going back to table 5–1, this implies that preference between c_6 and the "c_4 *versus* c_5 conditional lottery" is independent of the complementary profile, namely, c_3 and the "c_1 *vs.* c_2 conditional lottery". (The situation, and this argument, are a bit more complex when there are three or more contingent choices at a node like c_{4-6}, since in this case failure of transitivity requires randomized choice. According to the preceding argument, however, optimal randomized choice will be independent of choice at c_{1-3}.)

General Results

Despite their application to an apparently special case, the reasoning in the preceding subsection pertains generally.

PROPOSITION 1. Assumptions E, I and F imply Cancellation.

Proof. Cancellation, or sure-thing substitution (Fishburn, 1987) is the assertion that $f > g$ if and only if $f' > g'$ in the following table:

	A	A^c
f	f_0	x
g	g_0	x
f'	f_0	y
g'	g_0	y

for any consequences x and y and any consequence profiles f_0 and g_0, where A and A^c represent any partition of the states into exclusive, exhaustive, and nonempty events; the assertion is trivial if one of these events is empty. Since the full decision in question may offer other strategies, there may be additional rows in the table, so that the displayed portion is strategically equivalent to the subtree depicted in figure 5–3. By Assumption I, preferences must be the same in both such representations. If Cancellation failed, with for example, $f \geqslant g$ and $g' > f'$, a

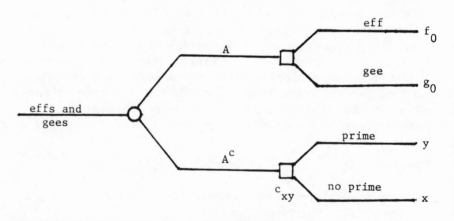

Figure 5–3.   Subtree for proof of proposition 1.

violation of Assumption F would also ensue: with the horizon constrained to c_{xy}, whatever preference exists (by Assumption E) between "eff" and "gee" must (by Assumption F) be unaffected by the simple extension of horizon to reflect the restoration of the distribution between primed and unprimed strategies. Hence no violation of cancellation can occur. ■

Savage's (1954) P2 is the "stronger" assertion that $f > g$, if and only if, $f' > g'$ in the context of a table like that in the preceding proof, except that P2 has x and y denoting profiles rather than individual consequences. That P2 is only superficially stronger follows from glancing at figure 5–3 and noting that x and y are, in the context of Assumption F, only summaries for extended-horizon profiles.

There are two related results worthy of note. The first concerns Fishburn's (1987) weakening of Savage's weak-order postulate P1 to require that $>$ and $\sim$ be transitive only on two-outcome acts. As his Theorem 2 shows, requiring transitivity on all acts forces SEU. But two-outcome acts generally become many-outcome acts as horizons are extended to the right. Thus Assumption F, in conjunction with Fishburn's weakened version of P1 and Savage's P2 − P6, imply SEU.

The second noteworthy fact concerns the Machina and Schmeidler (1990) weakening of Savage's axiomatization to imply existence of finitely additive subjective probability measures in the context of nonseparable preferences. They dispense with Savage's P2, impose P1, P3, P5, and P6, and strengthen P4 (=Weak Comparative Probability) to the following Strong Comparative Probability axiom: whenever A and B are exclusive events, h and h' are profiles, and x, x^*, y, y^* are *consequences* such that $x^* > x$ and $y^* > y$, then $f' > g'$ whenever $f > g$ and f, g, f', and g' are as specified by the following table:

	A	B	$(A \cup B)^c$
f	x^*	x	h
g	x	x^*	h
f'	y^*	y	h'
g'	y	y^*	h'

Now let $x = y$, $x^* = y^*$, and $B = \emptyset$, so that this table collapses to

	A	A^c
f	x^*	h
g	x	h
f'	x^*	h'
g'	x	h'

Note that an extension of the horizon beyond event A makes *profiles* out of the Consequences x and x^*, in which context the assertion that $f' > g'$ whenever $f > g$ is Savage's P2. Thus Assumption F, in conjunction with the Machina and Schmeidler axioms, also yield SEU.

TO SUMMARIZE:

PROPOSITION 2. Assumption F yields SEU in conjunction with the weakened Savage axioms of either Fishburn (1987) or Machina and Schmeidler (1990).

The second major observation in the preceding subsection, that a strong path-independence property of strategic preferences also follows, could be established using an elaborate general notation, but doing so adds nothing to the discussion of the example and hence will be omitted here.

Some Surviving Models of Preference

The "old-time religion" (Edwards, 1988) of SEU clearly satisfies all four applicable-technology-inspired assumptions, but it is not unique. To see why some generalizations of SEU are admissible, note that these assumptions contain neither Continuity nor the machinery necessary for characterizing subjective probabilities.

These omissions, or incompletenesses, suggest two generalizations of SEU that appear normatively satisfactory for technology. The first weakens or abandons Continuity: The expectation of a *vectorial* utility can be component-wise assessed, component-wise expected with respect to subjective probabilities, and component-wise maximized in a take-from-the-top fashion. This is called *lexicographic utility*; such a theory was envisioned by von Neumann and Morgenstern (1944), but was first worked out by Hausner (1954). See also Chipman (1960) and Fishburn (1971, 1982b). A related, nonstandard-analytic approach is due to Skala (1975). See LaValle (1978[Sec. 5.6], 1989) for elementary discussions, with (1989) containing a plug for this theory in decisions having strong ethical implications. The second generalization retains continuity, but relaxes existence of subjective probabilities, while maintaining an additive decomposition of holistic utility across the states. This is "state-dependent utility"; see Fishburn (1970, 1982b) and Karni (1985).

A merger of these two classes of generalization has been outlined by LaValle and Fishburn (1990a,b). It has some unexpected features, one of which is that subjective probabilities emerge, not as real numbers, but rather as matrices which may contain some negative elements.

The preceding generalizations of SEU do not exhaust all "technologically tame" possibilities; assuming continuity, Hammond (1988) demonstrates that *multiplicative*-across-states utility models are also consequentialist.

On Nonseparabilities

It appears that the only way that violations of cancellation or path independence can be justified is to restrict the application of (primarily) Assumption F by developing a theory of cogent horizons. Such a theory would have to address the reasons for existence of nonseparable preferences as a precondition for specifying the requisite horizon testing.

One type of nonseparability arises from the perceived relevance of "risks borne but not experienced" (Machina, 1989). With reference to a decision in normal form, it arises when intracolumn preferences $[f(s')$ *versus* $g(s')]$ depend potentially upon the complementary profile $\{f(s) = g(s): s \neq s'\}$, and a violation of Concellation results. Prescriptively, the specification of $f(s')$ and $g(s')$ can be elaborated to incorporate relevant features of the complementary profile, in which case the violation is rendered moot. Machina (1989) agrees, but cautions that addressing such psychologically fraught unobservables is fatal for descriptive purposes.

This type of nonseparability links consequences within the same row of a decision table. Such nonseparabilities are of primary concern to advocates of theories where preferences over strategies are transitive and the relative desirability of a strategy can be represented by some holistic utility that depends only upon the row in question. (See Fishburn (1989) for a listing of many such models.) The underlying psychological considerations giving rise to nonseparability of this type include disappointment, elation, and relief.

Another type of nonseparability links consequences within the same column of the decision table and is associated most prominently with feelings of regret; see Fishburn (1989), Loomes (1989), and references therein. Here again, explicit incorporation of regret considerations in the consequence definitions can eliminate the nonseparability. I return to this point below, noting for the present that regret arises due to choices foregone rather than risks surmounted, which accounts for my use of "paths not travelled" as the umbrella term.

Other types of nonseparability arise from concerns about flexibility in temporally extended (that is, important real) problems and about distributive equity (see Keeney (1992) and Machina's (1989) "Mom" problem). Inadequate inclusion of environmental background considerations in the "temporal risk" problem (see references in the Introduction) should be remedied either through reformulating the decision problem under consideration, redefining its consequences so as to explicitly account for flexibility et al., or both. As regards distributive equity, auxiliary analyses can be used to identify explicit courses of action that involve randomizing and produce superior consequences (for example, the act "flip a fair coin to allocate the candy" in the "Mom" problem).

I submit two arguments against incorporating regret, elation, disappointment, and similar considerations in prescriptive analyses to any significant extent, whether in explicit (but unobservable) descriptions of the consequences or in espousing a preference theory that produces choices accommodating such effects.

The first argument maintains that such considerations impose a very heavy modeling—and memory—burden. To introduce it, I focus on regret, which goes back to Allais (1953) if not to earlier but less psychologically-based notions of opportunity cost in economics and statistics. In addition to the modern, nonseparable treatments by Bell (1982), Loomes and Sugden (1982), and Fishburn (1982a), it has been argued at least as far back as Fellner (1965) that regret be explicitly included as an attribute of consequences within the separable context of expected utility. Raiffa (1968, p. 86) was initially cool to the idea but has warmed to it (1985). While serving as a research associate to Fellner, I was warm but have now cooled off for reasons that are stated below. However much the following discussion may cite regret, it is no less pertinent to same-row-linking attributes such as elation and disappointment; in fact, the following argument is very close to that of Bell (1985).

If you wish to include regret, rejoicing, disappointment, and similar emotions among preference-relevant attributes, then doing so will *inextricably link at least some of the consequences together* when the time comes to assess preferences. Varying the consequences for calibration purposes can be done only with great wariness if at all; in particular, even within separable-preference theory, changing the horizons may alter descriptions of, and preferences between, consequences at other end positions. Thus, a full temporal-resolution model may be necessitated.

To see why one may need a full temporal-resolution model, assume that figure 5–4 sketches the following choice problem. Suppose that Chance has already selected one of three exclusive and exhaustive states s_1, s_2 and s_3, and that you are forced to choose one of the three depicted ways that the news is broken to you. Also suppose that the temporal-risk

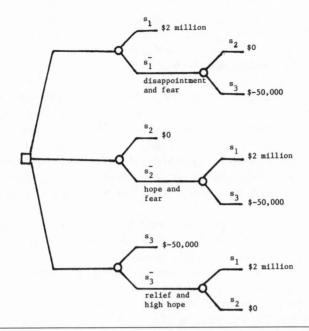

Figure 5–4.   Potential effects of revelation sequencing upon preferences.

problem of ties to the background environment really does not enter the picture, inasmuch as the first report will be delivered ten minutes after you choose and the second, if it is needed, will occur half an hour thereafter. If you let your preferences be governed by your feelings (as guessed in figure 5–4) during the half-hour interlude between reports, then you cannot reduce compound lotteries! For further discussion of considerations of this sort, see Bell (1985).

I note, however, that compound lotteries are automatically reduced in most nonseparable choice theories, and local preferences are assumed to vary with news to date in such a way as to amount to the same thing. A nonseparabilist who is not indifferent over all these choices in figure 5–4 is no better off than a separabilist.

It is necessary to elaborate on the horizon dependence of consequence-linking, preference-affecting attributes and how they entail full temporal treatment. Suppose in figure 5–1 that you want to include in the definition of c_0 some notion of regret at not having "taken the chance" a_1, depending of course on how a_1 would have turned out. But in that dependence lies the problem, since any definition of regret in c_0 begs the question of *horizon length and knowability of how paths not taken become successively elaborated.* If your tree's horizon stopped at c_{1-3} and c_{4-6}, your regret would presumably be different than if it went all the way to $c_{1}\text{-}c_{6}$.

Even worse is true, since the elaboration of paths since "Back Then" may also be relevant to regret. Your life as a chooser did not really start at "Now", and so information about how wonderfully some foregone investment in the past turned out could influence your preferences for positions in the current problem—in a possibly nonneutral manner as regards the currently available strategies. This implies that all such informational events would have to be brought into the tree in order to account for their effects upon your preferences, even though they provide no otherwise useful information for clarifying choices at subsequent act nodes.

These complications obtain with no less force to any other psychological attributes that link consequences together, and they pertain equally to nonseparable theories that deal at an observable level of consequence descriptions but account via nonseparability for interconsequential psychological effects.

In nonseparable theories, therefore, you really cannot make do at "Now" with some summarization of all paths not travelled, as well as the one travelled, since the continued evolution of paths not travelled will affect preferences during the evolution of the current decision. And, in the absence of an explicit theory of horizons, one cannot "restart" at an endpoint without bringing along the entire baggage of paths in the current tree as well as the other paths not travelled since "Back Then." All of this requires a fully temporal treatment, which is not practical in the context of the finite resources of attention than can be devoted to making any given decision, even an important one.

The second argument against succumbing to regret et al. notes that this heavy modeling burden is avoidable for decision makers with separable preferences *who school themselves not to experience consequence-linking psychological attributes.* From the perspective that a consequence is really nothing more than a position in your tree of experience, and that preferences are appropriately specified over alternative positions in this tree, the incentive to include regret et al. in position descriptions is somewhat mitigated.

These arguments are reminiscent of, and consistent with, the views expressed by R.A. Howard on various occasions, notably (1988, 1992); in the former address, he characterized worry and fear as *ex ante* harmful thoughts, and regret and disappointment as *ex post* harmful, counselling that their *prima facie* pertinence can be greatly reduced if not entirely eliminated by always keeping in mind the distinction between good/bad *decisions* and good/bad *outcomes*. From personal experience I can corroborate that knowing you have made the best *decision* possible under the circumstances can be of great sustenance if a bad *outcome* obtains—especially when you had thought that outcome very likely!

Conclusions

Four applicable-technology-motivated assumptions were shown in Proposition 1 to be inconsistent with violations of Cancellation and thus to cast doubt upon the normative/prescriptive usefulness of many of the generalizations of SEU developed over the past decade. And, as suggested by Proposition 2, axiomatic generalizations of Savage's theory which rely for the generalization upon a relationship restricted to consequences rather than to more general profiles of consequences appear to reduce to SEU once the horizon assumption implicit in the restriction is relaxed.

It was argued that the preferential linking of consequence positions in the tree one faces at any point in time stem from psychological considerations that, if given free rein, impose an enormous informational and modeling burden upon the decision maker. In the extreme, they imply that any differences whatsoever in the model are preference-affecting and hence the *ceteris* are never sufficiently *paribus* to permit even the variations required for preference and judgment calibration.

That preferential linkages must be confronted explicitly within the context of SEU or a separable (see "some surviving models of preference") generalization thereof rather than accomodated implicitly *via* a nonseparable model is an advantage: the explicit confrontation is conducive to disciplining oneself to think about one's basic values at a more fundamental and less context-dependent level, as Keeney (1988) in particular counsels.

Notes

1. I use the usual symbols $\geq$, $>$, $\sim$, and $\nsim$ to denote "is preferred or indifferent to," "is preferred to," "is indifferent to," and "is not indifferent to," respectively. In the context of a normal form, acts-*vs*-states table, $f(s)$ denotes the consequence (or outcome) of choosing act f when state s obtains.

References

Allais, M. (1953). "Le Comportement de L'homme Rationnel Devant le Risque: Critique des Posulats et Axiomes de L'ecole Americaine." *Econometrica*, 21, 503–546.

Becker, J.L., and R.K. Sarin (1989). "Decision Analysis Using Lottery-dependent Utility." *Journal of Risk and Uncertainty*, 2, 105–117.

Behn, R.D., and J.W. Vaupel (1982). *Quick Analysis for Busy Decision Makers*. Basic Books, New York.

Bell, D.E. (1982). "Regret in Decision Making Under Uncertainty." *Operations Research*, 30, 961–981.

Bell, D.E. (1985). "Disappointment in Decision Making Under Uncertainty." *Operations Research*, 33, 1–27.

Brown, R.V., Kahr, A.S., and C. Peterson (1974). *Decision Analysis for the Manager*. Holt, Rinehart and Winston, New York.

Burks, A.W. (1977). *Chance, Cause, Reason: An Inquiry into the Nature of Scientific Evidence*. University of Chicago Press, Chicago IL.

Camerer, C.F. (1989). "An Experimental Test of Several Generalized Utility Theories." *Journal of Risk and Uncertainty*, 2, 61–104.

Camerer, C.F. (1992). "Recent Tests of Generalizations of Expected Utility Theory." In W. Edwards (Ed.), *Utility Theories: Measurements and Applications*. Kluwer Academic Publishers, Boston, MA.

Chew, S.H. (1983). "A Generalization of the Quasilinear Mean with Applications to the Mearsurement of Income Inequality and Decision Theory Resolving the Allais Paradox." *Econometrica*, 51, 1065–1092.

Chipman, J.S. (1960). "The Foundations of Utility." *Econometrica*, 28, 193–224.

Edwards, W. (1988). *Videotaped Ramsey-Medalist Address*. TIMS/ORSA, Denver, CO.

Ellsberg, D. (1961). "Risk, Ambiguity, and the Savage Axioms." *Quarterly Journal of Economics*, 75, 643–669.

Epstein, L.G. (1980). "Decision Making and the Temporal Resolution of Uncertainty." *International Economic Review*, 21, 269–283.

Fellner, W. (1965). *Probability and Profit: A Study of Economic Behavior Along Bayesian Lines*. Richard D. Irwin, Homewood, IL.

Fishburn, P.C. (1970). *Utility Theory for Decision Making*. John Wiley & Sons, New York.

Fishburn, P.C. (1971). "A study of Lexicographic Expected Utility." *Management Science*, 17, 672–678.

Fishburn, P.C. (1982a). "Nontransitive Measurable Utility." *Journal of Mathematical Psychology*, 26, 31–67.

Fishburn, P.C. (1982b). *The Foundations of Expected Utility*. Reidel Publishing Company, Dordrecht, The Netherlands.

Fishburn, P.C. (1987). "Reconsiderations in the Foundations of Decision Under Uncertainty." *The Economic Journal*, 97, 825–941.

Fishburn, P.C. (1988). *Nonlinear Preference and Utility Theory*. The Johns Hopkins University Press, Baltimore MD.

Fishburn, P.C. (1989). "Generalizations of Expected Utility Theories: A Survey of Recent Proposals." In P.C. Fishburn and I.H. LaValle (Eds.), *Choice Under Uncertainty: Annals of Operations Research* (Vol. 19, pp. 3–28). Baltzer, Basel Switzerland.

Fishburn, P.C., and I.H. LaValle (1988a). "The Structure of SSB Utilities for Decision Under Uncertainty." *Mathematical Social Sciences*, 15, 217–230.

Fishburn, P.C., and I.H. LaValle (1988b). "Context-dependent Choice with Nonlinear and Nontransitive Preferences." *Econometrica*, 56, 1221–1239.

Gilboa, I. (1987). "Expected Utility with Purely Subjective Nonadditive Probabilities." *Journal of Mathematical Economics*, 16, 65–88.

Hammond, P.J. (1988). "Consequentialist Foundations for Expected Utility." *Theory and Decision*, 25, 25–78.

Harsanyi, J.C. (1987). "von Neumann-Morgenstern Utilities, Risk Taking, and Welfare." In G.R. Feiwel (Ed.), *Arrow and the Ascent of Modern Economic Theory*. New York University Press, New York.

Hausner, M. (1954). "Multidimensional Utilities." In R.M. Thrall, C.H. Coombs and M.L. Davis (Eds.), *Decision Processes*. Wiley, New York.

Hazen, G.B. (1987). "Does Rolling Back Decision Trees Really Require the Independence Axiom?" *Management Science*, 33, 807–809.

Howard, R.A. (1988). *Videotaped Ramsey-Medalist Address*. TIMS/ORSA, Denver, CO.

Howard, R.A. (1992). "In Praise of the Old Time Religion." In W. Edwards (Ed.), *Utility Theories: Measurements and Applications*. Kluwer Academic Publishers, Boston, MA.

Howard, R.A., and J.E. Matheson (Eds.), (1983). *The Principles and Applications of Decision Analysis*. Strategic Decisions Group, Menlo Park CA.

Kalai, E., and N. Megiddo (1980). "Path Independent Choices." *Econometrica*, 48, 781–784.

Karni, E. (1985). *Decision Making Under Uncertainty: The Case of State-dependent Preferences*. Harvard University Press, Cambridge, MA.

Keeney, R.L. (1988). "Value-Focused Thinking and the Study of Values." In D.E. Bell, H. Raiffa and A. Tversky (Eds.), *Decision Making: Descriptive, Normative, and Prescriptive Interactions*. Cambridge University Press, Cambridge UK.

Keeney, R.L. (1992). "On the Foundations of Prescriptive Decision Analysis." In W. Edwards (Ed.), *Utility Theories: Measurements and Applications*. Kluwer Academic Publishers, Boston, MA.

Keeney, R.L., and H. Raiffa (1976). *Decisions with Multiple Objectives: Preferences and Value Tradeoffs*. Wiley, New York.

Keller, L.R. (1992). "Properties of Utility Theories and Related Empirical Phenomena. In W. Edwards (Ed.) *Utility Theories: Measurements and Applications*. Kluwer Academic Publishers, Boston, MA.

Kreps, D.M., and E.L. Porteus (1978). "Temporal Resolution of Uncertainty and Dynamic Choice Theory." *Econometrica*, 46, 185–200.

Kreps, D.M., and E.L. Porteus (1979). "Dynamic Choice Theory and Dynamic Programming." *Econometrica*, 47, 91–100.

Kuhn, H.W. (1953). "Extensive Games and the Problem of Information." In H.W. Kuhn and A.W. Tucker (Eds.), *Contributions to the Theory Games, vol. II*. Princeton University Press, Princeton NJ.

La Valle, I.H. (1978). *Fundamentals of Decision Analysis*. Holt, Rinehart and Winston, New York.

La Valle, I.H. (1989). "New Choice Models Raise New Difficulties: Comment on Sarin." In I. Horowitz (Ed.), *Organization and Decision Theory*. Kluwer-Nijhoff, Dordrecht, The Netherlands.

LaValle, I.H., and P.C. Fishburn (1987a). "Decision Analysis Under States-additive SSB Preferences." *Operations Research*, 35, 722–735.

La Valle, I.H., and P.C. Fishburn (1987b). "Equivalent Decision Trees and Their Associated Strategy Sets." *Theory and Decision*, 23, 37–63.

LaValle, I.H., and P.C. Fishburn (1990a). *Lexicographic State-dependent Subjective Expected Utility*. Preprint. A.B. Freeman School of Business, Tulane University, New Orleans, LA.

La Valle, I.H., and P.C. Fishburn (1990b). *Linear Lexicographic State-dependent Utility*. Preprint. A.B. Freeman School of Business, Tulane University, New Orleans, LA.

LaValle, I.H., and K.R. Wapman (1986). "Rolling Back Decision Trees Requires the Independence Axiom!" *Management Science*, 32, 382–385

Loomes, G. (1989). "Predicted Violations of the Invariance Principle in Choice Under Uncertainty." In P.C. Fishburn and I.H. LaValle (Eds.), *Choice Under Uncertainty: Annals of Operations Research*, 19, 103–113. Baltzer Basel, Switzerland.

Loomes, G., and R. Sugden (1982). "Regret Theory: An Alternative Theory of Rational Choice Under Uncertainty." *The Economic Journal*, 92, 805–824.

Loomes, G., and R. Sugden (1987). "Some Implications of a More General Form of Regret Theory." *Journal of Economic Theory*, 41, 270–287.

Machina, M.J. (1984). "Temporal Risk and the Nature of Induced Preferences." *Journal of Economic Theory*, 33, 199–231.

Machina, M.J. (1985). "Stochastic Choice Functions Generated From Deterministic Preferences Over Lotteries." *The Economic Journal*, 95, 575–594.

Machina, M.J. (1987). "Choice Under Uncertainty: Problems Solved and Unsolved." *Journal of Economic Perspectives*, 1, 121–154.

Machina, M.J. (1989). "Dynamic Consistency and Non-expected Utility Models of Choice Under Uncertainty." *Journal of Economic Literature*, 27, 1622–1668.

Machina, M.J., and D. Schmeidler (1990). *A More Robust Definition of Subjective Probability*. Reprint. Department of Economics, University of California-San Diego, La Jolla, CA.

Machina, M.J., and R.P. Parks (1981). "On Path Independent Randomized Choice." *Econometrica*, 49, 1345–1347.

Markowitz, H. (1959). *Portfolio Selection: Efficient Diversification of Investments.* Yale University Press, New Haven CT.

Marschak J. (1963). "The Payoff-relevant Description of States and Acts." *Econometrica*, 31, 719–725.

McClennen, E.F. (1986). *Rationality and Dynamic Choice: Foundational Explorations.* Preprint. Department of Philosophy, Washington University, St. Louis MD.

McNeil, B.J., Pauker, S.G., Sox, H.C., Jr., and A. Tversky (1982). "On the Elicitation of Preferences for Alternative Therapies." *New England Journal of Medicine*, 306, 1259–1262.

Milnor, J.W. (1954). "Games Against Nature." In R.M. Thrall, C.H. Coombs and R.L. Davis (Eds.), *Decision Processes.* Wiley, New York.

Mossin, J. (1969). "A Note on Uncertainty and Preferences in a Temporal Context." *American Economic Review*, 59, 172–174.

Plott, C.R. (1973). "Path Independence, Rationality and Social Choice." *Econometrica*, 41, 1075–1091.

Pratt, J.W. (1988). "Aversion to One Risk in the Presence of Others." *Journal of Risk and Uncertainty*, 1, 395–413.

Pratt, J.W., and R.J. Zeckhauser (1987). "Proper Risk Aversion." *Econometrica*, 55, 143–154.

Quiggin, J. (1989). "Sure Things-Dominance and Independence Rules for Choice Under Uncertainty." In P.C. Fishburn and I.H. LaValle (Eds.), *Choice Under Uncertainty: Annals of Operation Research*, 19, 335–357. Baltzer, Basel Switzerland.

Raiffa, H. (1968). *Decision Analysis: Introductory Lectures on Choices Under Uncertainty.* Addison-Wesley, Reading MA.

Raiffa, H. (1985). "Back From Prospect Theory to Utility Theory." In M. Grauer, M. Thompson and A.P. Wierzbicki (Eds.), *Plural Rationality and Interactive Decision Processes.* Springer-Verlag Berlin.

Sarin, R.K. (1992). "What Now for Generalized Utility Theory?" In W. Edwards, (Ed.) *Utility Theories: Measurements and Applications.* Kluwer Academic Publishers, Boston, MA.

Savage, L.J. (1954). *The Foundations of Statistics.* Wiley, New York.

Schlaifer, R.O. (1969). *Analysis of Decisions Under Uncertainty.* McGraw-Hill, New York.

Schmeidler, D. (1989). "Subjective Probability and Expected Utility Without Additivity." *Econometrica*, 57, 571–578.

Sen, A.K. (1977). "Social Choice Theory: A Re-examination." *Econometrica*, 45, 53–89.

Skala, H.J. (1975). *Non-Archimedean Utility Theory.* Reidel, Dordrecht, The Netherlands.

Spence, M., and R. Zeckhauser (1972). "The Effect of the Timing of Consumption Decisions and the Resolution of Lotteries on the Choice of

Lotteries." *Econometrica*, 40, 401–403.

Tversky A., and D. Kahneman (1986). "Rational Choice and the Framing of Decisions." In R.M. Hogarth and M.W. Reder (Eds.), *Rational Choice*. The University of Chicago Press, Chicago IL.

von Neumann, J., and O. Morgenstern (1944). *Theory of Games and Economic Behavior*. Princeton University Press, Princeton NJ.

von Winterfeldt, D., and W. Edwards (1986). *Decision Analysis and Behavioral Research*. Cambridge University Press, New York.

Wakker, P.P. (1989). *Additive Representations of Preferences*. Kluwer Academic Publishers, Dordrecht, The Netherlands.

6 WHAT NOW FOR GENERALIZED UTILITY THEORY?

Rakesh K. Sarin

Expected Utility Revisited as a Normative Theory

In this chapter, we argue that a decision maker who does not maximize expected utility (or subjective expected utility) will necessarily violate at least one of the two rules of rational behavior in a dynamic decision context. By *dynamic decision context* we mean choice situations where some decisions are made after the resolution of some uncertainty. The field of decision analysis (see Raiffa, 1968) deals, to a large extent, with dynamic choice situations. An implication of our arguments, therefore, is that recent generalizations of expected utility theory do not constitute a coherent normative theory for decision analysis.

Suppose F, G, H, etc. are lotteries (simple probability distributions) defined over outcomes x. We assume that a person is able to rank order the lotteries from the most preferred to the least preferred including indifferences. Further, suppose an appropriate notion of continuity is satisfied. We use $\geqslant$ to denote "preferred or indifferent to". An immediate implication of the ordering and continuity assumptions is that there exists a real-valued function U such that for any F, G

$$F \geqslant G, \quad \text{if and only if,} \quad U(F) \geqslant U(G). \tag{1}$$

W. Edwards (ed.), UTILITY THEORIES: MEASUREMENTS AND APPLICATIONS. *Copyright © 1992. Kluwer Academic Publishers, Boston. All rights reserved.*

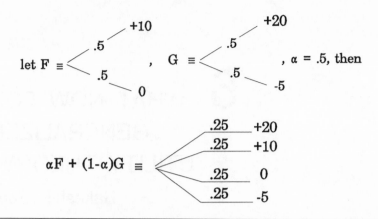

Figure 6–1.   Notation for lotteries.

We further restrict the preference functional U in (1) so that stochastically dominating lotteries (Quirk and Saposnik, 1962) are preferred. Strictly speaking, our results do not require this restriction. We, however, consider that the stochastic dominance property is normatively appealing and theories that do not satisfy it ought to be excluded as candidates for replacing the expected utility theory in decision analysis. We write $F >_{st} G$ and say that F stochastically dominates G. The function U is assumed to satisfy (2) for any F and G.

$$\text{If} \quad F >_{st} G \quad \text{then} \quad U(F) > U(G). \tag{2}$$

We label any theory that satisfies (1) and (2) as a *generalized utility theory*. Examples include Chew and MacCrimmon (1979), Machina (1982), Fishburn (1983), and Becker and Sarin (1987).

Expected utility theory (von Neumann-Morgenstern, 1947) is a special case of generalized utility theory. Suppose $\alpha F + (1 - \alpha)G, 0 \leq \alpha \leq 1$, represents a lottery with a probability distribution function $\alpha F + (1 - \alpha)G$. Note that though it may be easy to think of $\alpha F + (1 - \alpha)G$ as a two-stage lottery, we are working with only single stage lotteries so far. A numerical example in figure 6–1 illustrates the meaning of our notation $\alpha F + (1 - \alpha)G$.

Expected utility theory satisfies, in addition to (1) and (2),

$$U(\alpha F + (1 - \alpha)G) = \alpha U(F) + (1 - \alpha)U(G). \tag{3}$$

The function U is therefore restricted to be *linear in probabilities* in the expected utility theory. Hereafter, we will call a theory that satisfies (1) and (2) but *not necessarily* (3) as a generalized utility theory. If we denote F_x as a degenerate lottery in which outcome x occurs with probability 1, then from (3) it follows that if $F = \alpha F_x + (1 - \alpha)F_y$,

$$
\begin{aligned}
U(F) = U(\alpha F_x + (1 - \alpha)F_y) &= \alpha U(F_x) + (1 - \alpha)U(F_y) \\
&= \alpha u(x) + (1 - \alpha)u(y) \qquad (4) \\
&= E_F[u(x)].
\end{aligned}
$$

The question we examine here is: What additional assumptions are needed so that a function U that satisfies (1) and (2) also satisfies (4)? We will argue that in the context of decision analysis two reasonable assumptions about a decision maker's preferences restrict any generalized utility function to the functional form given by (4). Thus, in order to reject expected utility theory one must reject at least one of these two assumptions.

We will represent dynamic choice situations by a decision tree. In a decision tree, decisions are depicted by decision nodes (squares in figure 6–2) and random events are depicted by chance nodes (circles in figure 6–2). Decision nodes and chance nodes are arranged in chronological order. For notational economy we will call a decision that results in a probability distribution F over payoffs simply as decision F. Throughout, F, G, etc. represent conditional probability distributions—conditional upon all decisions and events prior to the decision node under consideration. To indicate the preference of F over G at a given decision node, we will cross out the branch representing G (see figure 6–2a,b).

ASSUMPTION 1. *Principle of Optimality.* If $F \geqslant G$ for some $\alpha > 0$ and H in figure 6–2a, then $F \geqslant G$ for every $\alpha' > 0$ and H' in figure 6–2b.

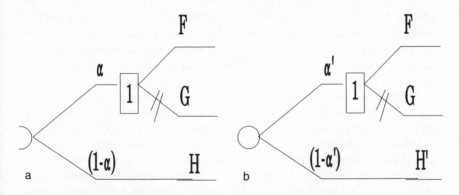

Figure 6–2a,b.   Lotteries illustrating the principle of optimality.

This assumption says that at decision node 1 in figure 6–2a, if a decision F (a decision whose outcome is given by lottery F) is preferred or indifferent to a decision G, then this preference order is maintained regardless of how one reaches the decision node where a choice between F and G needs to be made. Thus, the events that "did not happen" do not influence the choice between F and G.

This assumption has been attacked (see Machina, 1988) because it, along with some other assumptions, requires the separability of preference functionals across mutually exclusive events. But this is putting the cart before the horse. We cannot first make up our mind on an objective function (nonseparable preference function) and then proceed to reject a reasonable rule of behavior because it happens to be inconsistent with the assumed objective function.

McClennen (1988) has proposed a mechanism called the *resolute choice* to evaluate dynamic choices. Simply stated, the resolute choice requires that a decision maker consider the normal (or strategic) form of the decision tree, choose the most preferred strategy, and stick with those decisions throughout the tree that are contained in the originally chosen strategy. This is precisely what an expected utility maximizer would do. But, there is a catch. At *any* decision node, the preferred decision by an expected utility maximizer would coincide with the decision implied by the original strategy, even if the decision maker recalculates the optimal choice *anew* at the decision node under consideration. A generalized utility maximizer is forbidden to compute the optimal choice anew if he wishes to maintain the consistency between the original strategy and the newly computed optimal choice. Resolute choice, therefore, provides a technical escape from the inconsistency that may result if a generalized utility maximizer recalculates the optimal choice beginning at some intermediate decision node in the tree. The escape parachute, however, lands in quick sand. The extensive form of the decision tree loses its usefulness in analysis, the principle of optimality is violated, and the decision maker is forced to consider the entire past history in order to determine an optimal choice at the current decision node.

There is nothing wrong with the resolute choice in itself. It merely enforces the intuitive notion of dynamic consistency. Ironically, it is touted as a savior of generalized utility theory and as a workable normative theory in dynamic choice situations. When the dust settles, however, it will be recognized that resolute choice works only for the expected utility maximizer. This is because a generalized utility maximizer could improve his lot by not being resolute, but an expected utility maximizer cannot do so. Succinctly stated, under resolute choice, a generalized utility maximizer will face a direct conflict with the principle of optimality. As a result, at an intermediate decision node his choice between some two decisions will flip-flop, depending on the past history even if such history has no influence whatsoever on the probability distributions associated with these decisions.

To illustrate the principle of optimality, consider an example of a joint innovation marketing decision. Suppose an entrepreneur is working on an innovation. The entrepreneur realizes a lottery H if the innovation is unsuccessful. If, however, the innovation is successful, she could either sell it to a marketing firm or produce the product herself. The marketing firm offers her a fixed sum F to buy the rights to produce and market the product. If she produces and markets the product herself she would realize a lottery G. Should her choice between F and G depend on the likelihood (α) that she would be successful in developing the product or for that matter her payoffs if the innovation fails? We think not.

The principle of optimality stated above is a rule of behavior that most people, upon reflection, will choose to abide by for most decision situations. A closer scrutiny of the violation of this assumption will reveal that the problem was not properly formulated to reflect all dimensions of concern to the decision maker. To illustrate this principle precisely, suppose you are asked to participate in a game in which a coin is tossed. If the coin lands "heads" up, you receive a consolation prize. If the coin lands "tails" up, you enter the second stage of the game where you can choose to bet on whether the ball in a roulette game will land on red or black. Your choice for the bet on the roulette wheel will clearly depend on the prizes offered, if you do win, and on the relative probabilities that you assign to the events that the ball will land on red or black. Those who wish to reject the principle of optimality must show why your choice for the bet on the roulette wheel ought to depend on the amount of the consolation prize that you would have received had the coin landed heads in the first stage of the game. The argument in favor of the principle of optimality is simple but powerful: the decision to be on red or black should depend only on the consequence (probability distributions) associated with these bets. A rule which requires that choices at a decision node be governed by the events and outcomes that did not occur seems patently unreasonable. At this point, one need not jump the ship and abandon generalized utility models. In fact, as we will discuss later, it is possible to simultaneously keep the principle of optimality and a preference function that is nonlinear in probabilities if one has a reason to reject the assumption of *economic equivalence* discussed next.

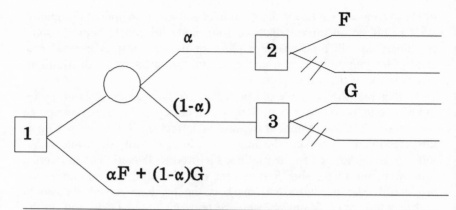

Figure 6–3.   Example of a two-stage gamble.

ASSUMPTION 2. *Economic Equivalence.* A two-stage decision in which a decision at the first stage leads with α chance to a decision F and with $(1 - \alpha)$ chance to a decision G in the second stage is equivalent to a single-stage decision $\alpha F + (1 - \alpha)G$.

We denote a two stage gamble shown in the upper branch at the decision node 1 of figure 6–3 as $\alpha \,\square\, F + (1 - \alpha) \,\square\, G$ and a single-stage gamble shown in the lower branch at the decision node 1 with our previous notation $\alpha F + (1 - \alpha)G$. Assumption 2 states that:

$$\alpha \,\square\, F + (1 - \alpha) \,\square\, G \sim \alpha F + (1 - \alpha)G.$$

In figure 6–4, an example demonstrating assumption 2 is shown.

Economic equivalence is compelling as a normative rule because decision strategies (choose F if decision node 2 in figure 6–3 is reached or choose G if decision node 3 is reached) associated with both the two-stage decision and the single-stage decision yield identical probability distributions over payoffs. This assumption may be violated in a descriptive setting because of *cognitive limitations*. A more potent cause of violation may be that, in some situations, the two-stage lottery and its economically equivalent single-stage lottery may invoke different *psychological concerns*. Because of these concerns, two economically equivalent lotteries may not be deemed psychologically equivalent even by a reflective decision maker. I prefer to regard economic equivalence is a normative rule but am willing to overrule it in a specific case. I see no contradiction in accepting "speaking the truth" and "do not hurt others" as normative

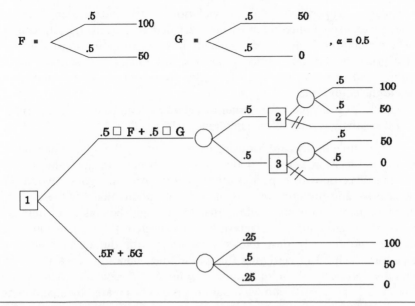

Figure 6–4. Example illustrating the principle of economic equivalence.

principles of behavior even though a deviation from these principles may be justified in some specific circumstances. A discussion of psychological aspects that impact economics of decisions is provided in the next section.

THEOREM 1. A generalized utility model given by (1) and (2) satisfies both the principle of optimality (assumption 1) and economic equivalence (assumption 2) only if

$$U(F) = E_F[u(x)].$$

Thus, two simple rules of rational behavior reduce every generalized utility theory to the expected utility form. Since every generalized utility theory proposed in the literature so far, or yet to be invented, will necessarily violate either assumption 1 or assumption 2, it seems futile to search for a normative theory from this class of theories unless one is willing to abandon one of these two assumptions. To see this incompatibility of a generalized utility theory with assumptions 1 and 2 transparently, consider the following property that every generalized utility theory must satisfy.

PROPERTY P. There exist some F, G, H and α such that $F > G$ and $\alpha F + (1 - \alpha)H < \alpha G + (1 - \alpha)H$.

Clearly, property P is just a violation of the independence axiom that generalized utility theories are designed to permit. The flexibility of a generalized utility theory gained through property P is achieved at a price. In dynamic choice situations, any theory that satisfies property P and ordering must violate either the principle of optimality or economic equivalence.

THEOREM 2. Principle of optimality, economic equivalence, Property P and transitivity cannot all be simultaneously satisfied.

This completes my case for using expected utility theory as a normative theory in decision analysis. I do, however, believe in the value of exploring relaxations of expected utility theory. And this goes beyond the descriptive and prescriptive uses of such relaxations that I will elaborate in subsequent sections. I believe that there could be classes of applications where an appropriate relaxation of expected utility theory may be deemed normatively desirable. An analogy with the development of algebra is helpful in clarifying this point. In common algebra the commutative property of multiplication is eminently reasonable. Who would say $37 \times 13 \neq 13 \times 37$ and what paradoxes can be created by abandoning this commutative property? But in vector analysis this property is discarded because it is not true for all vectors. Relaxation of the axioms of expected utility theory could be pursued for purely mathematical joy or because in some class of applications one or more of these axioms create an obstacle. A class of applications familiar to decision analysts where the independence assumption seems inappropriate is public risk equity, or more generally, applications where the marginal probability of an event is itself treated as an outcome.

Why Do People Violate Rules of Rational Behavior?

People (you and me included) violate rules of rational behavior because of *ignorance, cognitive limitations*, and *psychological concerns*.

In a study to explore future energy scenarios, I asked experts to estimate the probabilities of event A (nuclear slowdown), event B (oil restrictions), and the conditional probability of event B given event A. The events were precisely defined in the actual study. Typical numbers given by the experts were $p(A) = 0.8$, $p(B) = 0.8$, and $p(A/B) = 0.5$. This set of numbers is inconsistent because it implies $p(AB) = p(A/B)$ $p(B) = 0.4$, $p(A) + p(B) - p(AB) = 1.2$. In fact, $p(A/B)$ cannot be less than 0.75 if $p(A) = p(B) = 0.8$. I believe the error in this case occurred because even educated people do not fully understand the concept of conditional probability (proportion of B that is in A) and confuse it with causality. Ignorance is caused by incomplete understanding of the problem and related concepts. The issue here is not an imperfection of intuition due to an ongoing evolutionary process in the development of the brain. It is simply a misunderstanding about the definitions and the properties of the concepts used and sometimes a failure to recognize all relevant aspects of the problem. Errors caused by ignorance (failure to account for tax effects, portfolio effects, etc.) are easily corrected and, I believe, corrections are readily accepted by the decision maker.

A cursory glance at the loan terms offered by financial institutions (banks, mortgage firms) reveals a myriad of options that could overwhelm a person who is trying to decide which loan suits his needs best. Even in simpler situations, the effort of collecting information and evaluating all options is often not worth using optimal seeking procedures. Because of the cost of thinking, people learn to use simple rules or heuristics to make decisions. With repeated use these heuristics become habits and sometimes they interfere with reasoned choice even in important decisions. The impact of cognitive limitations of individual agents on their economic decisions was first explored by Simon (1957). The practice of decision analysis is considerably enhanced by psychologists' research (see Kahneman, Slovic and Tversky, 1982) exploring the biases in peoples' judgments caused by their cognitive limitations. The divide and conquer strategy employed in decision analysis to break the problem down into simple parts is intended to reduce the cognitive burden on the decision maker. Decision aids and counseling may go a long way in reducing the errors caused by cognitive limitations in important decisions.

Suppose you undergo a diagnostic test for which the results would indicate whether surgery would be required at a future date. Would you pay to know the results of the test immediately, rather than in a week, even though this information does not affect any of your economic or health decisions during this one week period? Many people may be willing to pay some amount just to relieve the anxiety. Some people arrive at the airport too early to be justified by economic risks of missing the plane and ensuing inconvenience. Psychological concerns such as anxiety, nervousness, regret, and fear play an important role in decision making. These concerns, though unaccounted for in the economics of decision, are real to a person and should be incorporated in the analysis.

A physicist was once offered a job that paid him three or four times what he was making. He refused the offer and gave the explanation, "After reading the salary, I've decided that I *must* refuse. The reason I have to refuse a salary like that is I would be able to do what I've always wanted to do—get a wonderful mistress, put her up in an apartment, buy her nice things . . . With the salary you have offered, I could actually *do* that, and I know what would happen to me. I'd worry about her, what she's doing; I'd get into arguments when I come home, and so on. All this bother would make me uncomfortable and unhappy. I wouldn't be able to do physics well, and it would be a *big mess*! What I've always wanted to do would be bad for me, so I've decided that I can't accept your offer." The physicist in this story was Nobel Laureate Richard P. Feynman, who was recruited by the University of Chicago to take Fermi's place. This example illustrates that even for important decisions there could be significant tradeoffs between economics and psychological concerns (self-control in this case).

Psychological concerns may not be alleviated by counseling or therapy as quickly as is often thought. To conquer anger or fear may require a life time. To control anxiety and regret is not much easier. It requires mental training akin to meditation to realize that the thoughts of "what could have been" are wasteful.

It seems to me that violations of the rules of rational behavior on the preference side, such as in the Allais paradox, occur due to cognitive limitations as well as psychological concerns. At a practical level, decision aids may be useful in reducing violations that occur due to cognitive limitations. Further, in a balanced approach, the economic costs for avoiding psychological concerns should be pointed out to the decision maker. Psychological studies sometimes tend to accentuate the role played by psychological concerns. This is done inadvertently by giving subjects too little time (and decision aids) so that the choice is guided more by emotional flashes and less by reflective thinking. On the other side, the normative theory requires people to have the temperament of "Buddha." It seems unclear, at this point, how normative theory ought to be modified to properly account for both psychology and economics of decision. It is obvious that in a prescriptive decision analysis, psychological concerns of the decision maker must be addressed.

Modeling Failure of the Independence Principle

There is now a rich body of empirical evidence that individuals' preferences do not obey the independence axiom (substitution principle) of expected utility theory (see Kahneman and Tversky, 1979). In light of this research, it may be unwise even for a rational agent (a marketing manager, for example) to assume that others are behaving rationally. A model that is closer to how people actually behave is useful in economic analysis in spite of its lack of normative appeal. The question here is not whether we can capture every nuance in a person's behavior—that will require a warehouse full of the biases and heuristics that psychologists have discovered. Instead we ask: How far can we go in accommodating choices that are inconsistent with expected utility model with small modifications to the original model? We offer here an engineering approach that retains some attractive properties (with respect to some applications) of expected utility model, permits types of analyses that have been found useful in economics and decision theory, and yet is capable of predicting empirically observed preference patterns that are found to be incompatible with the independence axiom.

Suppose outcome x is defined appropriately as final wealth position, or net liquid assets, or deviation from a status quo. Any generalized utility model given by (1) and (2) can be represented as

$$U(F) = E_F[u(x, c_F)], \qquad (5)$$

where $u(x, c_F)$ is a lottery dependent utility function. The parameter c_F depends on the lottery F and influences the degree of local risk aversion with respect to F. In (5) the utility of an outcome x is allowed to vary with the lottery in which the outcome occurs. In figure 6–5 utility functions that are used to evaluate lotteries F and G are shown. The utility function for lottery F is concave and for lottery G it s convex.

An intuitive interpretation for the model given by (5) is that the degree of cautiousness exhibited by a person depends on the lottery under consideration. The certainty equivalent of a lottery (0.9, \$1,000; 0.1, \$0) may be significantly less than its expected value (\$900) because of the sense of loss that one may experience if the outcome \$0 occurs. The utility function therefore employed in computing the expected utility of this lottery will be concave. For a lottery (0.01, \$1,000, 0.99, \$0), the sense of loss experienced if \$0 is the outcome is small because one expects this outcome. A person, in this case, may behave in a less cautious manner and refuse \$10 (the expected value of the lottery) as a payment to sell the lottery. The appropriate utility function for computing the expected utility of this lottery may be convex. A full development of this model is given in Becker and Sarin (1987).

The lottery dependent utility model satisfies property (P) and, there-fore, its use in decision analysis is tantamount to either rejecting the principle of optimality or economic equivalence (see Theorem 2). The principle of optimality is so basic that anyone who evaluates decisions

$$u(x,c_F)$$

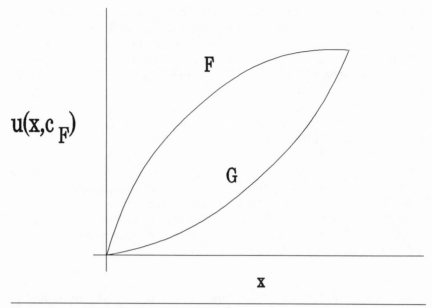

Figure 6–5. Two utility functions.

by their results must obey it. In some sense, the same argument could
be made for economic equivalence if only the economic results are of
interest to the decision maker. The psychological impact of two economically equivalent decision may, however, be quite different in a
person's frame of mind. Such a person may be counseled out of these
psychological concerns or, if the counseling fails, economic equivalence
must be abandoned. In a prescriptive setting, decision analysts must be
prepared to overrule the results of the analysis obtained by using a
normative model if sufficient justification exists. To illustrate this point
further consider the following example.

    Mr. "T" and Mr. "T'" are two stereotypical twins with identical utility
functions for monetary payoffs. Mr. T is tinkering with an innovation that
has 11/100 chance of being successful. If the innovation is unsuccessful
(89/100 chance), Mr. T receives nothing and loses nothing except a few
weekends of play. If the innovation does succeed, he has two options to
realize the fruits of his labor. One is to sell the rights of production and
marketing to an outside firm that will pay him $1M. Alternatively, Mr. T
could himself produce and market the product and this option will yield
$5M with a 10/11 chance and $0M with a 1/11 chance. The problem that

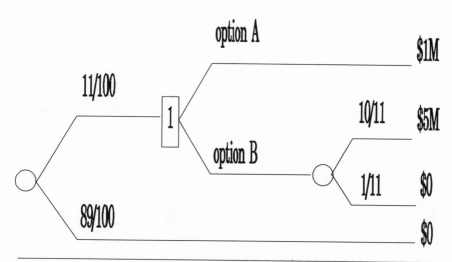

Figure 6–6. Mr. T's decision problem. Aversion of the Allais Paradox.

Mr. T faces is depicted in figure 6–6. Mr. T clearly prefers to sell the innovation to the outside firm (option A). The numbers used in this example are precisely those from the Allais paradox.

Mr. T' is also a tinkerer but he is trying to decide which of the two possible innovations (options C and D) he should pursue. He does not have time to pursue both. In figure 6–7 the problem faced by Mr. T' is depicted.

Mr. T' prefers to pursue option D. How can it be? Option C is economically equivalent to option A and option D is economically equivalent to option B. Since both Mr. T and Mr. T' have identical utility functions, one of them must be making a mistake. Upon further query, Mr. T affirms that if he were to be in his twin brother's shoes he too would prefer option D. Likewise, Mr. T' condones the choice made by Mr. T. Both agree that choices faced by them are really different in that the sense of loss experienced, if the outcome $0 occurs in option B, is significantly more than the sense of loss induced by the $0 outcome in option D. The two problems, though economically equivalent, are not psychologically equivalent for our twins.

It has been argued in the literature that normal and extensive forms of decision trees are merely two ways of depicting the decision problem. This superfluous latitude offered to an analyst by the decision methodology should not lead to different recommendations. I agree so long as the decision maker is willing to evaluate decisions only by their economic

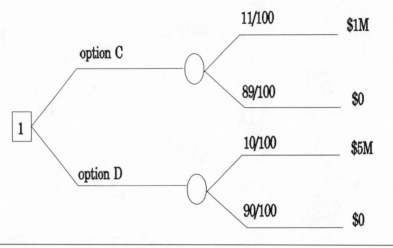

Figure 6−7.   Mr. T's decision problem.

results. Otherwise, the analyst must identify the *natural form* of the decision tree for the problem at hand. The natural form captures the way the decision maker frames the problem. In many cases the distinction among alternative frames of the problem may be inconsequential. In some cases, however, psychological concerns induced by the problem may only be captured by the natural form of the decision tree, and alternative forms that are economically equivalent may not be viewed as equivalent by the decision maker. This complicates the analysis but in some cases it may be worth the price.

In summary, generalized utility theories are primarily useful in descriptive or predictive research and applications. In prescriptive settings a generalized utility model could provide an important *diagnostic* role. I believe that in some cases, where psychological concerns of the decision maker so warrant, the dependence of utility on the lottery being evaluated may be permitted. This tolerance in no way diminishes the stature of expected utility theory as a normative theory of decisions under risk.

Subjective Expected Utility Theory

In the discussions so far, we have assumed that probabilities associated with events are well specified. We now turn to the situation where probabilities are not given and two decision makers could possibly assign different probabilities to the same event. Ramsey (1926, 1928) and Savage (1954) developed conditions under which both utilities and probabilities are derived from a decision maker's preferences. Further, a person who obeys these conditions must maximize subjective expected utility in choosing the most preferred act. We call a decision an act (denoted a, b, etc.) when its outcomes are contingent on events (denoted R, Y, W, etc.). We permit these event contingent outcomes to be lotteries.

In recent years, the empirical validity of subjective expected utility theory has come under attack. In response, several nonsubjective expected utility theories have been developed that accommodate the empirically observed preference patterns. I will first scrutinize the normative implications of these new theories and then discuss the descriptive aspects.

Specifically, I will discuss conditions that show nonsubjective expected utility theories have some undesirable implications in decision analysis. Such theories therefore cannot be accepted as normative for applications in dynamic decision settings.

We deal here with the class of theories that satisfy, for any bets a, b,

$$a \gtrsim b \text{ if and only if } U(a) \geq U(b). \qquad (6)$$

Examples of models that satisfy (6) include Schmeidler (1989), Gilboa (1987), Luce and Narens (1985), Hazen (1987), and Becker and Sarin (1989). An elementary exposition of these theories is given in Sarin (1990).

Consider events R, Y, W and bets a, b, a', b' as in figure 6–8, where $R \cap W = Y \cap W = \varnothing$. For an interpretation of these bets consider an urn with 30 red balls and 60 yellow or white balls in unknown proportions. We will denote bet a as $(x \, R \, y)$ and bet a' $(x \, RUW \, y)$ and so on.

Every nonsubjective expected utility theory given by (6) which is compatible with Ellsberg's paradox also satisfies the property Q below.

PROPERTY Q. For some outcomes $x > y$ and some events R, Y, W, such that $R \cap W = Y \cap W = \varnothing$, if $(x \, R \, y) > (x \, Y \, y)$ then $(x \, YUW \, y) > (x \, RUW \, y)$.

In fact, in order to resolve Ellsberg's paradox, which is often the motivation to develop a nonsubjective expected utility theory, property Q must be satisfied.

Suppose you are offered a choice between two bets depicted in figure 9.

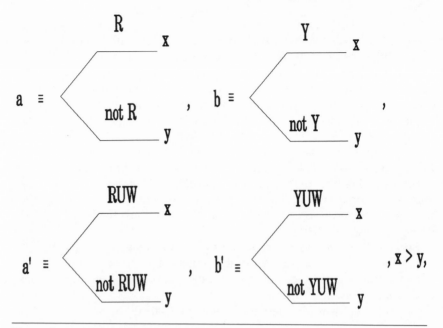

Figure 6–8.   Four bets.

Will your preference depend on whether $x = \$10$ or $\$100$ so long as $x > y$? We formalize this notion of independence of belief with the size of prizes.

ASSUMPTION 3. If $(x \; R \; y) > (x \; W \; y)$ for some $x > y$ and events R and W, then $(x' \; R \; y') > (x' \; W \; y')$ for all $x' > y'$.

We permit x and y to be lotteries in Assumption 3. We now restate the principle of optimality as it applies to bets rather than to lotteries (Assumption 1).

ASSUMPTION 4. For any bets a, b, if $a \geqslant b$, then $\alpha \; \square \; a + (1 - \alpha) \; \square \; c \geqslant \alpha \; \square \; b + (1 - \alpha) \; \square \; c$, for all $\alpha > 0$ and any bet c.

We have already discussed the reasonableness of the principle of optimality for decision analysis. Finally, economic equivalence is illustrated below with an example and then stated more formally.

You toss a fair coin and draw a ball from an urn containing red, yellow, and white balls. The decision tree on the L.H.S. in figure 6–10 depicts that you receive $\$100$ if either the coin lands Heads *and* the red ball is drawn or the coin lands Tails *and* the yellow ball is drawn.

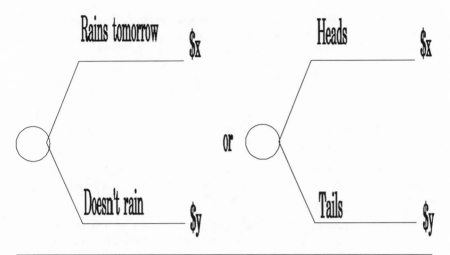

Figure 6–9.   Bets illustrating independence of beliefs from size of prices.

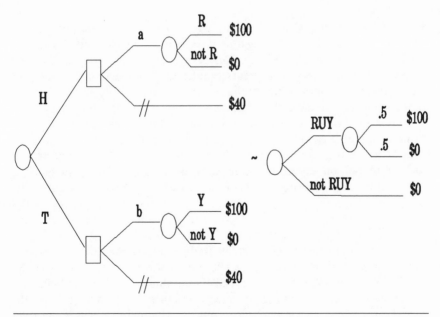

Figure 6–10.   Bets illustrating economic equivalence.

The decision tree on the R.H.S. in figure 6–10 depicts that if you do draw the red or the yellow ball, then you have a 0.5 chance of winning $100 and a 0.5 chance of winning $0.

ASSUMPTION 5. For any $x > y$, and $R \cap Y = \emptyset$, $0.5 \; \square$ $(x \, R \, y) + 0.5 \; \square \; (x \, Y \, y) \sim ((0.5x + 0.5y)RUY \, y)$.

Assumption 3, 4, and 5 seem appealing for a normative theory. These assumptions along with transitivity are sufficient to rule out every nonsubjective expected utility theory that explains Ellsberg's paradox.

THEOREM 3. Assumption 3, Transitivity, Principle of Optimality (Assumption 4), economic equivalence (Assumption 5), and Property Q cannot all be simultaneously satisfied.

Thus, an undesirable implication of any U given by (6) that resolves Ellsberg's paradox is that either the principle of optimality or economic equivalence must be abandoned.

Why Are People Ambiguity Averse?

Probabilities of all real world events are ambiguous to some degree. For perfectly symmetric devices such as dice, coins, and roulette wheels, we might agree on the probability of an event (six will comp up in the next throw of the die) and have great confidence in our estimate. When we lack information upon which to base our judgment about the probability of an event, we are naturally suspicious. A direct result of this suspicion is that people exhibit cautiousness in undertaking bets when they feel "shaky" about their odds of winning. In the famed Ellsberg urn, subjects do not know the proportion of yellow and white balls so they are reluctant to bet on either the yellow or white balls. This reluctance is reflected in their favoring to bet on an urn which contains 50 yellow and 50 white balls as they feel confident that the chance of winning is 0.5. The chance of winning is 0.5 even in the urn with the unknown proportion of yellow or white balls; however, subjects feel shaky (less confident, suspicious) about this chance. Incidentially, the example of the urn with unknown proportion of yellow or white balls was used by Keynes (1921, p. 75) to demonstrate his "weight of the argument" notion. Suspicion is the greatest when people fear being cheated or proven "wrong" after the fact. However, suspicion is reduced but not eliminated, even if the rules are such that cheating is not possible and the event probability is not revealed, for example, if a subject goes blindfolded to a pile of yellow and white balls (say 1,000 balls of each color mixed together) and picks 100 balls to put in an opaque urn. In the urn so constructed, the possibility of cheating by the experimenter is ruled out, but, the subject may still prefer to bet on an urn with a known proportion of yellow and white balls. Notice that even in the original Ellsberg urn, the possibility of cheating (strategic manipulation) occurs only if one assumes that the experimenter is somehow able to guess the color on which a subject will decide to bet on. It seems that the amount of knowledge upon which one forms a belief is a better determinant of suspicion. We will call a subjective probability more ambiguous if it is based on a lesser amount of knowledge and therefore a person has higher suspicion (low trust or confidence) in his estimate. Later we will define ambiguity precisely with respect to a class of applications. Two rules then explain aversion to ambiguity in probability.

Rule 1. Suspicion about the probability of an event decreases with the amount of knowledge upon which the probability estimate is based.

Rule 2. Cautiousness in betting on an event increases with the suspicion about the probability of the event.

Suppose a person is offered a choice between two bets. In the first bet the person gets $1,000 if he correctly picks the winner in the upcoming Super Bowl game. In the second bet, he gets $1,000 if he picks the winner in the upcoming cricket test match. For either of the two bets the person assigns a 0.7 chance of correctly picking the winning team. However, he is an ardent follower of football and considers himself a resident expert in assessing the strengths and weaknesses of the two teams in various departments. The cricket match had been his favorite in the past; however, he has not followed the game for the last ten years. His judgment about the probability of picking the winning team in the cricket match is based on how good the two teams were a decade ago. He is suspicious of his judgment as much could have changed in the period of ten years since he followed the game. Subjective expected utility theory predicts indifference between the two bets since in both the probability of winning is 0.7. An application of rules 1 and 2 will predict a preference for betting on the Super Bowl game. On what Nitsche (1892) called "intensitat" the two bets are equivalent but on "qualitat" the bet on the football game is superior (or at least more comforting) to the bet on the cricket test match.

It seems that for two equiprobable events involving epistemic uncertainty, people will prefer the one about which they have the most knowledge or least suspicion (the argument may not hold in the loss domain or with low probability events). This is not contrary to Tversky and Heath (1989), as their data involve comparisons between a subjective probability and a chance game. Though the chance game has the least suspicion, other attributes such as a preference for the skill game over the chance game influence the results.

Why are people influenced by the ambiguity in probability, and why do they not guide their choices by the probability of winning alone? At one level, the aversion to ambiguity may be due to our faulty instinct. We learn to avoid situations and people we do not trust. We mistakenly treat probability as an *outcome* and ambiguous probability as an outcome that we do not trust. It is rational not to delegate one's affairs to a person who one does not trust. It is wrong to carry over the same intuition and pay to avoid a probability even if it is based on scant information. Of course, one may discount the information from any source as one pleases or seek additional information if its value exceeds the cost. The point is that once one has determined the probability, based upon all available information, to reflect one's degree of belief, there is no superior (trustworthy) or inferior (untrustworthy) probability.

It is possible that the lack of trust in probability contributes to psychological concerns such as anxiety until the uncertainty resolves and self-blame due to hindsight. People often scrutinize their decisions and second-guess their choices. It is easier for mental health to attribute a poor outcome to bad luck than to a misjudgment. When one has plenty of information and trusts the probability, a poor outcome is likely to be attributed to bad luck. When one has low trust in the probability, one may mentally conjure up many scenarios that could have suggested an assignment of a different probability. In this case, it is difficult to acquit oneself of misjudgment. These mental excursions are minimal when one trusts the assigned probability. There are always reasons for selecting the other choice in difficult decisions. Ambiguity in probability contributes to this wavering of will. It requires self-discipline and persistent mental training to make decisions on relevant probabilities and payoffs and not to look back and play internal auditor once the preferred choice is made. Auditing one's decisions to learn for the future is worthwhile, but to lament on "what could have been" is wasteful. Nevertheless, if such psychological concerns are real for a decision maker, these ought to be respected and addressed in decision analysis.

Consider a principal-agent problem where the agent has considerable uncertainty about the probability of an event. For example, the agent assesses that it is equally likely that the probability of an event is 0.2 or 0.8 (for example, there are either 20 or 80 white balls in the urn). The principal observes only the true state (say 20 white balls). If the agent believes that the principal will base her evaluation on the observed state (20 white balls) and not recognize the uncertainty that he actually faced (20 or 80 white balls) at the time of the decision, then it is rational for him to incorporate ambiguity in probability in his decisions. In real situations the asymmetry of information, improper incentive structures, and need to justify one's actions may lead to ambiguity aversion. The problem is more serious when the principal resides within the agent himself. In football games and stock markets, people rarely seem surprised about the outcome since they construct arguments that are consistent with the observed outcome and ignore equally valid explanations that could have led to different outcomes. This hindsight bias causes a person to misjudge (ex post) the ex ante probability, leaving himself vulnerable to self-accusation. If one is suspicious about the probability ex ante, one may attribute a poor outcome to one's misjudgment about the probability. When suspicion about the probability is low, the poor outcome is more likely to be attributed to bad luck. This fear of being "wrong," howsoever economically irrational, leads to cautiousness.

An argument is sometimes made that a normative theory that permits risk aversion must be extended to permit ambiguity aversion since both attitudes come about due to cautiousness in dealing with uncertainty. The cautiousness toward uncertainty in payoffs is rational because the magnitudes involved could impact one's life style. It is rational not to accept a gamble that increases the wealth position by $100,000 with a 0.5 chance and decreases it by $50,000 with a 0.5 chance as the latter outcome might cause one to give up a house, a car, or a long dreamed vacation. The uncertainty in probability has no such economic implication although it could cause psychological discomfort to some. Suppose you are trying to decide between two medical procedures for your mother. The procedure with an ambiguous probability offers a higher chance of survival. Will you reject it because it could cause psychological discomfort to you? Should a manager, who is supposed to act on stockholders' behalf, launch a product with lower probability of success? Engineers, lawyers, and legislators make decisions that impact others. Do we want them to make decisions (choose a technology to build a bridge) with a lower success rate?

A necessary implication of ambiguity aversion is that a decision with lower probability of success will be preferred. The sacrifice in probability of success due to ambiguity aversion must be accounted for by a gain in some other dimension. When forced to think hard about this tradeoff, I believe, people will pay much less to avoid ambiguity than their unaided gut reaction will suggest. I will go along, if upon reflection, you are willing to accept a lower chance of an economic gain because ambiguity causes sleepless nights or anxiety to you. This is not a sufficient reason to abandon the subjective expected utility theory as a normative theory though the application of the theory requires a modification to respect your psychological concerns.

Modeling Ambiguity in Probability

In spite of its normative appeal, subjective expected utility theory is descriptively violated when the probability of an event is ambiguous. In developing a descriptive model to account for such preference, two distinct approaches may be pursued. In the first approach, a decision weight is associated with an event and this decision weight depends on the degree of ambiguity in the probability of the event. Thus, two events with identical probability may carry different decision weights. In the second approach, the utility of an outcome is modified to reflect regret associated with the outcome when event probability is ambiguous. Thus, the utility of a poor outcome, when one has high confidence in the estimated probability, is different than when one has low confidence. Presumably, in the latter case one experiences a higher degree of regret because the poor result can be attributed to a misjudgment about the estimated probability.

Consider a bet b in which a payoff x is received if an event e occurs and a payoff y if it does not occur $(x > y)$. The utility of bet b is given by:

$$U(b) = w(e)u(x) + (1 - w(e))u(y), \qquad (7)$$

where $w(e)$ is the decision weight associated with event e.

In order to obtain $w(e)$ one may first specify the random variable $\bar{p}_e$, the distribution of which is interpreted as a second order probability distribution. The decision weight $w(e)$ can be interpreted as the "probability equivalent" of the random variable $\bar{p}_e$. We introduce a function $\phi(\cdot)$ to compute the decision weight. We use

$$\phi(w(e)) = E[\phi(\bar{p}_e)]. \qquad (8)$$

Thus, $w(e) = \phi^{-1}E[\phi(\bar{p}_e)]$. A large number of the empirical observations reported in the literature about subject's preferences for p_e can be explained by model (8) by using an appropriate shape for ϕ. Concavity of

ϕ, for example, implies preference of $E[\tilde{p}_e]$ over $\tilde{p}_e$ (ambiguity aversion); convexity implies ambiguity seeking and linearity implies neutrality toward ambiguity. Similarly, subadditivity of decision weights ($w(e) + w(\text{not } e) < 1$) is obtained if ϕ is strictly concave. Several properties of ϕ and a measure of ambiguity aversion are discussed in Becker and Sarin (1989).

In the second approach the utility of bet b is given by

$$U(b) = pu(x/y) + (1 - p)u(y/x), \tag{9}$$

where p is the probability of event e and the utility of x depends both on the ambiguity of the event and the payoff y. The model (9) is reduced to model (7) under some preference conditions. The impact of ambiguity in model (9) is captured through a modification of utilities. This preference-based approach is more general than model (7) because aversion to ambiguity is allowed to depend on the relative magnitudes of payoffs as well as on the event. It is an empirical question whether this additional flexibility is useful for explaining observed preferences. This approach is fully developed in Sarin and Winkler (1989).

Conclusions

Individuals' unaided preferences over lotteries are often inconsistent with the predictions of the expected utility model. These inconsistencies may occur due to cognitive limitations or psychological concerns (anxiety, regret, etc.) invoked by the problem scenario.

In response to widespread observed violations of the expected utility theory, researchers in recent years have proposed several alternatives to the classical theory. These generalized utility theories possess desirable properties of transitivity, stochastic dominance, and yet, permit preference patterns that are incompatible with expected utility theory. It seems, on the surface, that this flexibility is bought at no additional price and there seems to be a temptation to regard such theories as legitimate replacements of expected utility theory. Such theories may indeed be superior to expected utility theory descriptively but their normative status seems unclear.

In this chapter, we show that two appealing assumptions about a decision maker's preferences rule out every generalized utility theory except expected utility theory. These assumptions are: *principle of optimality*, and *economic equivalence*.

We do not argue that an appropriate generalized utility theory will have no role as a normative theory in *any* application. After all, Euclidean geometry is appropriate for measurement along flat surfaces and some non-Euclidean geometry for curved surfaces. In decision analysis, however, generalized utility theories have undesirable implications and, therefore, these cannot be regarded as a normative substitutes for expected utility theory.

In a specific application, both economic and psychological concerns may be of relevance to the decision maker. Generalized utility theories could serve as an important *diagnostic* tool to uncover the reasons that lead to distortions in assessed utility and probability functions. This diagnostic potential of generalized utility theories has not been explored in the literature.

Modifications of subjective expected utility theory that accommodate aversion to ambiguity in probability also cause serious problems in decision analysis. Again, the principle of optimality and economic equivalence point to the supremacy of subjective expected utility theory as a normative theory in decision analysis.

Knowledge, or the amount of information upon which one bases assessments of probability (and even utility), clearly influences the confidence in one's action. Two actions with equal expected utilities could be far apart on this "confidence" dimension. In a prescriptive analysis, the economic sacrifice made to gain psychological comfort should be made transparent. Some people will indeed pay a price, even upon reflection, to alleviate psychological concerns; but, this price will often be lower than what a gut reaction (unaided choice) would suggest.

It is apparent that a gap between descriptive theory and normative theory will always exist. This is because peoples' unaided judgments and choices are influenced by ignorance, cognitive limitations, and psychological concerns. It is inappropriate to substitute a descriptive theory for a normative theory because of its flexibility or generality. It is equally inappropriate to continue to use a normative theory as an individual-level assumption about peoples' actual behavior as is the case in economics and other social sciences.

In recent years, there has been a renewed interest in empirically testing assumptions of expected utility theory and in developing alternative theories of decision making under risk and uncertainty. This vigorous activity has caused some doubts about the foundational assumptions of the classical theory. In spite of this unsettling effect, the field has gained a much better understanding of both normative and descriptive decision making. Research efforts of the empiricists and the modelers are continuing to evolve toward a common understanding and there seems to be more of a fusion between the two approaches than the parallelism of the past. This continual interaction of behavioral and theoretical research will be fruitful in enhancing our understanding of the role of economics and psychology in human decision making.

Acknowledgments

I am thankful to Rich Daniels, Ward Edwards, Irv LaValle, Peter Wakker, and Bob Winkler for providing constructive comments on an earlier draft of this chapter. The support for this research from the Decision, Risk and Management Science Program of the National Science Foundation is gratefully appreciated.

Appendix 1

PROOF OF THEOREM 1. Suppose $F \geqslant G$. By Assumption 1,

$$a \square F + (1 - a) \square H \geqslant a \square G + (1 - a) \square H.$$

By Assumption 2 and transitivity,

$$aF + (1 - a)H \geqslant aG + (1 - a)H.$$

Thus, a consequence of Assumptions 1 and 2 is that the independence assumption holds and, hence, the generalized utility model is restricted to the expected utility form.

PROOF OF THEOREM 2. Suppose $F > G$. By property P, there exist a and H such that:

$$aF + (1 - a)H < aG + (1 - a)H. \qquad (A1)$$

By Assumption 1, for any a and H,

$$a \square F + (1 - a) \square H > a \square G + (1 - a) \square H.$$

By Assumption 2 and transitivity,

$$aF + (1 - a)H > aG + (1 - a)H,$$

which is incompatible with (A1).

PROOF OF THEOREM 3. Suppose for some $x > y$, $(x \ R \ y) > (x \ Y \ y)$. Then, by Assumption 4,

$$0.5 \square (x \ R \ y) + 0.5 \square (x \ W \ y) > 0.5 \square (x \ Y \ y) + 0.5 \square (x \ W \ y).$$

By transitivity, and Assumption 5,

$$((0.5x + 0.5y)\ RUW\ y) > ((0.5x + 0.5y)\ YUW\ y).$$

By Assumption 3,

$$(x\ RUW\ y) > (x\ YUW\ y),$$

which contradicts property Q.

References

Becker, J.L., and R.K. Sarin (1987). "Lottery Dependent Utility." *Management Science*, 33(11), 1367–1382.

Becker, J.L., and R.K. Sarin (1989). "Economics of Ambiguity in Probability." Working paper. The Fuqua School of Business, Duke University.

Bell, D.E. (1982). "Regret in Decision Making Under Uncertainty." *Operations Research*, 30, 961–981.

Chew, S.H., and K.R. MacCrimmon (1979). "Alpha-nu Choice Theory: An Axiomatization of Expected Utility." Working paper, No. 686. Faculty of Commerce, University of British Columbia.

Fishburn, P.C. (1983). "Transitive Measurable Utility." *Journal of Economic Theory*, 31, 293–317.

Gilboa, I. (1987). "Expected Utility with Purely Subjective Non-additive Probabilities." *Journal of Mathematical Economics*, 16, 65–88.

Hazen, G.B. (1987). "Subjectively Weighted Linear Utility." *Theory and Decision*, 23, 261–282.

Kahneman, D., and A. Tversky (1979). "Prospect Theory: An Analysis of Decision Under Risk." *Econometrica*, 47, 263–291.

Kahneman, D., Slovic, P. and A. Tversky (1982). *Judgment Under Uncertainty: Heuristics and Biases*. Cambridge University Press, New York.

Keynes, J.M. (1948). *A Treatise on Probability*. Macmillan and Co. (First Edition, 1921).

Luce, R.D., and L. Narens (1985). "Classification of Concatenation Structures According to Scale Type." *Journal of Mathematical Psychology*, 29, 1–72.

Machina, M. (1982). "Expected Utility Analysis Without the Independence Assumption." *Econometrica*, 50, 277–323.

Machina, M. (1988). "Dynamic Consistency and Non-expected Utility Models of Choice Under Uncertainty." Working paper. Department of Economics, University of California, San Diego.

McClennen, E. (1988). "Dynamic Choice and Rationality." In B. Munier (Ed.), *Risk Decision and Rationality*. Reidel, Dordrecht, Holland.

Nitsche, A. (1892). "Die Dimensionen der Wahrscheinlichkeit und die Evidenz der Ungewissheit." *Vierteljahrsschr. f. Wissensch. Philos.*, 16, 20–35.

Quirk, J.P., and R. Saposnik (1962). "Admissibility and Measurable Utility Functions." *Review of Economic Studies*, 29, 140–146.

Raiffa, H. (1968). *Decision Analysis: Introductory Lectures on Choice Under Uncertainty*. Addison-Wesley, Reading, MA.

Ramsey, F.P., "Truth and Probability," (1926), and "Further Considerations," (1928), in *The Foundations of Mathematics and Other Logical Essays*. Kegan Paul, London: and Harcourt Brace New York. (1931)

Sarin R.K. (1990). "Analytical Issues in Decision Methodology." In I. Horowitz (Ed.), *Organization and Decision Theory*. Kluwer Academic Publishers, Boston, MA.

Sarin, R.K., and R.L. Winkler (1992, in press). "A Preference-based Approach for Choice Under Ambiguity." Journal of Risk and Uncertainty, 5(4).

Savage, L.J. (1954). *The Foundations of Statistics*. Wiley, New York.

Schmeidler, D. (1989). "Subjective Probability and Expected Utility Without Ambiguity." *Econometrica*, 57, 571–587.

Simon, H. (1957). *Models of Man: Social and Rational*. Wiley, New York.

Tversky, A., and C. Heath (1990) "Ambiguity and Competence in Choice Under Uncertainty." Working paper No. 19. Stanford University.

von Neumann, J., and O. Morgenstern, (1953). *Theory of Games and Economic Behavior*, (3rd ed.) Wiley, New York.

7 THE INDEPENDENCE AXIOM VERSUS THE REDUCTION AXIOM: MUST WE HAVE BOTH?

Uzi Segal

Introduction

Since the early 18th Century, expected utility theory became the leading theory in explaining behavior of decision makers under uncertainty. For most of this time it was used as a purely descriptive theory. For example, Ramsey (1931) explicitly assumed that people evaluate a risky prospect by its expected utility. He expressed this idea in the following words:

> I suggest that we introduce as a law of psychology that his [the decision maker's] behavior is governed by what is called the mathematical expectation; that is to say that, if p is a proposition about which he is doubtful, any goods or bads for whose realization p is in his view a necessary and sufficient condition enter into his calculations multiplied by the same fraction, which is called the 'degree of his belief in p'.

This theory changed its status sometime in the late forties when different authors tried to give it an axiomatic basis, that is, a set of decision rules implying expected utility maximization. Some of the early axiomatizations were suggested by von Neumann and Morgenstern (1947), Marschak (1950), and Samuelson (1952).

These sets of axioms were usually considered normative, that is, rules that must be obeyed by "rational" decision makers. The common belief is (or at least was) that violating these rules implies that decision makers are willing to give something for nothing, a violations of the most sacred rule in Economics, that more is better. But axioms have another important role, which is their descriptive value. A certain theory may or may not be used by decision makers. Although we may find by chance a behavioral violation of a theory, it may be considered an insignificant mistake. However, if we find that people systematically violate one of the rules that necessarily follow from a certain theory, then this evidence will probably carry more value. Moreover, it should be easier to find counterexamples to well-defined rules than to the theory itself. This approach has also a positive value. Obviously, it is impossible to verify the validity of a theory by any finite number of observations. However, if we can isolate some rules and test them directly, then we will be presumably more willing to accept them. If these rules imply a certain decision theory, we are then thus bound to accept the theory as well.

Undoubtedly, the existence of an axiomatic basis for expected utility theory helped those who claimed that decision makers do not follow it to find behavioral departures from this theory. The first, and by far the most famous type of nonexpected utility behavior, was suggested by Allais (1953) shortly after the first axiomatizations were found. Since then a lot of other evidence against this theory was accumulated. (See, for example, Ellsberg, 1961; Kahneman and Tversky, 1979; MacCrimmon and Larsson, 1979.) Obviously, if a certain set of axioms implies a certain theory, and empirical evidence fails to support this theory, then one or more of these axioms must be violated.

Some axioms have more appeal than others, thus, we would prefer to try to keep these axioms at the cost of the less appealing ones. Moreover, if a certain axiom is widely used, not only in theories of decision making under uncertainty, but in general decision problems as well, then we will probably be more reluctant to abandon it. This is one of the reasons why economists are so unwilling to give up the transitivity axiom. Since the continuity and completeness axioms carry a similar, or even a higher value, the only disposable axiom is the independence axiom.

Let X, Y, and Z be lotteries. According to the independence axiom, the lottery $aX + (1 - a)Z$ is preferred to the lottery $aY + (1 - a)Z$ if and only if X is preferred to Y. The normative justification for this axiom is that if X is preferred to Y, it should also be so when receiving these lotteries becomes uncertain. Recent authors in the field of decision theory are of course well aware of the normative appeal of this axiom, but claim that whether we like it or not, decision makers do not accept it. In other words, even if nonexpected utility theories cannot be used on normative grounds because they violate the independence or the transitivity axioms (for the latter, see Fishburn, 1983; Loomes and Sugden, 1986; MacCrimmon and Larsson, 1979), they are still superior to expected utility as descriptive theories.

But do decision makers really violate the independence axiom? After all, the idea that a preference relation should not depend on outcomes that were never realized is very compelling even on a purely behavioral basis. Moreover, this rule appears in a lot of other areas of economic theory. Indeed, there is not much difference between the reasoning behind this axiom and the justification for the axiom of revealed preferences (Samuelson, 1938) or Arrow's rule of independence of irrelevant alternatives. This does not mean that decision makers necessarily follow this axiom, but it raises the theoretical price we have to pay to exclude it.

I claim below that most of the evidence against expected utility theory, as well as some other evidence, can be analyzed as a violation of the reduction of compound lotteries axiom. Moreover, in an appropriate setting, this axiom has less normative value than is usually believed. This analysis follows closely the one presented in Segal (1990), where the model is more formally presented. Of course, it is nicer to have a model in which this axiom is accepted. But it is my belief that releasing the reduction axiom is the lesser of the many other evils we may choose.

This point appears in several former works. Luce and Narens (1985) analyze, among other things, a model where multi-stage uncertainty is different from a single-stage uncertainty with the same compound probabilities. Luce (1988) gives an axiomatization of the rank dependent model (Quiggin, 1982) based on the assumption that in some cases, the *order* at which uncertainty is resolved makes no difference to the decision maker. For different axiomatizations of the same model, based on other versions of order indifference, see Segal (1989), and Chew (1989). For some references to the experimental literature, see Segal, 1990.

The chapter is organized as follows. In the next section I discuss two-stage lotteries with the reduction of compound lotteries axiom and the (compound) independence axiom. Section three analyzes a Dutch book in support of the reduction axiom. In section four I show how this approach may be useful in analyzing some empirical evidence dealing with two-stage lotteries. The Ellsberg paradox is discussed in section five. Section six concludes with some further remarks on the independence axiom.

Two-Stage Lotteries

There are situations where uncertainty is resolved in more than one stage. This may be because some real time elapses between the point when the uncertainty begins to be resolved and the point where all the uncertainty is resolved, or because the decision maker's concept of the uncertainty is multi-stage, even if no real time is involved. In this section I describe the formal structure of such lotteries. For a more detailed discussion see Segal (1990).

Let L_1 be the set of lotteries with outcomes in a bounded interval $[-M, M]$. That is, $L_1 = \{(x_1, p_1; \ldots; x_n, p_n): x_1, \ldots, x_n \in [-M, M], p_1, \ldots, p_n \geq 0, \text{ and } \Sigma p_i = 1\}$. Elements of L_1 are denoted X, Y, etc. We usually assume that the outcomes of these lotteries are monetary outcomes. Let $\succeq_1$ be a complete, transitive, monotonic, and continuous preference relation on L_1. We say that $X \succ_1 Y$ if $X \succeq_1 Y$ but not $Y \succeq_1 X$ and that $X \sim_1 Y$ if $X \succeq_1 Y$ and $Y \succeq_1 X$. A function $V: L_1 \to I\!R$ is said to represent the order $\succeq_1$ if $V(X) \geq V(Y)$ if and only if $X \succeq_1 Y$. For $X \in L_1$, let $CE(X)$, the certainty equivalent of X, be defined by $X \sim_1 (CE(X), 1)$.

A two-stage lottery is a lottery where the outcomes are tickets for simple lotteries in L_1. Formally, let $L_2 = \{(X_1, q_1; \ldots; X_m, q_m): X_1, \ldots, X_m \in L_1, q_1, \ldots, q_m \geq 0, \Sigma q_i = 1\}$. Elements of L_2 are denoted A, B, etc. A preference relation on L_2 is denoted $\succeq_2$. We assume throughout that such a preference relation is complete and transitive. Two subsets of L_2 are of special interest. Let $\Delta = \{(X, 1): X \in L_1\} \subset L_2$. Δ is the set of all two-stage lotteries which have no uncertainty in the first stage—the decision maker knows that with probability one he will receive a ticket for lottery X. In other words, all the uncertainty is resolved in the second stage. Let $\Gamma = \{((x_1, 1), p_1; \ldots; (x_n, 1), p_n): (x_1, p_1; \ldots; x_n, p_n) \in L_1\}$. Γ is the set of all lotteries where all the uncertainty is resolved in the first stage. With probability p_i the decision maker knows that he has won a ticket for the lottery $(x_i, 1)$, that is, a sure gain of x_i dollars. In other words, both Γ and Δ are L_1 type spaces. Let $X = (x_1, p_1; \ldots; x_n, p_n) \in L_1$ be a simple, one-stage lottery. Define the two lotteries $\gamma_X \in \Gamma$ and $\delta_X \in \Delta$ as follows:

$$\gamma_X = ((x_1, 1), p_1; \ldots; (x_n, 1), p_n)$$
$$\delta_X = ((x_1, p_1; \ldots; x_n, p_n), 1).$$

The preference relation $\succeq_2$ on L_2 induces two $\succeq_1$-type relations on L_1 in the following way:

$$X \succeq_\Gamma Y \text{ if and only if } \gamma_X \succeq_2 \gamma_Y;$$
$$X \succeq_\Delta Y \text{ if and only if } \delta_X \succeq_2 \delta_Y.$$

The preference relation $\geqslant_\Gamma$ $[\geqslant_\Delta]$ is the induced order over simple lotteries whose uncertainty is resolved in the first second stage. These two orders are not necessarily the same. The following theorem claims that they are the same, if and only if, the decision maker does not care for the resolution timing of the uncertainty concerning a one-stage lottery. Formally:

THEOREM 1. $\geqslant_\Gamma \equiv \geqslant_\Delta$ *if and only if for every* X, $\gamma_X \sim_2 \delta_X$.

PROOF. Suppose that $\geqslant_\Gamma \equiv \geqslant_\Delta$, and let $X = (x_1, p_1; \ldots; x_n, p_n) \in L_1$. There is a number x such that $X \sim_\Gamma (x, 1)$ and, hence, $X \sim_\Delta (x, 1)$. By the definitions of $\geqslant_\Gamma$ and $\geqslant_\Delta$ it follows that

$$X \sim_\Gamma (x, 1) \Rightarrow \gamma_X = ((x_1, 1), p_1; \ldots; (x_n, 1), p_n) \sim_2 ((x, 1), 1)$$
$$X \sim_\Delta (x, 1) \Rightarrow \delta_X = ((x_1, p_1; \ldots; x_n, p_n), 1) \sim_2 ((x, 1), 1).$$

Hence $\gamma_X \sim_2 \delta_X$.

Suppose now that for every X, $\gamma_X \sim_2 \delta_X$, and let $X, Y \in L_1$. By the definitions of $\geqslant_\Gamma$ and $\geqslant_\Delta$ it follows that

$$X \geqslant_\Gamma Y \Leftrightarrow \gamma_X \geqslant_2 \gamma_Y \Leftrightarrow \delta_X \geqslant_2 \delta_Y \Leftrightarrow X \geqslant_\Delta Y. \quad \square$$

I assume throughout that for every X, $\gamma_X \sim_2 \delta_X$; that is, that the two induced orders $\geqslant_\Gamma$ and $\geqslant_\Delta$ are the same.

The next question is how do people compare different two-stage lotteries. It is reasonable to assume that when confronted with a choice between two-stage lotteries, a decision maker will try to simplify the choice problem by transforming them into simpler, one-stage lotteries. This can be done in at least two ways. The first method, using the reduction of compound lotteries axiom, is objective in the sense that it is independent of the decision maker's preferences and is based on the laws of probability theory. The other method is based on the compound independence axiom and is subjective in the sense that different decision makers will transform the same two-stage lottery into different one-stage lotteries. These two methods are formally defined below.

REDUCTION OF COMPOUND-LOTTERIES AXIOM (RCLA). Let

$$X_j = (x_1^j, p_1^j; \ldots; x_{n_j}^j, p_{n_j}^j) \in L_1, j = 1, \ldots, m$$

and let $A = (X_1, q_1; \ldots; X_m, q_m) \in L_2$. Define

$$X_A = (x_1^1, p_1^1 q_1; \ldots; x_{n_1}^1, p_{n_1}^1 q_1; \ldots; x_1^m, p_1^m q_m; \ldots; x_{n_m}^m, p_{m_1}^m q_m).$$

Then the decision maker is indifferent between A and γ_{X_A}.

This axiom suggests that a decision maker is indifferent between a two-stage lottery and its actuarial equivalent one-stage lottery, where all the uncertainty is resolved in the first stage. By our previous assumptions, it is also indifferent to the same one-stage lottery when all the uncertainty is resolved in the second stage. By using the transitivity axiom and RCLA, we can now uniquely extend a preference relation $\succsim_1$ on L_1 to a preference relation $\succsim_2$ on L_2 in the following way. For a given $\succsim_1$, define $\succsim_\Gamma (\equiv\succsim_A) \equiv\succsim_1$ and let $A, B \in L_2$. By RCLA, $A \sim_2 \gamma_{X_A}$, $B \sim_2 \gamma_{X_B}$. By transitivity,

$$A \succsim_2 B \Leftrightarrow \gamma_{X_A} \succsim_2 \gamma_{X_B} \Leftrightarrow X_A \succsim_\Gamma X_B \Leftrightarrow X_A \succsim_1 X_B.$$

It follows from the above discussion that, if we do not make any further assumptions on the preference relation $\succsim_2$, then the reduction of compound lotteries axiom does not impose any restrictions at all on the preference relation $\succsim_1$ on simple lotteries. Next, I show an alternative way to extend a preference relation $\succsim_1$ on L_1 to a preference relation $\succsim_2$ on L_2.

COMPOUND INDEPENDENCE AXIOM (CIA). Let

$$A = (X_1, q_1; \ldots ; X_m, q_m) \in L_2$$

and define $CE_A(X_i) \in I\!R$ by

$$(CE_A(X_i), 1) \sim_A X_i, \quad i = 1, \ldots, m.$$

Then, the decision maker is indifferent between A and the lottery $((CE_A(X_1), 1), q_1; \ldots ; (CE_A(X_m), 1), q_m) \in \Gamma.$[1]

This axiom suggests the following procedure for simplifying a two-stage lottery $A = (X_1, q_1; \ldots ; X_m, q_m)$. First, replace each of the simple lotteries X_i by its certainty equivalent under the order $\succsim_A$, which is a $\succsim_1$-type relation. This procedure transforms the two-stage lottery into an element of Γ (an isomorphic set to L_1). Moreover, given CIA, each preference relation $\succsim_1$ on L_1 can be uniquely extended to a preference relation $\succsim_2$ on L_2 to satisfy $\succsim_\Gamma (\equiv\succsim_A) \equiv\succsim_1$. Indeed, given an order $\succsim_1$ and a pair of two-stage lotteries A and B in L_2, transform each one of them to a lottery in Γ by using the above procedure with $\succsim_A \equiv \succsim_1$. Next compare these two lotteries by using $\succsim_\Gamma \equiv \succsim_1$. We have thus proved the following theorem:

THEOREM 2. *Each preference relation $\succsim_1$ on L_1 has two unique extensions to $\succsim_2$ on L_2 satisfying $\succsim_\Gamma \equiv \succsim_A \equiv \succsim_1$. One by using RCLA, the other by using CIA.*

It is well known that a (continuous and transitive) preference relation $\geqslant_2$ satisfies both RCLA and CIA, if and only if, it can be represented by an expected utility functional. That is, there exists a function $u: I\!R \to I\!R$ such that the orders $\geqslant_\Gamma \equiv \geqslant_A$ can be represented by the functional

$$V(x_1, p_1; \ldots; x_n, p_n) = \sum_{i=1}^{n} p_i u(x_i) \qquad (1)$$

This representation theorem can be tracked down back to von Neumann and Morgenstern (1947), but it first appeared in such a form in Samuelson (1952). The axiomatization of Marschak (1950) is similar, but the distinction between RCLA and CIA is not as clear as it is in Samuelson's work. (The domain of Marschak's, as well as Herstein and Milnor's (1953) axioms, is L_1.) Although it has many different versions, the following is the axiom usually used to obtain expected utility:

DEFINITION. Let $X = (x_1, p_1; \ldots; x_n, p_n)$ and $Y = (y_1, q_1; \ldots; y_m, q_m)$ and let $\alpha \in [0, 1]$. Then $\alpha X + (1 - \alpha)Y = (x_1, \alpha p_1; \ldots; x_n, \alpha p_n; y_1, (1 - \alpha)q_1; \ldots; y_m, (1 - \alpha)q_m)$.

MIXTURE INDEPENDENCE AXIOM (MIA). For every $X, Y, Z \in L_1$ and for every $\alpha \in [0, 1]$, $X \geqslant_1 Y$, if and only if, $\alpha X + (1 - \alpha)Z \geqslant_1 \alpha Y + (1 - \alpha)Z$.

Of course, if the decision maker's preference relation satisfies both RCLA and CIA, then it must also satisfy MIA. The importance of Theorem 2 above is in showing that the compound independence axiom by itself is not equivalent to the mixture independence axiom. Moreover, the way the independence axiom is usually defended fits better the *compound* rather than the *mixture* independence axiom. The common argument in favour of the independence axiom is as follows.

Suppose that a decision maker is indifferent between the two simple lotteries X and Y, and consider the following two lotteries A and B. Lottery A yields with probability α a ticket for (the simple) lottery X and with probability $1 - \alpha$ a ticket for the lottery Z. The lottery B is the same as A, only that X is replaced by Y. If the event whose probability is $1 - \alpha$ happens, both A and B yield the same outcome, Z. They differ only if the α-event happens, where A yields X and B yields Y. Since the decision maker prefers X to Y he should also prefer A to B.

A careful examination of this last justification shows that it really supports the *compound* and not the mixture independence axiom. The crucial difference between the two is that the latter identifies the two-stage lottery A with the one-stage lottery $aX + (1 - a)Z$. These two lotteries are equally attractive only if the decision maker cares only for the probabilities of final outcomes and not for the way uncertainty is resolved. Some may consider any violation of RCLA a mistake. The next section presents this argument, and rejects it.

The Dutch Book Argument

Consider the following "Dutch book" in favor of the law of conditional probabilities. Let S and T be two events, and suppose that the decision maker (henceforth the bookie) has the following beliefs: $P(S) = p$, $P(T|S) = q$, but $P(S \cap T) \neq pq$, say $P(S \cap T) = r < pq$. Since he believes that $P(S) = p$, he is willing to put \$$p$ on S; that is, he is willing to pay \$$p$ for a lottery ticket that pays \$1 if S happens (and nothing otherwise).[2] Similarly, he is willing to for \$$r$ "sell" tickets for a gamble paying \$1 if the event $S \cap T$ happens. A smart bettor will now offer the bookie to put \$$pq$ on S, thus winning \$$q$ if S happens. Also, the bettor will put \$$r$ on the event $S \cap T$. If S does not happen, the game is over and the bettor's net gain is $pq - r > 0$. If S happens, the bettor pays \$$q$, which he now asks the bookie to put on T (recall that the bookie believes the probability of this event, given that S had happened, to be q). If T does not happen, the game is over. If T happens, the bettor pays \$1, which he receives back from the bookie since $S \cap T$ happened. In other words, whatever happens, the bettor's net gain is $pq - r$ dollars. The only way the bookie can avoid such a Dutch book is by following the law of conditional probabilities, hence RCLA.

This argument, if true, proves that bookies *must* follow RCLA. If they also satisfy the compound independence axiom, then it follows that they must be expected utility maximizers (provided, of course, they satisfy continuity and transitivity). However, the above argument crucially depends on the assumption that for small bets bookies behave like expected value maximizers. This is true when they follow expected utility and the utility function is differentiable. It is *not* necessarily true when they maximize some other utility functionals. I show that this is so by means of a counterexample.[3] The first step in the above Dutch book asserts that since the bookie is willing to put \$$pq$ on S, and he is willing to accept \$$r$ on $S \cap T$, then he is also willing to do both. The following table presents the outcomes in these three gambles ($S \backslash T$ is the event "S but not T" and $\neg S$ is the event "not S"):

Event (probability)	$S \cap T$ (r)	$S \setminus T$ $(p - r)$	$\neg S$ $(1 - p)$
Bet on S	$q - pq$	$q - pq$	$-pq$
Accept a bet on $S \cap T$	$r - 1$	r	r
Both	$r - 1 + q - pq$	$r + q - pq$	$r - pq$

Suppose that the decision maker has anticipated utility-type preferences (Quiggin, 1982) with a linear utility function (Yaari, 1987). Let $x_1 \leq \ldots \leq x_n$. According to the anticipated utility model,

$$V(x_1, p_1; \ldots; x_n, p_n) = \sum_{i=1}^{n} u(x_i)\left[f\left(\sum_{j=0}^{i} p_j\right) - f\left(\sum_{j=0}^{i-1} p_j\right)\right] \qquad (2)$$

Where $p_0 = 0$, the function f is strictly increasing and continuous, $f(0) = 0$, and $f(1) = 1$. When the utility function u is linear, this function reduces to

$$V(x_1, p_1; \ldots; x_n, p_n) = \sum_{i=1}^{n} x_i\left[f\left(\sum_{j=0}^{i} p_j\right) - f\left(\sum_{j=0}^{i-1} p_j\right)\right] \qquad (3)$$

The values of the above three lotteries are therefore given by:

Bet on S: The lottery is $(-pq, 1 - p; q - pq, p)$. Its value is given by

$$-pqf(1 - p) + (q - pq)[1 - f(1 - p)] = q[1 - p - f(1 - p)]$$

Accept a bet on $S \cap T$: The lottery is $(r - 1, r; r, 1 - r)$. Its value is given by

$$(r - 1)f(r) + r[1 - f(r)] = r - f(r)$$

Play both: The lottery is $(r - 1 + q - pq, r; r - pq, 1 - p; r - pq + q, p - r)$. Its value is given by

$$\begin{aligned} (r - 1 + q - pq)f(r) &+ (r - pq)[f(r + 1 - p) - f(r)] \\ &+ (r - pq + q)[1 - f(r + 1 - p)] = r - f(r) + q[1 - p + f(r) \\ &- f(r + 1 - p)] \end{aligned}$$

It is possible to find examples for a function f such that the bookie is willing to play each of the separate gambles (that is, he is willing to bet on S and to sell on $S \cap T$) but not both. For example, let $p = q = 0.5$, $r = 0.2$, and let $f(0.2) = 0.19$, $f(0.5) = 0.49$, and $f(0.7) = 0.72$. It is easy to verify that the value of the first two lotteries is positive, but that of the third one is negative.

It is sometimes claimed that Dutch book arguments are irrelevant, because once a decision maker realizes that a Dutch book is offered he will refuse to participate, even if each offer by itself is desirable to him. It is important to note that the arguments above are different in nature. Even if he is unaware of the Dutch book he will not suffer from it as it is against his (nonexpected utility) preferences to participate in all the lotteries offered to him in the first round. Also observe that this behavior is consistent with RCLA. As claimed in Theorem 2 above, all preference relations (including anticipated utility theory) are consistent with RCLA *or* CIA (but not both). It is also possible that the bookie violates RCLA and follows CIA (or neither).

The Empirical Evidence

As claimed in previous sections, decision makers may violate RCLA or CIA (or both). But do they follow any of these two axioms? It is of course impossible to prove that people obey a certain decision rule, since the set of different alternatives is infinite. Nevertheless, it supports the behavioral validity of an assumption to find out that subjects do not systematically violate it. Several studies show that decision makers violate RCLA. On the other hand, some empirical evidence indicates that most people tend to obey the compound (but not the mixture) independence axiom.

We assume throughout the rest of the chapter that for a given preference relation $\geq_2$, the induced orders $\geq_\Gamma$ and $\geq_\Delta$ are the same $\geq_1$-type order. Moreover, whenever two simple one-stage lotteries are compared, this order is used. To simplify notation I will, therefore, use $\geq$ to denote all these preference relations. Moreover, whenever a simple lottery X is mentioned, it is supposed to be the lottery $\gamma_X \in \Gamma \subset L_2$.

Consider the following decision problem taken from Kahneman and Tversky (1979):

Problem 1: Choose between $X_1 = (3000, 1)$ and $Y_1 = (0, 0.2; 4000, 0.8)$.

Problem 2: Choose between $X_2 = (0, 0.75; 3000, 0.25)$ and $Y_2 = (0, 0.8; 4000, 0.2)$.

Problem 3: Choose between $A = (0, 0.75; X_1, 0.25)$ and $B = (0, 0.75; Y_1, 0.25)$.

The lotteries in problems 1 and 2 are simple lotteries. The lotteries in problem 3 are two-stage lotteries. Kahneman and Tversky found that most subjects prefer X_1 to Y_1 but Y_2 to X_2. Such behavior, by itself, already violates expected utility theory and the mixture independence axiom. Let $Z = (0, 1)$, that is, a sure gain of 0 dollars. Trivially, $X_2 = 0.25X_1 + 0.75Z$ while $Y_2 = 0.25Y_1 + 0.75Z$. By MIA, $X_1 \gtrsim Y_1$, if and only if, $X_2 \gtrsim Y_2$, hence a violation of this axiom.

By RCLA, $A \sim X_2$ and $B \sim Y_2$, hence $Y_2 > X_2$ implies $B > A$. By CIA, on the other hand, $A \gtrsim B$, if and only if, $X_1 \gtrsim Y_1$, hence $X_1 > Y_1$ implies $A > B$. Kahneman and Tversky found that most subjects prefer A to B, in agreement with CIA, but not with RCLA.

Other violations of the reduction of compound lotteries axiom were reported by Ronen (1971) and Snowball and Brown (1979), although, as reported by Keller (1985), these violations may depend on the way the problems are formed. Next, I show how another empirical evidence can be modeled as a violation of RCLA. It is based on findings by Schoemaker (1987).

Consider the lottery $(x, p; 0, 1 - p)$ and suppose that the decision maker does not know the exact values of x and p. Assume further that he knows that both are the outcomes of random processes. The probability p may be $\frac{1}{4}$, $\frac{1}{2}$, or $\frac{3}{4}$, with probability $\frac{1}{3}$ each. The value of the prize x may be 20, 50, or 80, with probability $\frac{1}{3}$ each. The expected value of p is $\frac{1}{2}$, and that of x is 50.[4] The decision maker may now choose one of the two following options:

OPTION A: $p = \frac{1}{2}$ and the value of x is as before;

OPTION B: $x = 50$ and the value of p is as before.

Each of these two options can be modeled as a two-stage lottery, where

$$A = ((20, \tfrac{1}{2}; 0, \tfrac{1}{2}), \tfrac{1}{3}; (50, \tfrac{1}{2}; 0, \tfrac{1}{2}), \tfrac{1}{3}; (80, \tfrac{1}{2}; 0, \tfrac{1}{2}), \tfrac{1}{3})$$

$$B = ((50, \tfrac{1}{4}; 0, \tfrac{3}{4}), \tfrac{1}{3}; (50, \tfrac{1}{2}; 0, \tfrac{1}{2}), \tfrac{1}{3}; (50, \tfrac{3}{4}; 0, \tfrac{1}{4}), \tfrac{1}{3}).$$

By RCLA, the lottery A is transformed into $X = (0, \tfrac{1}{2}; 20, \tfrac{1}{6}; 50, \tfrac{1}{6};$ $80, \tfrac{1}{6})$, while B is equally attractive as $Y = (0, \tfrac{1}{2}; 50, \tfrac{1}{2})$. Obviously, X is a mean preserving spread of Y, hence risk averse decision makers will prefer Y to X, and by RCLA, B to A. Schoemaker found that most people prefer A to B; that is, they prefer to know that the value of p is $\frac{1}{2}$ with uncertainty concerning the value of x, to the elimination of this uncertainty while making the value of p random. Note that this result does not depend on any specific value function. It follows that in this example RCLA and risk aversion contradict each other.

Consider now the same problem while using CIA. According to this approach, lotteries A and B are equally as attractive as the one-stage lotteries X' and Y', respectively, where

$$X' = (\text{CE}(20, \tfrac{1}{2}; 0, \tfrac{1}{2}), \tfrac{1}{3}; \text{CE}(50, \tfrac{1}{2}; 0, \tfrac{1}{2}), \tfrac{1}{3}; \text{CE}(80, \tfrac{1}{2}; 0, \tfrac{1}{2}), \tfrac{1}{3})$$

$$Y' = (\text{CE}(50, \tfrac{1}{4}; 0, \tfrac{3}{4}), \tfrac{1}{3}; \text{CE}(50, \tfrac{1}{2}; 0, \tfrac{1}{2}), \tfrac{1}{3}; \text{CE}(50, \tfrac{3}{4}; 0, \tfrac{1}{4}), \tfrac{1}{3}).$$

It turns out that within the anticipated utility model, risk aversion is not inconsistent with the preferences $X' > Y'$, (hence, by CIA, with $A > B$).[5] By Equation (2), the values of the lotteries X' and Y' are given by

$$V(X') = u(20)[1 - f(\tfrac{1}{2})]f(\tfrac{1}{3}) + u(50)[1 - f(\tfrac{1}{2})][f(\tfrac{2}{3}) - f(\tfrac{1}{3})]$$
$$+ u(80)[1 - f(\tfrac{1}{2})][1 - f(\tfrac{2}{3})],$$

$$V(Y') = u(50)\{[1 - f(\tfrac{1}{4})]f(\tfrac{1}{3}) + [1 - f(\tfrac{1}{2})][f(\tfrac{2}{3}) - f(\tfrac{1}{3})]$$
$$+ [1 - f(\tfrac{3}{4})][1 - f(\tfrac{2}{3})]\}.$$

The anticipated utility model represents risk aversion, if and only if, the utility function u and the probability transformation function f are concave (see Chew, Karni, and Safra, 1987). It is possible to find examples for concave u and f such that $V(X') > V(Y')$. For a further discussion of this explanation, see Segal, (1990). For a different analysis of this problem, see Schoemaker, (1987).

Ambiguous Probabilities

Consider the following problem (Ellsberg, 1961). An urn contains ninety balls, out of which exactly thirty are black. Each of the remaining sixty balls is colored either red or blue, but no further information about the composition of the urn is available. Consider the following four random variables. In each of them, one ball is to be drawn at random.

Gamble	Black (30)	Red (60)	Blue
X	100	0	0
Y	0	100	0
Z	100	0	100
W	0	100	100

Savage's (1954) sure thing principle may be applied to these random variables. Let S be an event, and let X^*, Y^*, Z^*, and W^* be four random variables such that if S happens, $X^* = Z^*$, $Y^* = W^*$ and if "not S" happens, then $X^* = Y^*$ and $Z^* = W^*$. By the sure thing principle, $X^* \geqslant$

Y^*, if and only if, $Z^* \geqslant W^*$. This principle implies that in the above table, $X \geqslant Y$, if and only if, $Z \geqslant W$. (To see this, let S be the event "the color of the ball is black or red.") Most subjects prefer X to Y but W to Z, (see Becker and Brownson, 1964; Ellsberg, 1961; MacCrimmon and Larsson, 1979).

Violations of the sure thing principle prove that decision makers do not maximize expected utility. If the Ellsberg paradox is just such a violation, then it does not differ in principle from the Allais paradox, and as such, should be solved by all recent nonexpected utility theories. The paradox exists, however, in all theories where random variables are evaluated by outcomes and probabilities. Denote the (subject's subjective) probability of the event "the color of the ball is black" by p and the probability that it is red by q. Since the outcomes in all four lotteries are either 100 or 0, a decision maker satisfying the monotonicity assumption should rank these lotteries by the probability of winning the high outcome 100. The preference $X > Y$, therefore, implies $p > q$. Similarly, $W > Z$ implies $1 - p > 1 - q$. These two inequalities clearly contradict each other.

This violation of monotonicity becomes even clearer in the following example. There are two urns. Urn number 1 contains one hundred balls, out of which fifty are blue and fifty are red. Consider the following two random variables (in both cases, one ball is to be drawn at random):

X': Win 100 if the color of the ball is red, 0 if it is blue;
Y': Win 100 if the color of the ball is blue, 0 if it is red.

Both random variables can be written as $(100, \frac{1}{2}; 0, \frac{1}{2})$, hence they are equally attractive.

Urn number 2 contains one hundred balls, each of them is either blue or red. No further information about this urn is available. Consider the following two random variables (here too, one ball is to be drawn at random):

Z': Win 100 if the color of the ball is red, 0 if it is blue;
W': Win 100 if the color of the ball is blue, 0 if it is red.

Translating both random variables into lotteries, we get

$$Z' = (100, \text{Pr(red)}; 0, \text{Pr(blue)});$$
$$W' = (100, \text{Pr(blue)}; 0, \text{Pr(red)}).$$

Suppose that the decision maker is indifferent to the choice between these last two lotteries. It follows that Pr(red) = Pr(blue). Otherwise, if Pr(red) > Pr(blue), then $Z' > W'$, and if Pr(red) < Pr(blue), then $W' >$

Z'. Since each ball in the second urn is either blue or red, it follows that $\Pr(\text{blue}) = \Pr(\text{red}) = \frac{1}{2}$. The two lotteries Z' and W' are thus identical, and $Z' = W' = X' = Y' = (100, \frac{1}{2}; 0, \frac{1}{2})$. Therefore, the decision maker must also be indifferent between X' and Z'. Most decision makers are indifferent between X' and Y' and also between Z' and W', but prefer X' to Z'. (See above references.)

Several recent works argue that the Ellsberg paradox can be explained by using nonadditive probabilities (see Fishburn, 1983; Gilboa, 1987; Schmeidler, 1989). According to this approach, $S \cup T = \emptyset$ does not imply $\Pr(S \cup T) = \Pr(S) + \Pr(T)$. (Note that the above discussion assumed that for an event S, $\Pr(S) + \Pr(\text{not } S) = 1$.) In Segal (1987) I showed that this paradox can be explained if one assumes CIA while rejecting RCLA. Intuitively, it is clear that decision makers do not consider the random variable Z' equivalent to the lottery $(100, \frac{1}{2}; 0, \frac{1}{2})$. I believe that most subjects will agree that the probability that we draw a blue ball out of urn 2 is $\frac{1}{2}$. Most of them will probably say that this event is, nevertheless, different from drawing a blue ball out of urn 1. The fact that the number of blue and red balls in the second urn is unknown (and therefore, from the decision maker's point of view, is by itself a random variable), induces a natural compound lottery representation of the two random variables Z' and W'.

Let S_i, $i = 0, \ldots, 100$, be the event "urn 2 consists of i red and $100 - i$ blue balls." If the number of red balls is i, then the decision maker faces the lottery $E_i = \left(100, \dfrac{i}{100}; 0, \dfrac{100 - i}{100}\right)$. Let $p_i = \Pr(S_i)$. The random variable Z' can thus be represented as the two-stage lottery C, where $C = (E_0, p_0; \ldots; E_{100}, p_{100})$. By RCLA, this two-stage lottery is equally attractive as the simple, one-stage lottery

$$\left(100, \sum_{i=0}^{100} \frac{p_i i}{100}; 0, 1 - \sum_{i=0}^{100} \frac{p_i i}{100}\right).$$

There is no reason to assume that the probability of winning 100 in this lottery is not $\frac{1}{2}$.[6] Clearly, this is what people mean by saying that the probability of the event "the color of a random ball out of urn 2 is blue" is $\frac{1}{2}$. Therefore, if RCLA is used, there is no difference between the two-stage lottery C and the one-stage lottery Z'. In other words, this approach fails to explain the paradox.

Suppose, however, that decision makers use the compound independence axiom. According to this approach, they replace each of the lotteries E_i by its certainty equivalent, $\text{CE}(E_i)$. The lottery C is thus transformed into the one-stage lottery $(CE(E_0), p_0; \ldots; CE(E_{100}), p_{100})$. Note, that this lottery yields 101 different prizes. (Of course, the probability of some of them may be zero.) Assume, for example, that the decision maker is an anticipated utility maximizer (see Equation (2) above) where $u(x) = x$ and $f(p) = \dfrac{e - e^{1-p}}{e - 1}$. Assume further that $p_{50} = \frac{1}{2}$, $p_{25} = p_{75} = \frac{1}{4}$, and for all other values of i, $p_i = 0$. In other words, the decision maker believes that the number of red balls in urn 2 may be 25, 50 or 75, with probabilities $\frac{1}{4}$, $\frac{1}{2}$, and $\frac{1}{4}$, respectively.

The anticipated utility of the lottery $(100, \frac{1}{2}; 0, \frac{1}{2})$ is $u(100)[1 - f(\frac{1}{2})] = 37.75$. The values of the lotteries E_{25}, E_{50}, and E_{75} are 16.53, 37.75, and 65.01, respectively. Since $u(x) = x$, these are also the certainty equivalents of these lotteries. It thus follows that the random variable Z' is equally attractive as the lottery $(16.53, \frac{1}{4}; 37.75, \frac{1}{2}; 65.01, \frac{1}{4})$. The anticipated utility of this lottery is

$$16.53 f(\tfrac{1}{4}) + 37.75[f(\tfrac{3}{4}) - f(\tfrac{1}{4})] + 65.01[1 - f(\tfrac{3}{4})] = 34.83$$

which is less than 37.75, the value of the lottery $(100, \frac{1}{2}; 0, \frac{1}{2})$. For further discussion of this interpretation see Segal (1987).

Some Remarks on the Independence Axiom[7]

One of the common vindications of expected utility theory, besides its usefulness, is that it is based on normatively appealing assumptions. Special attention was given to the independence axiom, which became almost synonymous with the theory itself. It was first formulated by Samuelson in a lecture he gave in Paris in 1952, and in an article in *Econometrica* in the same year. Its formal presentation, as suggested by Samuelson, is as follows:

> *Strong independence*: If lottery ticket $(A)_1$ is (as good or) better than $(B)_1$, and lottery ticket $(A)_2$ is (as good or) better than $(B)_2$, then the even chance of getting $(A)_1$ or $(A)_2$ is (as good or) better than an even chance of getting $(B)_1$ or $(B)_2$. This is simply a version of what Dr. Savage calls the "sure thing principle." Whether heads or tails comes up, the A lottery ticket is better than the B lottery ticket; hence it is reasonable to say that the compound (A) is definitely better than the compound (B) (Samuelson, 1952; p. 672).

Note that this is exactly the compound independence axiom used throughout this chapter. Moreover, Samuelson himself was aware of the fact that it requires an additional reduction rule and outlined it separately (p. 671, Section 4).

Following Samuelson, it is commonly believed that Savage's sure thing principle and the independence axiom are equivalent. The sure thing principle deals with random variables. This principle can be reformulated for lotteries in the following way. Let

$$X = (x_1, p_1; \ldots ; x_n, p_n; w_1, s_1; \ldots ; w_k, s_k)$$
$$Y = (y_1, q_1; \ldots ; y_m, q_m; w_1, s_1; \ldots ; w_k, s_k)$$
$$Z = (x_1, p_1; \ldots ; x_n, p_n; z_1, r_1; \ldots ; z_h, r_h)$$
$$W = (y_1, q_1; \ldots ; y_m, q_m; z_1, r_1; \ldots ; z_h, r_h).$$

Then $X \geqslant Y$, if and only if, $Z \geqslant W$. As this version of the sure-thing principle compares one-stage lotteries in L_1 and CIA compares two-stage lotteries in L_2, these two axioms are equivalent only in the presence of RCLA. As a result of this confusion, the independence axiom is today unjustly rejected on normative and descriptive grounds, while normative arguments and empirical evidence prove it to be a very natural decision rule to be used for evaluating two-stage lotteries.

The best known evidence against the expected utility hypothesis is the Allais paradox. Allais (1953) found that most people prefer $X_1 = (0, 0.9;$ 5 million, 0.1) to $Y_1 = (0, 0.89;$ 1 million, 0.11), but $Y_2 = (1$ million, 1) to $X_2 = (0, 0.11;$ 1 million, 0.89; 5 million, 0.1), while by expected utility theory, $X_1 \geqslant Y_1$, if and only if, $X_2 \geqslant Y_2$. Such behavior certainly contradicts MIA (see Machina, 1982, p. 287). Let $X = (0, \frac{1}{11};$ 5 million, $\frac{10}{11})$, $Y = (1$ million, 1), and $Z = (0, 1)$. By MIA, $X_1 = 0.11X + 0.89Z > Y_1 = 0.11Y + 0.89Z$ if and only if $X_2 = 0.11X + 0.89Y > Y_2 = 0.11Y + 0.89Y$, while by the Allais paradox, $X_1 > Y_1$ but $Y_2 > X_2$. Beyond doubt, however, this argument does not prove a behavioral violation of CIA, unless one assumes RCLA. Indeed, nonexpected utility theories like Chew's (1983) weighted utility or Quiggin's (1982) anticipated utility may be consistent with CIA, but they are not contradicted by the Allais paradox.

One may argue that the mixture and the compound independence axioms have the same normative justification. This, in my view, is false. The rationale for CIA is that if X is preferred to Y, than it should be preferred to Y even when receiving X or Y becomes uncertain and other prizes are possible. This argument cannot justify MIA, as there is no initial preference relation between half lotteries like (0, 0.01; 5 million, 0.1; —) and (1 million, 0.11; —). Similarly, we usually assume that the bundle of commodities $(x_1, x_2, \ldots, x_n)$ is preferred to $(y_1, x_2, \ldots, x_n)$, if and only if, $x_1 > y_1$, because there is a well defined natural order on quantities of commodities. However, we do not necessarily assume that $(x_1, x_2, x_3, \ldots, x_n)$ is preferred to $(y_1, y_2, x_3, \ldots, x_n)$, if and only if, $(x_1, x_2, y_3, \ldots, y_n)$ is preferred to $(y_1, y_2, y_3, \ldots, y_n)$, because there is not initial natural order on the half bundles $(x_1, x_2, \text{---})$.

In this chapter I interpret the compound independence axiom as a mechanism that transforms two-stage lotteries into one-stage lotteries. This results from using the certainty equivalents of the possible outcomes in the compound lotteries. According to this approach, CIA and RCLA should not be used together. Indeed, if the decision maker uses RCLA, then CIA becomes meaningless, because he never really considers two-stage lotteries as such. This approach proves itself to be useful in obtaining alternative axiomatizations for expected utility and anticipated utility theories (see Segal, 1990), and in proving the existence of Nash equilibrium with nonexpected utility preferences (see Dekel, Safra, and Segal, 1991). This is so because, like consequentialism (Hammond, 1988), it makes preferences dynamically consistent in a natural way. For another view on Dynamic consistency in decision theory, see Machina (1989).

Acknowledgments

I am grateful to Ward Edwards and two anonymous referees for helpful suggestions and comments.

Notes

1. For a different formal analysis of this axiom see Luce and Narens (1985) and Luce (1988).

2. We ignore here the issue of risk aversion. To be more precise, the bookie is willing to pay $p - \varepsilon$ for this lottery ticket. The argument works nonetheless—see Border and Segal (1990).

3. The example works because the preference relation represents "first order" risk aversion—see Segal and Spivak (1990).

4. This is a simplified version of the actual example used by Schoemaker.

5. This result may hold true in other nonexpected utility models as well.

6. This is certainly true if the decision maker has symmetric beliefs about the urn, but it may be true in more general cases as well.

7. This section is based on Section 6 in Segal (1990).

References

Allais, M. (1953). "Le Comportement de L'homme Rationnel Devant le Risque, Critique des Postulates et Axiomes de L'ecole Americaine." *Econometrica*, 21, 503–546.

Becker, S.W., and F.O. Brownson (1964). "What Price Ambiguity? Or the Role of Ambiguity in Decision Making." *Journal of Political Economy*, 72, 62–73.

Border, K., and U. Segal (1990). "Dutch Book Arguments and Subjective Probability." Mimeo, Department of Economics, University of Toronto.

Chew, S.H. (1983). "A Generalization of the Quasilinear Mean with Applications to the Measurement of Income Inequality and Decision Theory Resolving the Allais Paradox." *Econometrica*, 51, 1065–1092.

Chew, S.H. (1989). "Axiomatic Generalization of the Quasilinear Mean and the Gini Mean." Working paper Department of Economics. Tulane University.

Chew, S.H., Karni, E., and Z. Safra (1987). "Risk Aversion in the Theory of Expected Utility with Rank-dependent Probabilities." *Journal of Economic Theory*, 42, 370–381.

Dekel, E., Safra, Z., and U. Segal (1991). "Existence of Nash Equilibrium with Non-expected Utility Preferences." *Journal of Economic Theory*, 55, 229–246.

Ellsberg, D. (1961). "Risk, Ambiguity, and the Savage Axioms." *Quarterly Journal of Economics*, 75, 643–669.

Fishburn, P.C. (1983). "Ellsberg Revisited: A New Look at Comparative Probability." *The Annals of Statistics*, 11, 1047–1059.

Gilboa, I. (1987). "Expected Utility with Purely Subjective Non-additive Probabilities." *Journal of Mathematical Economics*, 16, 65–88.

Hammond, P. (1988). "Consequentialist Foundations for Expected Utility." *Theory and Decision*, 25, 25–78.

Herstein, I.N., and J. Milnor (1953). "An Axiomatic Approach to Measurable Utility." *Econometrica*, 21, 291–297.

Kahneman, D., and A. Tversky (1979). "Prospect Theory: An Analysis of Decision Under Risk." *Econometrica*, 47, 263–291.

Keller, L.R. (1985). "Testing of the 'Reduction of Compound Alternatives' Principle." *Omega*, 13, 349–358.

Loomes, G., and R. Sugden (1986). "Disappointment and Dynamic Consistency in Choice under Uncertainty." *Review of Economic Studies*, LIII, 271–282.

Luce, R.D. (1988). "Rank-dependent Subjective Expected-utility Representations." *Journal of Risk and Uncertainty*, 1, 305–332.

Luce, R.D., and L. Narens (1985). "Classification of Concatenation Measurement Structures According to Scale Type." *Journal of Mathematical Psychology*, 29, 1–72.

MacCrimmon, K.R., and S. Larsson (1979). "Utility Theory: Axioms Versus 'Paradoxes'." In M. Allais and O. Hagen (Eds.), *Expected Utility Hypotheses and the Allais Paradox*. Reidel, Dordrecht The Netherlands.

Machina, M.J. (1982). "'Expected Utility' Analysis Without the Independence

Axiom." *Econometrica*, 50, 277–323.

Machina, M.J. (1989). "Dynamic Consistency and Non-expected Utility Models of Choice Under Uncertainty." *Journal of Economic Literature*, XXVII, 1622–1668.

Marschak, J. (1950). "Rational Behavior, Uncertain Prospects, and Measurable Utility." *Econometrica*, 18, 111–141.

Quiggin, J. (1982). "A Theory of Anticipated Utility." *Journal of Economic Behavior and Organization*, 3, 323–343.

Ramsey, F.P. (1931). "Truth and Probability." In *Foundations of Mathematics and Other Logical Essays*. K. Paul, Trench, Trubner and Co, London UK.

Ronen, J. (1971). "Some Effects of Sequential Aggregation in Accounting on Decision-making." *Journal of Accounting Research*, 9, 307–332.

Samuelson, P.A. (1938). "A Note on the Pure Theory of Consumer's Behaviour." *Economica*, V(17), 61–71.

Samuelson, P.A. (1952). "Probability, Utility, and the Independence Axiom." *Econometrica*, 20, 670–678.

Savage, L.J. (1954). *The Foundations of Statistics*. Wiley, New York.

Schmeidler, D. (1989). "Subjective Probability and Expected Utility Without Additivity." *Econometrica*, 57, 571–587.

Schoemaker, P. (1987). "Preferences for Information of Probabilities Versus Payoffs: Expected Utility Violations Involving Two-stage Lotteries." Mimeo, School of Business, University of Chicago.

Segal, U. (1987). "The Ellsberg Paradox and Risk Aversion: An Anticipated Utility Approach." *International Economic Review*, 28, 175–202.

Segal, U. (1989). "Order Indifference and Rank Dependent Probabilities. Department of Economics, University of Toronto. Mimeo.

Segal, U. (1990). "Two-stage Lotteries Without the Reduction Axiom." *Econometrica*, 58, 349–377.

Segal, U., and A. Spivak (1990). "First Order Versus Second Order Risk Aversion." *Journal of Economic Theory*, 51, 111–125.

Snowball, C., and D. Brown (1979). "Decision Making Involving Sequential Events: Some Effects of Disaggregated Data and Dispositions Toward Risk. " *Decision Sciences*, 10, 527–546.

von Neumann, J., and O. Morgenstern (1947). *Theory of Games and Economic Behavior* (2nd ed.). Princeton University Press, Princeton NJ.

Yaari, M.E. (1987). "The Dual Theory of Choice Under Risk." *Econometrica*, 55, 95–115.

IV WHAT SHOULD DESCRIPTIVE DECISION MODELS LOOK LIKE? WHAT DO THEY DESCRIBE?

8 RATIONAL VERSUS PLAUSIBLE ACCOUNTING EQUIVALENCES IN PREFERENCE JUDGMENTS

R. Duncan Luce

Introduction

Many different qualitative axiomatizations exist for preferences over uncertain alternatives (gambles) that all lead to the well-known subjective expected utility (SEU) or to expected utility (EU) representations (see Fishburn, 1982, 1989). In one way or another each of these axiomatizations embodies four fundamentally different principles of rationality, together with some further assumptions, that entail a considerable richness to the domain of gambles. Moreover, these four principles are each implied by the representation.

Aside from the more-or-less extended philosophical discussions about the logical status and actual rationality of these postulates, a gradually growing literature has focussed upon their descriptive accuracy. One comprehensive analysis is that MacCrimmon and Larsson (1979), and Hogarth and Reder (1986) compiled a number of papers on the subject. This empirical literature is not free from controversy because it is harder than one might first anticipate to provide unambiguous empirical evidence that bears on just a single principle without explicitly or, more often, implicitly invoking some of the others. Depending upon which

W. Edwards (ed.), UTILITY THEORIES: MEASUREMENTS AND APPLICATIONS.
Copyright © 1992. Kluwer Academic Publishers, Boston. All rights reserved.

principles one believes to have survived these tests, one develops alternative, more descriptive theories. In some cases these theories are simply generalizations of EU or SEU in the sense that some principles are abandoned, others accepted, and nothing inherently new and restrictive is added. In other cases, however, alternative postulates are invoked, which no one claims to be aspects of rationality, but rather are suggested as more-or-less plausible descriptive principles or heuristics that actual decision makers may follow despite their acknowledged "irrationality."

My goals in this expository paper are :

- To remind the reader of the four principles underlying SEU[1].
- To indicate which ones I am convinced are descriptively inaccurate and so must be abandoned in a descriptive theory, and why I think so.
- To describe a weighted utility representation in which the weights depend not only on the event underlying the consequence but also on the relation of that consequence to both the status quo and the other consequence. This representation resembles SEU in some respects but does not imply the unwanted principles. Moreover, it generalizes prospect theory (Kahneman and Tversky, 1979), the binary rank-dependent (or dual-bilinear) theory of Luce and Narens (1985), and the general rank-dependent theory of Luce (1988). It is related to the original rank-dependent theory of Quiggin (1982) and later versions due to Gilboa (1987), Schmeidler (unpublished), and Yaari (1987). Much of this research is summarized in Wakker (1989).
- To list several plausible postulates that result in that representation, but with the extra, and some may feel undesirable, wrinkle that utility is additive over the joint receipt of gambles.

The Four Principles of Rationality Underlying SEU

Probably the most basic principle is *transitivity* of preference for choices between pairs of alternatives: if $a \geq b$, that is, a is at least as preferable as b, and $b \geq c$, then $a \geq c$. The standard argument given for transitivity, at least for strict preferences, is that an intransitive person can be made to serve as a money pump. For indifference, it is far less clear that people should be transitive if there is a threshold separating preferences from indifferences. Alternative postulates have been proposed (see Fishburn, 1985), but effectively meshing intransitive indifference with the other principles has proved relatively intractable.

The second principle is a form of dominance that can be described as follows: if a consequence in a gamble is replaced by a more preferred consequence (where this more preferred consequence may itself be a gamble), then the resulting gamble is preferred to the original one, and vice-versa. This goes under many names, such as "independence," but mostly these terms refer to it in conjunction with one or another accounting equivalence, discussed below, and so I avoid using them. My preferred term is the mathematical *monotonicity*, although dominance is good—except for the fact it is readily confused with the next principle. Cancellation, another mathematical term, is sometimes used, apparently always in isolation from other principles.

The third is generally called *stochastic dominance*, when probabilities are known. There seems to be no agreed upon term for uncertain events. Perhaps *likelihood dominance* is suitable. For binary gambles (with just two consequences), it says that if a new gamble is formed by making the more preferred consequence more likely, then the modified gamble will be preferred to the original one.

The last principle of rationality asserts *indifference between formally equivalent framings* of a gamble. For a general discussion of framing, see Tversky and Kahneman (1981, 1986). A major consequence of this postulate, and the one used in the theories, is that one can always reduce a compound gamble—one in extensive (or tree) form—to a one-stage, formally equivalent normal form; the extensive form and its corresponding normal form are indifferent in preference.

For money gambles with known probabilities, the last principle means that such gambles can be treated as random variables, and economists especially have grown so accustomed to this simplifying feature that they typically postulate a family of random variables as the domain over which preferences are defined. This has been the case for almost all versions of the rank-dependent theories that have arisen in the 1980s; see below for some of the references. It should always be recognized that this familiar step either limits the theory to gambles in normal form—I call them first-order gambles below—or if applied to higher-order or compound gambles, it implicitly invokes the fourth, and very strong, principle of rationality.

In the absence of known probabilities, the assumption of no framing effects continues to be very strong. It implies the following concept of *accounting equivalences*:[2] two gambles are judged indifferent if they give rise to the same consequences under the same conditions, ignoring the order in which different events are realized. Several examples of such equivalences are discussed below.

As long as the domain of gambles is sufficiently rich, both in consequences and in chance events, these four principles are sufficient to prove that there exists a real valued function U over gambles that is order-preserving and a finitely additive probability measure P over events such that the U value of a gamble is the expected value of the U values of its primitive consequences relative to P. To be quite explicit for the binary case, let $a \circ_E b$ denote the gamble in which a is the consequence, if the event E occurs, and b otherwise, then U satisfies:

$$U(a \circ_E b) = P(E)U(a) + [1 - P(E)]U(b). \qquad (1)$$

Further, each of the rationality principles is implied by such a representation. It is important to recognize that this not only means that transitivity, monotonicity, and likelihood dominance are implied by the representation, as is widely acknowledged, but also, that all possible accounting equivalences are also implied. This says that any two extensive forms having the same normal form are seen to be equivalent and so indifferent.

Which Principles Fail Descriptively

The empirical literature concerning these principles is too complex to be summarized here in detail. Rather, I focus on what, over time, has come to be regarded as the major evidence against each principle.

The sharpest evidence against transitivity arises from two classes of experiments. One is the often replicated preference reversal experiment (see Bostic, Herrnstein, and Luce, 1990; Grether and Plott, 1979; Hamm, 1980; Karni and Safra, 1987; Lichtenstein and Slovic, 1971, 1973; Lindman, 1971; Mowen and Gentry, 1980; Pommerehne, Schneider, and Zweifel, 1982; Reilly, 1982; Slovic and Lichtenstein, 1983; Tversky, Sattath and Slovic, 1988; Tversky, Slovic, and Kahneman, 1990). Basically it has this form. Within a larger context of selecting and evaluating gambles, pairs of gambles are embedded that have the features that the two members of each pair have the same expected value and one member of the pair, called the $-gamble, has a small probability of a reasonably large payoff and the other, called the P-gamble, has a far larger probability of a considerably more modest payoff. Some one-third to one-half of subjects (of various types) choose the P-gamble when the choice is presented, but, nevertheless, assign an appreciably larger money value to the $-gamble than to the P-gamble. If one assumes, as seems to have been done, that the assigned money values represent choice indifferences, then these observations violate choice transitivity. Recently, several authors, using quite different experimental procedures, have raised considerable doubt about the assumed equivalence between judged and choice indifferences, which raises doubts about the degree to which these studies actually provide any evidence against the transitivity of choices (Bostic et al., 1990; Tversky et al., 1988, 1990). If these doubts are sustained, then the assumption of transitivity need not be discarded on the basis of apparent preference reversals. But, equally important, if judged indifference cannot be explained in terms of choices, then we must develop an explicit theory for judged indifferences. Such an additional theory is essential since such judgments of money equivalents play an important role in many applied contexts including much of the work carried out by decision analysts.

Tversky (1969) carried out a systematic study of the intransitivities that can be generated when successive pairs of alternatives in a chain of them differ only slightly in the probabilities, which small difference is apparently ignored in favor of the consequences, but between the ends of the chain the probability difference is far too large to ignore. This phenomenon has been replicated and further studied by Budescu and Weiss (1987), Lindman and Lyons (1978), Montgomery (1977), and Ranyard (1977). It appears to be a pervasive failure of transitivity that is due primarily to insufficient attention being paid to small differences. Researchers differ in the weight they give to these demonstrations. From a theoretical perspective, it appears to be somewhat messy to take it into account—for example, it has proved difficult to combine any kind of structure with the ordinal generalization of weak orders to semi- or interval-orders.

In sum, although some evidence questions the descriptive accuracy of transitivity, I along with many other theorists, believe that it is accurate enough to assume as a first, and certainly a normatively compelling, approximation.

Turning to monotonicity, the major phenomenon usually interpreted as evidence against it is the Allais paradox, again a highly robust finding. For a detailed discussion largely from an economic perspective, see Allais and Hagen (1979). I need not describe it again, except to point out that it has been demonstrated only when the gambles are presented in normal, not extensive, form. This means that what is demonstrated to be false is the combination of monotonicity and the reduction, via an accounting equivalence, from extensive to normal form. Little experimentation has been done on monotonicity when the extensive form is retained, but what exists supports monotonicity (Keller, 1985; Kahneman and Tversky,

1979). If that is correct, then the paradox really only proves that people do not perceive formally equivalent gambles as indifferent. Although descriptive validity of monotonicity is far from certain, in my opinion, there is no compelling reason at present to reject it. Furthermore, many commentators feel it is on a par with transitivity as an unambiguous principle of rational behavior.

Likelihood dominance was first made descriptively suspect by Ellsberg (1961) by means of the *gedanken paradox*, now named after him, and nothing since then has made it look more satisfactory. Since the main role of likelihood dominance in the theory is to establish the finite additivity of the probability measure, dropping it forces one to representations in which probabilities are replaced by weights with somewhat weaker properties than those of probability. Tversky (1967) ran an empirical study quite different from the Ellsberg paradox that showed the incompatibility of SEU and additive weights.

Finally, there are the accounting equivalences—including the many reductions from extensive to normal form. Actually, and perhaps surprisingly, very little data exists on such equivalences. When the problem of universal accounting is clearly formulated, most psychologists are deeply suspicious as to whether such insights into the structure of gambles are very widespread. Certainly, anyone who has taught decision theory is aware that many students have grave difficulty in seeing through the structure of any, beyond the simplest, accounting equivalences. It is in this respect that subjects' rationality is most bounded, to use a phrase first introduced by Simon (1955, 1978). I believe theorists should be very circumspect in postulating accounting equivalences, and experimentalists need to seek out those (few, I suspect) that appear descriptively valid. Which they are make a good deal of difference in the resulting theory.

One problematic feature of these accounting equivalences is how to interpret the order in which events are carried out. The classes of theories being discussed do not include time as a variable, but quite clearly, any empirical realization of a decision tree does have a strong temporal aspect. This is a clear failing of the modeling.

A mathematically disturbing aspect of giving up on the reduction to normal form is that a full theory for binary gambles does not extend in any automatic way to gambles with three distinct consequences, and one for three consequences does not extend in any simple way to either two or four, and so on. Thus, I first describe some binary theories that generalize binary SEU, and then turn to a generalization to finite, first-order gambles that is of a slightly different character.

Event Commutativity and Binary
Rank-dependent Representations

The first utility paper in which the idea of rank dependence appeared is Quiggin (1982); it provided a rank-dependent generalization of expected utility theory of von Neumann and Morgenstern. (Yaari (1987) gave a somewhat different axiomatization that leads to a special case of Quiggin.) The basic idea of Quiggin's rank-dependent representation is as follows: When the events are rank ordered according to preference for the consequences that are attached to them by the gamble, then the utility of the gamble is calculated to be a weighted average of the utilities of the money consequences with the weights being constructed as follows. The weight associated to the ith event is the difference between two similar terms. The first is a fixed function of the probability of the union of that i^{th} event together with all inferior events. The second is that same function of the probability of the union of all inferior events. Such "expectations" with nonadditive weights of this type are examples of Choquet (1953 to 54) integrals, as seems first to have been recognized by Schmeidler (unpublished). These integrals are described fully in Chapter VI of Wakker (1989).

Two types of modification of this axiomatization have appeared subsequently. Schmeidler (unpublished) and Gilboa (1987) give rank-dependent generalizations of Savage's (1954) subjective-expected utility in which decisions are defined over a fixed set of states of nature of unknown probabilities. There the weights are the difference of non-additive measures on the two sets of events, which again are Choquet integrals. Luce and Narens (1985) and Luce (1988) explore the generalization to events, also with unknown probability, but instead of acts over a fixed set of states, each gamble is conditional on some individual event such as the toss of a coin, a throw of a die, or the unknown composition of colored balls in an urn. It generalizes mixture space ideas. The work being discussed here generalizes these last two papers to theories that are both rank- and sign-dependent, and so I shall focus only on them.

It should be emphasized that, unlike SEU, where all the accounting equivalences hold, the issue of how the domain of gambles is formulated is extremely important. The lack of empirical realism in the Savage-type formulation becomes acute in the rank-dependent theories.

Luce and Narens (1985) looked into the question of finding the most general interval-scale theory of binary utility on the following assumptions: indefinite iterations of binary gambles and a preference ordering that is transitive and connected (weak order), monotonic, and satisfies two of the simplest accounting equivalences, namely,

1. *Idempotence*: for all consequences a and events E

$$a \circ_E a \sim a; \tag{2}$$

2. *Event Commutativity*: for all consequences a and b and events E and F,

$$(a \circ_E b) \circ_F b \sim (a \circ_F b) \circ_E b. \tag{3}$$

The first of these is a triviality. The second simply says that if a is the consequence when E and F both occur, and b is the consequence otherwise, then it is immaterial in which order E and F are carried out. The main doubt is not subjects' ability to see through the logic, which they seem to do, but a possible preference in having one event run before the other.

Luce and Narens showed (see also Luce, 1988, for a refinement in the use of event commutativity) that together with some more technical assumptions about the richness of the domain, these assumptions imply the existence of an order preserving utility function U and two weighting functions $S_>$ and $S_<$ that map events into $(0, 1)$ such that for all consequences a and b and events E

$$U(a \circ_E b) = \begin{cases} S_>(E)U(a) + [1 - S_>(E)]U(b), \text{ if } a \geqslant b \\ S_<(E)U(a) + [1 - S_<(E)]U(b), \text{ if } a \leqslant b. \end{cases} \tag{4}$$

This representation is said to be *rank dependent*, (RD), because the weights depend upon the rank order of the consequences. In other respects, it is much like SEU. It entails transitivity, monotonicity, idempotence, and event commutativity, but not the other accounting equivalences of SEU theory.

The number of weights can be reduced from two to one by adding a further rational accounting equivalence that may well be descriptively accurate, namely,

$$a \circ_E b \sim b \circ_{\neg E} a. \tag{5}$$

This forces the relation:

$$S_>(E) + S_<(\neg E) = 1.$$

A general rank-dependent theory for gambles with any finite number of distinct consequences is given in Luce (1988), but since it is a special case of the representation of Eq. (11) below, I do not attempt to describe it here.

The key empirical issue about this iterated binary rank-dependent theory is the three simple accounting equations (2), (3), and (5), but there is little to report yet on this. However, widespread belief and indirect evidence suggests that the representation of Eq. (4) is inadequate because it fails to reflect the very distinctive role played by the status quo in decision making. There is no place for that in a purely rank-dependent theory, so we turn to a generalization that admits a special role for the status quo.

Rank- and Sign-dependent Utility

Gains, Losses, and the Status Quo

Everyone speaks of gains and losses, and almost everyone reacts to them differently. For example, the intuitive concept of riskiness—although not the formal Pratt-Arrow definition that is widely accepted by economists—seems to focus largely on losses (Luce and Weber, 1986; Weber, 1988). As early as 1952, Markowitz discussed the form of the utility function on either side of no change from the status quo. Edwards (1962) pointed out that if the weights fail to add to 1, for which he adduced empirical reasons, then, necessarily, the representation of utility is as a ratio, not an interval scale. This invited speculation about the (invariant) zero of such a scale, and Edwards suggested that the status quo was a natural possibility. Probably the most extensive recent such discussion is that of Kahneman and Tversky (1979), whose prospect theory assigns to the status quo a very special role. In particular, there is a major difference in computing the utility of gambles whose consequences are both on the same side of the status quo from those that span it. Indeed, their theory exhibits both a rank-dependent aspect as well as a sign-dependent one.

My purpose here is, first, to describe more fully the nature of weighted linear representations that are both rank-and sign-dependent, and then to describe one way to arrive at that representation using some "plausible" accounting equivalences that are based on having an operation of joint receipt of gambles. General results about concatenation structures with singular points, like maxima, minima, and no change from the status quo, are worked out in Luce (in press), and the utility results described below are in Luce (1991) and Luce and Fishburn (1991). It should be noted that when a structure has singular points, its representation is as a ratio scale rather than an interval scale. Thus, forms far more general than weighted averages are possible. They are fully characterized for the binary case, but not more generally. These have not yet been investigated with the context of preferences among gambles, but these richer possibilities should not be ignored.

The RSD Representation of Preferences Between Binary Gambles

Let e denote no change from the status quo. Purely formally, one can generalize the rank-dependent representation to take into account both the relation of a to b and each to e. This yields:

$$U(a \circ_E b) = \begin{cases} U(a)S_>^+(E) + U(b)[1 - S_>^+(E)], & \text{if } a \geqslant b \geqslant e \\ U(a)S_<^+(E) + U(b)[1 - S_<^+(E)], & \text{if } b \geqslant a \geqslant e \\ U(a)S_>^+(E) + U(b)[1 - S_>^-(E)], & \text{if } a \geqslant e \geqslant b \\ U(a)S_<^-(E) + U(b)[1 - S_<^+(E)], & \text{if } b \geqslant e \geqslant a \\ U(a)S_>^-(E) + U(b)[1 - S_>^-(E)], & \text{if } e \geqslant a \geqslant b \\ U(a)S_<^-(E) + U(b)[1 - S_<^-(E)], & \text{if } e \geqslant b \geqslant a \end{cases} \quad (6)$$

I refer to this as a rank- and sign-dependent utility representation (RSD) (Luce, 1991).

Note that, like prospect theory, the RSD representation is unique up to multiplication by a positive constant, and so it is a ratio scale theory, not an interval scale one. This arises because of the highly special role of the consequence e, which is totally unlike any other consequence. By setting $a = b = e$ in the representation, it is easy to see that either the weights are independent of sign, resulting in the purely rank dependent representation, or $U(e) = 0$.

Relation of Binary RSD Utility to Other Theories

The four weighting functions can be collapsed into fewer number by various assumptions. If the weights are independent of sign:

$$S_i^+ = S_i^-, \quad i = >, <. \quad (7)$$

then RSD-utility reduces to the RD representation.

If the weights are independent of order:

$$S_>^j = S_<^j, \quad j = +, -. \quad (8)$$

then RSD-utility reduces to a purely sign-dependent representation (which can be shown to lead to an implausible prediction).

If the diagonals are equated:

$$S_>^+ = S_<^- \quad \text{and} \quad S_<^+ = S_>^-. \tag{9}$$

then the result is a slight generalization of Kahneman and Tversky's prospect theory for binary gambles. It reduces exactly to binary prospect theory by adding the rational accounting equivalence (5). For the RSD-model, this is equivalent to:

$$S_>^j(E) = S_<^j(\neg E) = 1, \quad j = +, -.$$

Letting $S_>^+ = S$, the representation becomes

$$U(a \circ_E b) = \begin{cases} U(a)S(E) + U(b)[1 - S(E)], & \text{if } a \geqslant b \geqslant e \text{ or } e \geqslant b \geqslant a \\ U(a)S(E) + U(b)S(\neg E), & \text{if } a \geqslant e \geqslant b \text{ or } b \geqslant e \geqslant a, \quad (10) \\ U(a)[1 - S(\neg E)] + U(b)S(\neg E), & \text{if } b \geqslant a \geqslant e \text{ or } e \geqslant a \geqslant b \end{cases}$$

which is binary prospect theory.

A RSD Representation for First-Order Gambles

As was earlier noted, once we abandon the assumption of universal accounting equivalences, the binary theory does not automatically extend to a theory of gambles of any finite size. One needs to consider carefully the general form of the representation, explore its relation to the binary theory, and axiomatize it. In this subsection, I describe one proposal (Luce and Fishburn, 1991) that is a natural generalization of prospect theory and that agrees with the general RD theory of Luce (1988) for gambles whose consequence are either all gains or all losses.

Let $\mathscr{E}$ denote an algebra of events[3] and $\mathscr{C}$ a set of pure consequences, such as money or consumer items, but not gambles. Within $\mathscr{C}$, let e be a special consequence that intuitively should be thought of as no change from the status quo or, more generally, from an aspiration level. It is the null consequence.

A first-order gamble is a function g from a finite partition $\{E_j\}$ of $E \in \mathscr{E}$ into $\mathscr{C}$. A second-order gamble is a mapping into the set of the first-order, including the pure consequences. Let $\mathscr{G}$ denote all the first-order gambles, as well as those gambles of second-order, characterized below by the axioms. Preference over $\mathscr{G}$ is written $\geqslant$.

Suppose g is a first-order gamble based on the partition $\{E_j\}$ of an event E. Denote by $E(+)$ the union of all subevents that give rise under g to a gain; by $E(0)$, the union of events giving rise to the null consequence e; and by $E(-)$, the union of events giving rise to a loss.

The representation involves an order preserving utility function U over $\mathcal{G}$ and weighting functions S^i into $[0, 1]$ over event pairs (D, E) with $D \subseteq E$. Suppose that g is a first-order gamble defined on the partition $\{E_1, \ldots, E_{m-1}, E_m, E_{m+1}, \ldots, E_n\}$ and $g(E_j)$ is the consequence associated to E_j. Suppose the subevents have been labelled from best to worst, that is, $g(E_j) > g(E_{j+1})$, $j = 1, \ldots, n - 1$, and $g(E_m) = e$. Then,

$$U(g) = \left[\sum_{j=1}^{m-1} U[g(E_j)]W^+(E_j) \right] S^+[E(+)\,|\,E]$$

$$+ \left[\sum_{j=m+1}^{n} U[g(E_j)]W^-(E_j) \right] S^+[E(-)\,|\,E]. \qquad (11)$$

where the weights W^i, $i = +, -$, are explicit functions of the S^i, which I need not write here. Further, if h is a second-order gamble on a partition $\{E^+, E^0, E^-\}$ such that $h(E^+) = h^+$ is a first-order gamble of pure gains, $h(E^0) = e$, and $h(E^-) = h^-$ is a first-order gamble of pure losses, then

$$U(h) = U(h^+)S(E^+\,|\,E) + U(h^-)S^-(E^-\,|\,E). \qquad (12)$$

This representation, like that of prospect theory that it generalizes, partitions any gamble involving both gains and losses into those two parts, and the weights assigned to them do not generally add to 1. If one focuses on just gains, then the representation is a pure rank-dependent one of the type discussed in Luce (1988) in which the weights W^+ do add to 1. The same is true of the losses.

As written, this representation does not imply that gambles are strictly monotonic increasing in consequences, except for the binary gamble. For monotonicity to hold for all first-order gambles, it is necessary and sufficient that there exists function S^i over events such that

$$S^i(D\,|\,E) = S^i(D)/S^i(E).$$

An Axiomatization of RSD Utility

Additivity of Utility Over the Joint Receipt of Consequences

Let $\oplus$ be a binary operation over the underlying space of alternatives, where $g \oplus h$ denotes the joint receipt of both g and h, whether they are gambles or pure consequences. An experimental realization of $\oplus$ is the duplex gambles first employed by Slovic and Lichtenstein (1968). The axiomatic theory that I describe involves the joint axiomatization of $\oplus$

along with more usual properties of gambles. (Tversky and Kahneman (in press) cite an axiomatization that avoids introducing $\oplus$.) One feature of the resulting utility function, U, is that in the presence of other assumptions below it is highly restricted in form, as is derived in Luce and Fishburn (1991). The simplest special case that was studied in Luce (1991) and leads to the easiest to describe results, has U additive over $\oplus$, that is,

$$U(a \oplus b) = U(a) + U(b). \tag{13}$$

Such an assumption of additivity goes contrary to a good deal of accepted belief, but with the flexibility provided by sign- and rank-dependent weights, it may not be as troublesome as one first thinks. I give one example below having to do with the asymmetry of gains and losses.

Before going into that, however, explicit mention should be made of the basic "irrationality" embodied in the additivity assumption. Given the joint receipt of two gambles, a and b, a rational analysis would say that they should first be convolved, and then, that the normal form gamble be subjected to a utility analysis. The additivity hypotheses says otherwise: each gamble is evaluated separately and one simply adds the resulting utilities. For example, many of us buy both car and house insurance. Do you convolve the risks before making your decisions about the coverage to take? I have yet to find anyone who claims to do so. Each is evaluated in isolation as a distinct risk.

A number of applications of the binary additive RSD theory are given in Luce (1991). Included are definitions of buying and selling price in terms of $\oplus$. These are shown to be different from one another and also different from choice indifference under RSD theory, although not in some of its special cases, such as prospect theory. It follows readily from these definitions why people buy both lotteries and insurance. It also follows that judged indifferences will differ from choice indifference if subjects are in fact stating either a buying or a selling price. Finally, it is shown how to use money gambles to estimate the four weighting functions provided one has a suitable way of establishing choice indifferences.

Form of the Utility Function for Money

In the presence of some of the other axioms given below, additive utility for money can be shown to have the following power function representation (Luce, in 1991): There exist positive constants $k(j)$ and $\beta(j)$, $j = +$, $-$, such that for real x, y

$$U(x) = \begin{cases} k(+)x^{\beta(+)}, & \text{if } x > e, \\ -k(-)(-x)^{\beta(-)}, & \text{if } x < e. \end{cases}$$

For many purposes, this appears to permit adequate flexibility. In particular, it does not establish any special symmetry between gains and losses unless one makes the added assumption that for money $x \oplus y = x + y$. In that case, utility is simply proportional to money. One might first think that this assumption is automatic, but a great deal depends upon the exact interpretation given to $\oplus$. For example, if one thinks of it as successive receipt in time, then it is not so clear that first gaining x and then losing it is the same as $x - x = 0$. Even with this assumption, the RSD theory retains much asymmetry of gambles, as discussed in the next subsection. Using the more general form for U that they derived, Luce and Fishburn arrive at a second, interesting class of utility functions for money that have the property of initially exhibiting diminishing marginal utility but, after a point, changing over to growing marginal utility.

Asymmetry of Reflected Gambles With a Symmetric Utility Function

In contrast to prospect theory, *additive* RSD utility does not require any special assumptions about the asymmetry of U for gains and losses in order to accommodate the observed asymmetry of positive and negative gambles. Suppose U of money is symmetric in the sense that:

$$U(\$ - x) = -U(\$x).$$

Consider additive RSD utility applied to $x > y > e$,

$$U(x \circ_E y) + U(-x \circ_E -y) = [U(x) - U(y)][S_>{}^+(E) - S_<{}^-(E)],$$

which is zero, and so

$$-U(x \circ_E y) = U[-(x \circ_E y)] = U(-x \circ_E -y),$$

if and only if the basic property giving rise to prospect theory obtains, namely, Eq.(9). Thus, the following three suppositions are inconsistent:

1. prospect theory,
2. additive utility that is symmetric for money, and
3. the existence of an asymmetry between a gamble and its reflection.

But if prospect theory is not assumed, then gambling decisions may exhibit such an asymmetry without having to impose an asymmetry on the utility function itself.

The Major Axioms for Additive RSD Utility of Finite First-Order Gambles

The axioms that lead to the representation of Eqs. (11) and (12) are grouped into three distinct classes, the first of which consists of three structural ones. The first structural axiom assumes that $\langle \mathscr{G}, \geqslant \rangle$ is a continuum. The second says that for each gamble there is a pure consequence (for example, a sum of money) that is indifferent to it. And the third, which defines the extent to which second-order gambles must be involved, begins with any first-order gamble g, constructs its formally equivalent, second-order, sign-partitioned one, g_2, that partitions g into subgambles over $E(+)$, $E(0)$, and $E(-)$, and asserts that g_2 is a gamble in $\mathscr{G}$.

As an example, suppose E is an event (such as the toss of a die) having a partition into six subevents E_i, $i = 1, \ldots, 6$, and let g be the gamble:

event:	E_1	E_2	E_3	E_4	E_5	E_6
consequence:	\$10	1	0	-5	-25	-100

Then g_2 is the following second-order gamble:

$$E(+) = E(0) = E(-) =$$

event:	$E_1 \cup E_2$	E_3	$E_4 \cup E_5 \cup E_6$
consequences:	$g(+)$	0	$g(-)$

where $g(+)$ and $g(-)$ are the two (conditional) gambles:

event:	E_1	E_2	and	E_4	E_5	E_6
consequence:	\$10	1		\$$-5$	-25	-100

The second group of axioms captures several aspects of rationality. The first assumes that *binary* gambles exhibit monotonicity in the consequences. As was remarked earlier, this also appears to be reasonably descriptive. We do not know if more general monotonicity is also descriptive, but we do not need that assumption to arrive at Eqs. (11) and (12).

The second rationality condition postulates three things: transitivity of preference; that $\langle \mathscr{G}, \oplus, e \rangle$ is a mathematical group[4]; and monotonicity between the binary operation of joint receipt, $\oplus$, and the preference ordering, $\geqslant$. This with the continuum assumption implies the existence of an order preserving function U on $\mathscr{G}$ that is additive over the operation $\geqslant$, which was discussed earlier. As was noted there, Luce and Fishburn (1991) do give a somewhat less restrictive axiomatization and representation, but it is sufficiently complex that we do not go into here.

The third rationality axiom is an accounting equivalence, namely, that for any gamble g, its second-order, sign-partitioned equivalent form g_2 is in fact indifferent to it, that is, $g \sim g_2$. I am not aware of any data on this assumption, but I believe that it is fairly natural for people to reframe gambles by partitioning them according to gains and losses, as in the above example.

The last rationality assumption is a form of distribution relating gambles to the operation $\oplus$. It turns out to be the source of rank dependence in the theory. Nonetheless, as stated, it seems highly rational and non-objectionable. Define $\ominus$ in terms of $\oplus$ as follows: for $c > b$, $d \sim c \ominus b$ if $c \sim b \oplus d$. In the presence of the assumptions made so far, one can show that $c \ominus b$ always exists. If g is a first-order gamble consisting of only gains and c is the smallest gain, then let g' denote the gamble generated from g by subtracting c (using $\ominus$) from each consequence of g. The assertion is that g is indifferent to $g' \oplus c$. A similar statement holds for any first-order gamble with only losses, subtracting the smallest loss from all of the others. This assumption was discussed informally by Kahneman and Tversky (1979), and to some degree it seems a highly rational reframing. It is a special case of Pfanzagl's (1959) *consistency principle*.

The description "plausible" of my title refers both to the consistency principle, which while rational in some sense, certainly goes beyond the traditional axioms of rationality, and the next assumption which we have called a *decomposition axiom*. It involves an assertion of indifference between gambles, but unlike the superficially similar rationality assertions, the gambles involved in these indifferences are not formally equivalent. The attempt is to capture something that is heuristic and descriptive, but nonrational.

The decomposition axiom says that any second-order, sign-partitioned gamble is judged indifferent to the joint receipt of two independent gambles, one of which is the subgamble of gains on $E(+)$ pitted against the null consequence on $E(0) \cup E(-)$ and the other of which is the subgamble of losses on $E(-)$ pitted against the null consequence on $E(+) \cup E(0)$. This assumption, in effect, postulates a major point of nonrationality on the part of decision makers in dealing with gambles having both positive and negative consequences.

Returning to our previous example, this decomposition axiom says that the given g is indifferent to the joint receipt of:

$$E(+) =$$

event:	$E_1 \cup E_2$	$E_3 \cup E_4 \cup E_5 \cup E_6$
consequence:	$g(+)$	0

together with

$$E(-) =$$

event:	$E_1 \cup E_2 \cup E_3$	$E_4 \cup E_5 \cup E_6$
consequence:	0	$g(-)$

This assumption requires experimental exploration to see just how descriptive it actually is. Data in Slovic and Lichtenstein (1968) support it in the sense that most of their subjects failed to distinguish between a binary gamble with a gain and a loss and the joint receipt of the gain versus nothing and the loss versus nothing (so-called, duplex gambles).

One can show that the axioms just listed imply the representation given in Eqs. (11) and (12), and that the representation implies all but the structural ones. Specifically, it implies all of the rationality assumptions together with the last, nonrational assumption.

The theory has not yet been extended to general, higher-order or compound gambles. The difficulty in doing so resides in my uncertainty about how to cope with compound gambles whose component gambles each include both gains and losses. To be specific, suppose g and h are first-order gambles that each involve gains and losses, and suppose $g > e > h$. Consider the second-order gamble f on the event partition $\{G, E, H\}$ such that $f(G) = g$, $f(E) = e$, and $f(H) = h$. It is not obvious to me whether we should generalize Eq. (12) to apply in this case, that is

$$U(f) = U(g)S^+(G \mid G \cup E \cup H) + U(h)S^-(H \mid G \cup E \cup H),$$

or whether f should be replaced by its equivalent first-order gamble which then is partitioned into gains and losses and Eq. (12) applied, or something else. Some data probably would be helpful in guiding the generalization.

Acknowledgments

This chapter is a slight revision of Luce (1990). Its preparation was supported in part by a National Science Foundation grant IRI-8996149 to the University of California, Irvine. I wish to thank Ward Edwards, Mark Machina, an anonymous referee, and others for helpful comments; Jerome Busemeyer for bringing several empirical studies on intransitivity of preference to my attention; and Paul Slovic for bringing to my attention the relevance of Slovic and Lichtenstein (1968) to the decomposition axiom described in the chapter.

Notes

1. The ones for EU are closely similar, but make explicit use of the probabilities that are present.
2. The term apparently was first used in Luce and Narens (1985).
3. $\mathscr{E}$ is a collection of subevents of an event such that if E, $F \in \mathscr{E}$, then $\neg E$, $E \cup F \in \mathscr{E}$.
4. $\oplus$ is associative, e is the identity, and inverses exist.

References

Allais, M., and O. Hagen (eds.) (1979). *Expected Utility Hypothesis and the Allais' Paradox*. Reidel, Dordrecht, The Netherlands.

Bostic, R., Herrnstein, R.J., and R.D. Luce (1990). "The Effect on the Preference-reversal Phenomenon of Using Choice Indifference." *Journal of Economic Behavior and Organization*, 13, 193–212.

Budescu, D.V., and W. Weiss (1987). "Reflection of Transitivity and Intransitive Preferences: A Test of Prospect Theory." *Organizational Behavior and Human Decision Processes*, 39, 184–202.

Choquet, G. (1953–54). "Theory of Capacities." *Annales de l'Institut Fourier*, 5, 131–295.

Edwards, W. (1962). "Subjective Probabilities Inferred from Decisions." *Psychological Review*, 69, 109–135.

Ellsberg, D. (1961). "Risk, Ambiguity, and the Savage Axioms." *Quarterly Journal of Economics*, 75, 643–669.

Fishburn, P.C. (1982). *The Foundations of Expected Utility*. Reidel, Dordrecht, The Netherlands.

Fishburn, P.C. (1985). *Interval Orders and Interval Graphs*. Wiley, New York.

Fishburn, P.C. (1989). "Retrospective on the Utility Theory of von Neumann and Morgenstern." Journal of Risk and Uncertainty, 2, 127–157.

Gilboa, I. (1987). "Expected Utility with Purely Subjective Non-additive Probabilities." *Journal of Mathematical Economics*, 16, 65–88.

Grether, D.M., and C.R. Plott (1979). "Economic Theory of Choice and the Preference Reversal Phenomenon." *The American Economic Review*, 69, 623–638.

Hamm, R.M. (1980). "The Conditions of Occurrence of the Preference Reversal Phenomenon." *Dissertation Abstracts International*, 40, 5848–5849.

Hogarth, R.M., and M.W. Reder (Eds.) *Rational Choice*. University of Chicago Press, Chicago. IL.

Kahneman, D., and A. Tversky (1979). "Prospect Theory: An Analysis of Decision Under Risk." *Econometrica*, 47, 263–291.

Karni, E., and Z. Safra (1987). "'Preference Reversals' and the Observability of Preferences by Experimental Methods." *Econometrica*, 55, 375–385.

Keller, L.R. (1985). "The Effects of Problem Representation on the Sure-thing and Substitution Principles." *Management Science*, 31, 738–751.

Lichtenstein, S., and P. Slovic (1971). "Reversals of Preference Between Bids and Choices in Gambling Decisions." *Journal of Experimental Psychology*, 89, 46–55.

Lichtenstein, S., and P. Slovic (1973). "Response-induced Reversals of Preference in Gambling: An Extended Replication in Las Vegas." *Journal of Experimental Psychology*, 101, 16–20.

Lindman, H.R. (1971). "Inconsistent Preferences Among Gambles." *Journal of Experimental Psychology*, 89, 390–397.

Lindman, H.R., and J. Lyons (1978). "Stimulus Complexity and Choice Inconsistency Among Gambles." *Organizational Behavior and Human Performance*, 21, 146–159.

Luce, R.D. (1988). "Rank-dependent, Subjective Expected-utility Representations." *Journal of Risk and Uncertainty*, 1, 305–332.

Luce, R.D. (1991). "Rational Versus Plausible Accounting Equivalences in Preference Judgments." *Psychological Science*, 1, 225–234.

Luce, R.D. "Generalized Concatenation Structures that are Translation Homogeneous Between Singular points." *Mathematical Social Sciences*.

Luce, R.D., and P.C. Fishburn (1991). "Rank- and Sign-dependent Linear Utility Models for Finite First-order Gambles." Journal of Risk and Uncertainty, 4, 29–59.

Luce, R.D., and L. Narens (1985). "Classification of Concatenation Structures According to Scale Type." *Journal of Mathematical Psychology*, 29, 1–72.

Luce, R.D., and E.U. Weber (1986). "An Axiomatic Theory of Conjoint, Expected Risk." *Journal of Mathematical Psychology*, 30, 188–205.

MacCrimmon, K.R., and S. Larsson (1979). "Utility Theory: Axioms Versus 'paradoxes'." In Allais and Hagen (1979), pp. 333–409.

Markowitz, H. (1952). "The Utility of Wealth." *Journal of Political Economy*, 60, 151–158.

Montgomery, H. (1977). "A Study of Intransitive Preferences Using a Think Aloud Procedure." In H. Jungerman and G. de Zeeuw (Eds.), *Decision Making and Changes in Human Affairs*. Ridel, Dordrecht, The Netherlands.

Mowen, J.C., and J.W. Gentry (1980). "Investigation of the Preference-reversal Phenomenon in a New Product Introduction Task." *Journal of Applied Psychology*, 65, 715–722.

Pfanzagl, J. (1959). "A General Theory of Measurement—Applications to Utility." *Naval Research Logistics Quarterly*, 6, 283–294.

Pommerehne, W.W., Schneider, F., and P. Zweifel (1982). "Economic Theory of Choice and the Preference Reversal Phenomenon: A Reexamination." *The American Economic Review*, 72, 569–574.

Quiggin, J. (1982). "A Theory of Anticipated Utility." *Journal of Economic Behavior and Organization*, 3, 324–343.

Ranyard, R.H. (1977). "Risky Decisions Which Violate Transitivity and Double Cancellation." *Acta Psychologica*, 41, 449–459.

Reilly, R.J. (1982). "Preference Reversal: Further Evidence and Some Suggested

Modifications in Experimental Design." *The American Economic Review*, 72, 576–584.

Savage, L.J. (1954). *The Foundations of Statistics*. Wiley, New York.

Schmeidler, D. (unpublished). Working papers at the University of Pennsylvania, Tel-Aviv University, and University of Minnesota, 1984.

Simon, H.A. (1955). "A Behavioral Model of Rational Choice." *Quarterly Journal of Economics*, 69, 99–118.

Simon, H.A. (1978). "Rationality as Process and as Product of Thought." *The American Economic Review: Papers and Proceedings*, 68, 1–16.

Slovic, P., and S. Lichtenstein (1968). "Importance of Variance Preferences in Gambling Decisions." *Journal of Experimental Psychology*, 78, 646–654.

Slovic, P., and S. Lichtenstein (1983). "Preference Reversals: A Broader Perspective." *The American Economic Review*, 73, 596–605.

Tversky, A. (1967). "Additivity, Utility, and Subjective Probability." *Journal of Mathematical Psychology*, 4, 175–201.

Tversky, A. (1969). "Intransitivity of Preferences." *Psychological Review*, 76, 31–48.

Tversky, A., and D. Kahneman (1981). "The Framing of Decisions and the Psychology of Choices." *Science*, 211, 453–458.

Tversky, A., and D. Kahneman (1986). "Rational Choice and the Framing of Decisions." *Journal of Business*, 59, S251–S278. Also in Hogarth and Reder (1986), pp. 67–94.

Tversky, A., and D. Kahneman (in press). "Advances in Prospect Theory: Cumulative Representation of Uncertainty." *Journal of Risk and Uncertainty*.

Tversky, A., Sattath, S., and P. Slovic (1988). "Contingent Weighting in Judgment and Choice." *Psychological Review*, 95, 371–384.

Tversky, A., Slovic, P., and D. Kahneman (1990). "The Causes of Preference Reversal." *The American Economic Review*, 80, 204–217.

von Neumann, J., and O. Morgenstern (1947). *The Theory of Games and Economic Behavior*. Princeton University Press, Princeton, NJ.

Wakker, P. (1989). *Additive Representations of Preferences*. Kluwer, Dordrecht. The Netherlands.

Weber, E.U. (1988). "A Descriptive Measure of Risk." *Acta Psychologica*. 69, 185–203.

Yaari, M.E. (1987). "The Dual Theory of Choice Under Risk." *Econometrica*, 55, 95–115.

9 RECENT TESTS OF GENERALIZATIONS OF EXPECTED UTILITY THEORY

Colin F. Camerer

Introduction

To accomodate patterns of preference that violate expected utility (EU), many theories have been developed in which the EU axioms are weakened or replaced. All these theories were developed to explain the same small body of evidence (of which the Allais paradoxes are the most famous); new studies are needed to distinguish among the theories.

I will review several such studies, all of them experimental. The goal is to give a fresh snapshot of where EU, and the competing theories designed to replace it, describe actual choices poorly. Readers can judge for themselves whether EU fails badly enough to require replacement, and which replacement theories are worth exploring.

The picture that emerges from the new data is clear, but not simple. The findings are roughly summarized in six stylized facts, each of them based on several studies. No alternative theory emerges unscathed; each is contradicted by at least one stylized fact. Two of the essential features of prospect theory (which were mentioned in earlier work too)— nonlinear weighting of low probabilities, and utility defined over gains and losses rather than final wealth—can explain all but one fact. The

W. Edwards (ed.), UTILITY THEORIES: MEASUREMENTS AND APPLICATIONS.

new studies provide more evidence that those features are crucial in an adequate descriptive theory.

Indifference Curves in Triangle Diagrams

Triangle Diagrams

Predictions and data can be usefully displayed in the triangle diagram developed by Marschak (1950) and put to good use by Machina (1982, 1987), then others (Sugden, 1986; Weber and Camerer, 1987).

Fix three gambles X_L, X_M, X_H (the subscripts represent *low*, *medium*, *high*) such that $X_L < X_M$ (X_M is preferred to X_L), $X_M < X_H$, and $X_L < X_H$. (In most of the studies the X's are degenerate gambles with certain outcomes, like 0, \$5, or \$10).

We are interested in the set of compound gambles that consist of "probability mixtures" in which each of the three gambles occurs with objective probabilities p_L, p_M, p_H.[1] Compound gambles are denoted by $p_L X_L + p_M X_M + p_H X_H$. Since the three probabilities add to one, we can graph them in a two-dimensional $p_L - p_H$ space. (The third dimension, p_M, is implicitly defined by $p_M = 1 - p_L - p_H$, and can be measured by the vertical or horizontal distance from a point to the hypotenuse.) The set of feasible probabilities is a triangle bounded by the lines $p_L = 0$ (the left edge), $p_M = 0$ (the hypotenuse), and $p_H = 0$ (the lower edge).

Compound gambles cannot be represented in a triangle diagram if their outcomes are themselves gambles. However, suppose two-stage compound lotteries are equal in preference to reduced single-stage gambles, with the probabilities of stages leading to a particular outcome multiplied together and added. If this reduction assumption holds—a controversial question, discussed further below—we can plot the single-stage counterparts in place of the compound gambles. (Reduced single-stage gambles will be denoted by $(p_L, X_L; p_M, X_M; p_H, X_H)$, where the X's are certain outcomes.)

Predictions of Some Theories About Indifference Curves

Most generalized utility theories make different predictions about the shape of indifference curves that connect equally preferred gambles.[2] The predictions and functional forms of several theories are summarized below and in figures 9–1a to 9–1h and table 9–1. Each theory will be mentioned briefly. Camerer (1989) gives more details.

Expected utility depends on three axioms: ordering (completeness and transitivity of preferences), continuity, and independence. Completeness guarantees that any two points in the triangle are either on the same indifference curve or on two different curves. Transitivity guarantees that indifference curves do not cross *within* the triangle (Fishburn, 1984). Continuity guarantees that there are no open spaces in the indifference map.

The ordering and continuity assumptions do not restrict the shapes of indifference curves very much, but independence does. Stated formally:

(Compound) Independence: If $X < Y$, then $pX + (1 - p)Z < pY + (1 - p)Z$. for all $p > 0$, Z

Remember that $pX + (1 - p)Z$ is a compound gamble because X and Z might be gambles too. The statement of independence just given is therefore labelled "compound independence" by Segal (1990). Independence over reduced gambles is a slightly different assumption, written:

(Reduced) Independence:[3]
   If $(p_1,X_1; \ldots ; p_n,X_n) < (q_1,Y_1; \ldots q_m,Y_m)$,
   then $(rp_1,X_1; \ldots ;rp_n,X_n; (1 - r)Z) < (rq_1,Y_1; \ldots ;rq_m,Y_m; (1 - r)Z)$
   for all $r > 0$, Z.

Reduced independence is the same as assuming *both* compound independence *and* reduction (equivalence between compound gambles and their reduced single-stage counterparts). In this volume, Luce suggests that compound independence (which he calls "monotonicity") is more intuitively plausible than the mental "accounting" required for the reduction assumption to hold. Indeed, when compound independence is tested without assuming reduction, by displaying gambles in compound form, mixed evidence suggests there are fewer violations than of reduced-form independence.[4] Almost all the experiments described below test the reduced-form version of independence.

Returning to axioms, in the special case in which we take Z to be X or Y, independence reduces to a property called "betweenness:"

Betweenness: If $X < Y$, then $X < pX + (1 - p)Y < Y$ for all $p\varepsilon(0,1)$

(If Y is preferred to X, every probability mixture of X and Y is *between* them in preference.) Betweenness implies that indifference curves are straight lines. Independence implies that curves are parallel straight lines (as in figure 9–1a).

The functional form for EU (for discrete lotteries) is:

$$U(\Sigma p_i x_i) = \Sigma p_i u(x_i). \tag{1}$$

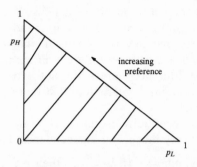

Figure 9-1a.   Indifference curves assuming expected utility.

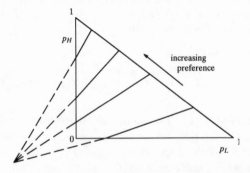

Figure 9-1b.   Indifference curves assuming weighted utility $(W(X_M) < 1)$.

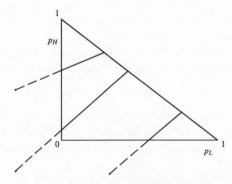

Figure 9-1c.   Indifference curves assuming implicit weighted utility.

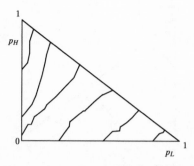

Figure 9–1d.   Indifference curves assuming the fanning-out hypothesis.

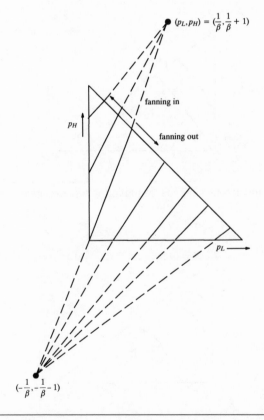

Figure 9–1e.   Indifference curves assuming disappointment theory ($\beta > 0$).

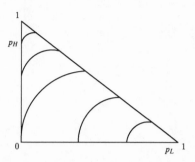

Figure 9–1f.   Indifference curves assuming expected utility with rank-dependent probabilities (*g*(*p*) concave).

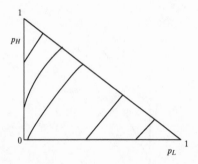

Figure 9–1g.   Indifference curves assuming lottery-dependent expected utility (*h*(*x*) concave).

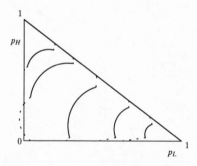

Figure 9–1h.   Indifference curves assuming prospect theory.

Weighted utility theory (Chew and MacCrimmon, 1979a; Chew, 1983; compare Fishburn, 1984; Bordley and Hazen, forthcoming) assumes a weakened form of independence, which implies that indifference curves are straight lines that meet at a point outside the triangle (see figure 9-1b, in which $w(x_M) < 1$). The functional form is:

$$U(\Sigma p_i x_i) = \Sigma p_i w(x_i) u(x_i) / \Sigma p_i w(x_i). \tag{2}$$

An even weaker theory, called implicit weighted utility by Chew (1989), or *implicit EU* by Dekel (1986), depends on betweenness rather than independence, so it implies only that curves are straight lines (which are positively-sloped, and don't cross over, as in figure 9-1c). Its functional form is:

$$U^* = U(\Sigma p_i x_i) = \Sigma p_i u(x_i, U^*). \tag{3}$$

In weighted utility theory, the curves may "fan out," becoming steeper as one moves from the lower right corner (or southeast) to the upper left corner (or northwest), or "fan in," becoming less steep to the northwest. Steeper indifference curves correspond to more risk-averse behavior: the steeper the curve, the more p_H a person demands in order to accept a unit increase in p_L.

In his "fanning out hypothesis," Machina (1982) conjectured that curves fan out throughout the triangle, but he did not assume curves are straight lines (figure 9–1d). Fanning out can be defined formally. Suppose a gamble X stochastically dominates Y; then X lies to the northwest of Y in the triangle.[5] Indifference curves fan out if their slope at X, or the slope of their tangent line, is greater than the slope at Y. (Fanning in is the opposite: the slope at X is *smaller* than at Y.) Intuitively, if people are more risk-averse toward gambles that are better (in the sense of stochastic dominance), their indifference curves will fan out.

In one variant of implicit EU, indifference curves in the northwest of the triangle fan in, meeting at a northeast point, while curves in the southeast fan out, meeting at a southwestern point. Chew (1985) originally derived such a theory and named it semi-weighted utility. Independently, Gul (1991) derived a slightly more restrictive theory from considerations of disappointment. (Neilson, in press, proposed an even more general "mixed-fanning" hypothesis.) Indifference curves for Gul's disappointment theory are shown in figure 9–1e. The functional form is

$$U(\Sigma p_i x_i) = \gamma(\alpha) \sum_{x_i > \Sigma p_i x_i} u(x_i) p_i / \alpha + (1 - \gamma(\alpha)) \sum_{x_i < \Sigma p_i x_i} u(x_i) p_i / (1 - \alpha)$$

where

$$\gamma(\alpha) = \alpha/(1 + (1 - \alpha)\beta) \qquad \alpha = \sum_{x_i > \Sigma \, p_i x_i} p_i$$

If $\beta > 0$ then indifference curves fan out in the southeast corner and fan in in the northwest corner; $\beta < 0$ is opposite.

In *expected utility with rank-dependent probability weights* (Chew, 1984; Hey, 1984; Quiggin, 1982, 1985; Segal, 1987, 1989; Yaari, 1987; compare Green and Jullien, 1988; Luce 1988), probabilities are weighted before an expected utility is calculated. The weights depend on the rank-order of the outcomes. Suppose $x_1 < x_2 < \ldots < x_n$. The functional form is:

$$U(\Sigma p_i x_i) = \sum_{i=1}^{n} u(x_i)\left[g\left(\sum_{j=1}^{i} p_j\right) - g\left(\sum_{j=1}^{i-1} p_j\right)\right]. \qquad (5)$$

With rank-dependent probability weights, indifference curves will not be straight lines unless the probability transformation function $g(p)$ is p. Their curvature will depend on $g(\cdot)$. A concave $g(\cdot)$ expresses risk-aversion because probabilities of lowest ranked outcomes are overweighted; a convex $g(\cdot)$ expresses risk-preference by overweighting the highest ranked outcomes. If $g(\cdot)$ is concave, indifference curves are steepest in the lower left hand corner, fan out to the southeast and fan in to the northwest, and are parallel at the hypotenuse (Roell, 1987; Camerer, 1989), as in figure 9–1f. (A convex $g(\cdot)$ has the opposite properties.)

Lottery-dependent utility theory (Becker and Sarin, 1987) assumes only stochastic dominance, ordering, and continuity. The theory is quite general:

$$U(\Sigma p_i x_i) = \Sigma p_i u(x_i, c_F) \quad \text{where } c_F = \Sigma h(x_i) p_i. \qquad (6)$$

Becker and Sarin (1987) suggest an exponential form for the utility function $u(x_i, c_F)$ which makes the theory more precise and useful. For that specific form, indifference curves fan out. Preferences are quasi-convex (curves are concave) if $h(\cdot)$ is concave (Camerer, 1989, p. 73), as in figure 9-1g.

Nonlinear weighting theories. There are several variants of EU in which probabilities are weighted nonlinearly. Denote the weight attached to p by $\pi(p)$. Such theories predict a form

$$U(\Sigma p_i x_i) = \Sigma \pi(p_i) u(x_i). \qquad (7)$$

The earliest tests of EU considered theories of this kind (Preston and Baratta, 1948; Mosteller and Nogee, 1951) and found some evidence that low probabilities (less than 0.2 or so) were underweighted and higher probabilities were overweighted. Edwards (1953, 1954a) found overweighting of specific probabilities, especially 0.5, but such "probability preferences" appear somewhat context-specific (cf. Edwards, 1954b).

Some variants of the form in (7) have been proposed by Bernard (1964), Karmarkar (1978), and Viscusi (1989). Handa (1977) proposed no specific form for $\pi(p)$ (but he assumed $u(x) = x$).

Karmarkar suggests $\pi(p_i) = (p_i/1 - p_i)^a/[(1 + (p_i/1 - p_i)^a)$. When $a = 1$, $\pi(p) = p$ so the theory reduces to EU. When $a > 1$ probabilities below 0.5 are underweighted and probabilities above 0.5 are overweighted; the opposite is true when $a < 1$.

In Viscusi's theory, $\pi(p) = (\lambda q + \xi p)/(\lambda + \xi)$, where q is a prior belief about the probability p. (And $\pi(1) = 1$, $\pi(0) = 0$.) The weight $\pi(p)$ is the Bayesian posterior of an event from an updating process in which people act as if they observed λ trials in which the event occurred with a relative frequency q and ξ trials where the event occurred with a relative frequency p. Thus, in the limiting case where $\xi \gg$, λ $\pi(p)$ converges to p.

Prospect theory (Kahneman and Tversky, 1979) departs from EU most dramatically. (It is not strictly a mathematical generalization of EU as the other theories are, but compare Luce, 1988.) In prospect theory, carriers of value are gains and losses from a reference point (compare Markowitz, 1952). Indifference curves may vary with the choice of reference point so that there is no distinct set of curves. But it is useful to compare a variant of the theory that ignores reference point switches and embodies other features of prospect theory with the theories described above. Assuming the reference point is zero, and ignoring editing and coding stages, the value of a gamble is:

$$V(\Sigma p_i x_i) = \pi(p_1)v(x_1) + \pi(p_2)v(x_2). \tag{8}$$

If $p_1 + p_2 = 1$ and both x_i have the same sign (with $|x_1| < |x_2|$), then

$$V(\Sigma p_i x_i) = (1 - \pi(p_2))v(x_1) + \pi(p_2)v(x_2). \tag{8'}$$

The decision weight function $\pi(p)$ is hypothesized (based on experimental observation) to overweight low probabilities and underweight high probabilities, to be subadditive ($\pi(p) + \pi(1 - p) < 1$) and subproportional ($\pi(pq)/\pi(p)$ converges to 1 as p converges to 0). Also $\pi(0) = 0$ and $\pi(1) = 1$.

Prospect theory indifference curves have several unusual properties. Since the decision weight function $\pi(p)$ is assumed to be nonlinear, the curves will indeed be curved, perhaps dramatically (see figure 9–1h). If $\pi(p)$ is convex throughout most of the p range (as the data suggest), curves will fan out toward the southeast and fan in toward the northwest (as in expected utility with rank-dependent probabilities). If $\pi(p)$ is highly nonlinear near 0 and 1 (or discontinous), curves will change slope and shape dramatically at the edges; choices inside the triangle will violate EU less than choices involving gambles on the edges. When gambles involve losses rather than gains, indifference curves will be flatter (reflecting risk-seeking for losses, or "reflection" of risk attitudes at the reference point), and their shape will be a reflection of the gain-gamble curves around the 45-degree line.

The experiments that follow test various elements of prospect theory in different combinations. Most experiments *do not* test reflection or loss-aversion because they use gambles in only one domain, gains or losses. Those experiments test only the nonlinear probability weighting assumption in prospect theory, which is shared by many other theories. Some experiments compare gambles over gains with gambles over losses to test reflection, but they do not test loss-aversion.

Properties of Indifference Curves: Curvature, Slope, and Fanning

Loosely speaking, indifference curves have three geometric properties: curvature, slope, and fanning. Every theory differs in some part of the triangle in its predictions about these properties (as table 9–1 and figures 9–1a to 9–1h show).

Curvature, slope, and fanning naturally express three different aspects of individual attitudes about choices:

1. Curvature expresses *attitude toward randomization*. If people do not mind randomizing among objects they are indifferent toward, like gambles or gender of children, they will obey betweenness (which implies that indifference curves are straight lines). The degree of curvature in their curves can be approximated by the frequency and regularity of violations of betweenness.
2. The slope of an indifference curve at a point expresses *attitude toward risk*. Slope measures how much p_H a person needs to be compensated for an increase in p_L (or the "price" of risk). Risk attitude is measured by the fraction of subjects choosing the less risky gamble in a pair.
3. Fanning expresses *variation in attitude toward risk* (or slope) throughout the triangle. Since risk attitude in EU is embodied solely in the utility function, the marginal rate of substitution of p_H for p_L should be constant in each triangle. All other theories permit risk attitude to

Table 9-1. Predictions of Competing Theories About Properties of Indifference Curves

Theory	Functional form of U^* — continuous $U^*(F(x))$	discrete $U^*(\sum p_j;x_j)$	Straight Lines?	Fanning Out?	Fanning In?	Miscellaneous
Expected Utility	$\int u(x)dF(x)$	$\sum p_i u(x_i)$	Yes	No	No	Curves parallel
Weighted Utility	$\dfrac{\int u(x)w(x)dF(x)}{\int w(x)dF(x)}$	$\dfrac{\sum p_i w(x_i)u(x_i)}{\sum p_i w(x_i)}$ $\quad w(X_m)<1$ $\quad w(X_m)>1$	Yes	Yes	No	Curves meet in a point
Implicit Expected Utility	$\int u(x, U^*)dF(x)$	$\sum p_i u(x_i, U^*)$	Yes	No	Maybe	Only testable; Property is betweenness
Fanning Out Hypothesis	$\dfrac{-U''(x;F)}{U'(x;F)} \geq \dfrac{-U''(x;G)}{U'(x;G)}$ if	$F(x) \leq G(x)$ for all x	Maybe	Yes	No	Movements to northwest cause steeper slopes
Disappointment (semiweighted utility)	$\gamma(\alpha)\displaystyle\int_{x_i>F(x)}\dfrac{u(x_i)dF(x)}{\alpha} + (1-\gamma(\alpha))\displaystyle\int_{x_i<F(x)}\dfrac{u(x_i)dF(x)}{(1-\alpha)}$	$\gamma(\alpha)\displaystyle\sum_{xi>\sum p_{si}}\dfrac{u(x_i)p_i}{a} + (1-(\alpha))\displaystyle\sum_{xi<\sum p_{si}}\dfrac{u(x_i)p_i}{(1-\alpha)}$ $\quad(\beta>0)$ $\quad(\beta<0)$	Yes / Yes	Lower right / Upper left	Upper left / Lower right	Curves meet in one of two points
Lottery-Dependent Utility	$\int u(x, c_F)dF(x)$ $\quad c_F = \int h(x)dF(x)$	$\sum p_i u(x_i, c_F)$ $\quad c_F = \sum h(x_i)p_i$ $\quad h$ concave $\quad h$ convex	No / No	Yes / Yes	No / No	Curves concave / Curves convex
Prospect Theory	$\pi(p_x)v(x) + \pi(p_y)v(y)$ $(1 - \pi(p_y))v(x) + \pi(p_y)v(y)$	$p_x + p_y < 1$ or x or $0 < y$; $p_x + p_y = 1$ and $0 < x < y$ or $y < x < 0$	No	Lower edge	Left edge, hypotenuse	Parallel along $P_H = (1 - P_L)/2$ (gains), $P_L = (1 - P_H)/2$ (losses)
Rank-Dependent Utility	$\int u(x)d[g(F(x))]$	$\displaystyle\sum_{i=1}^{n} u(x_i)\left[g\left(\sum_{j=1}^{i} p_j\right) - g\left(\sum_{j=1}^{i-1} p_j\right)\right]$ $\quad g$ concave $\quad g$ convex	No / No	Lower edge / Left edge	Left edge / Lower edge	Parallel along hypotenuse

vary, *as if* people are using different utility functions throughout the triangle.

However, each theory proposes a different motive for variation in risk attitude. In prospect theory and rank-dependent theory, variation arises from nonlinear weighting of probabilities. In weighted utility and the fanning out hypothesis, variation arises from a link between risk attitude and quality of gambles faced (a kind of "income effect," in economic terms).

The degree of fanning, or risk attitude variation, is measured by violations of EU in choosing between pairs in different parts of triangle. Each theory predicts different patterns of variation (see table 9–1).

The Common Ratio and Common Consequence Effects

The most widely-replicated evidence of EU violation is the "common ratio" and "common consequence" effects introduced by Allais (1953). Figure 9-1i illustrates them.

In the common consequence problem, subjects choose one gamble from pair A and one gamble from pair B. In the example, $A_1 = (1, 1$ million francs) and $A_2 = (0.10, 5\,\text{m}; 0.89, 1\,\text{m})$. By removing the "common consequence" of $(0.89, 1\,\text{m})$ from both gambles (and substituting a payoff of 0 for the $1\,\text{m}$), a new pair is constructed in which $B_1 = (0.11, 1\,\text{m})$ and $B_2 = (0.10, 5\,\text{m})$. Under EU, preferences shouldn't depend on a common consequence so $A_1 > A_2$ should imply $B_1 > B_2$. But many subjects choose the sure million francs $(A_1 > A_2)$ then take $B_2 > B_1$, violating independence. (A common rationale is that both B_1 and B_2 are unlikely to pay off and B_2 offers a higher gain.)

Graphically, the lines connecting A_1 with A_2 and B_1 with B_2 in figure 9-1i are parallel. If indifference curves are parallel, then preference for A_i predicts preference for B_i too.

The common ratio effect works similarly, using pairs C and D. Note that the lines connecting the gambles in each pair are again parallel; so, if $C_1 > C_2$, then $D_1 > D_2$. The "common ratio" label comes about because the winning probabilities in C_1 and C_2 (1 and 0.8) are multiplied by the same number, 0.05, to derive the winning probabilities in D_1 and D_2 (0.05 and 0.04); winning probabilities have a common ratio in the two pairs (1/0.8 or 0.05/0.04).

Evidence of common ratio and common consequence effects is systematically reviewed by MacCrimmon and Larsson (1979), Camerer

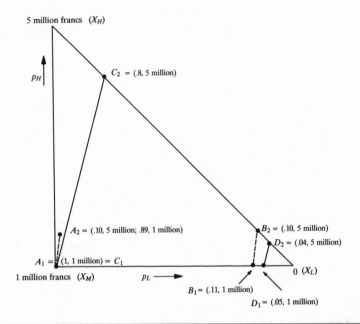

Figure 9–1i.   Allais's common consequence $(A_1 > A_2, B_2 > B_1)$ and common ratio $(C_1 > C_2, D_2 > D_1)$ effects.

(1989), and others. The studies described below mostly use variants of these two problems in new areas of the triangle to distinguish among competing theories.

Data From a New Experiment

In Camerer (1989) I described a large experiment using pairwise choices between gambles in all parts of the triangle (testing for a variety of common consequence effects). A second experiment was run to test further implications of some theories. I will report this second experiment in detail because it is new and also illustrates many of the methods used by others.

In the second experiment, all the gambles were located *inside* the triangles (for reasons explained below, stylized fact #1). The second experiment also tested a curious property called "bisector parallelism:" Even if probabilities are weighted nonlinearly (as in prospect theory and

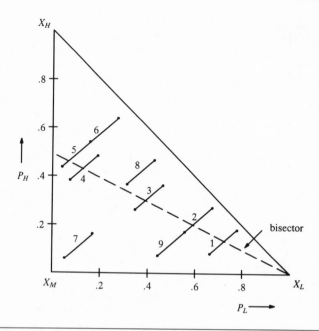

Figure 9–2. Gamble pairs used in the new experiment.

other theories), indifference curves should be parallel along the bisector of the triangle, $p_H = (1 - p_L)/2$, when gambles involve gains or mixed gains and losses.[6] (When gambles involve losses, parallelism holds along $p_L = (1 - p_H)/2$.) Rank-dependent probability weights do *not* predict that property.

In the new experiment, three gamble pairs straddling the bisector were used to test for bisector parallelism. If the nonlinear weighting theories are true, there should be fewer EU violations in these three pairs than in comparable pairs away from the bisector.

Experimental Methods

Each subject was shown twelve or eighteen pairs of gambles (in single-stage form) from three sets of nine pairs. The probabilities for each pair are given in table 9–2 and shown in a triangle diagram in figure 9–2. Each pair was a common consequence problem, a choice between a gamble $G = (p_L, p_M, p_H)$ and a gamble $(p_L + 0.10, p_M - 0.20, p_H +$

Table 9-2.   Gamble Pairs Used in the New Experiment

Pair	less risky gamble			more risky gamble		
Number	P_L	P_M	P_H	P_L	P_M	P_H
1	0.65	0.25	0.10	0.75	0.05	0.20
2	0.55	0.30	0.15	0.65	0.10	0.25
3	0.35	0.40	0.25	0.45	0.20	0.35
4	0.05	0.55	0.40	0.15	0.35	0.50
5	0.05	0.50	0.45	0.15	0.30	0.55
6	0.15	0.30	0.55	0.25	0.10	0.65
7	0.05	0.90	0.05	0.15	0.70	0.15
8	0.35	0.30	0.35	0.45	0.10	0.45
9	0.45	0.50	0.05	0.55	0.30	0.15

0.10) with 0.20 of the probability mass from p_M shifted from the middle outcome X_M to each of the extreme outcomes X_L and X_H. Three payoff levels (X_L, X_M, X_H) were used: large gains (0; \$10,000; \$25,000); small gains (0; \$5; \$10); and losses (−\$10; −\$5; 0). These payoffs enable us to test whether violations of EU vary with the size of the payoffs (as weighted utility, fanning out, and lottery-dependent utility allow) and whether choices for losses are different than choices for gains (as prospect theory suggests).

Since the transformation of the initial gamble G shifts probability mass away from p_M, a "mean-preserving spread" for the small gain and loss gambles, we will call the original gamble in each pair "less risky" and call the transformed gamble "more risky." Note that the less risky gamble in a pair is always to the lower left of the more risky gamble.

Gamble pairs were shown on separate sheets of paper (see Camerer, 1989, Appendix). Gambles were operationalized as random drawings of tickets that were uniformly distributed from 1 to 100. All choices were hypothetical.[7] Subjects were recruited from undergraduate and M.B.A. classes in quantitative methods.

Results: Between-Subjects Analysis

Figures 9-3 to 9-5 are triangle diagrams with X_L, X_M, X_H shown on the corners. Thin lines connect the two gambles in a pair (reproducing the lines showing the gambles in each pair in figure 9-2). In figures 9-4 and 9-5 the thin lines are iso-expected value lines.

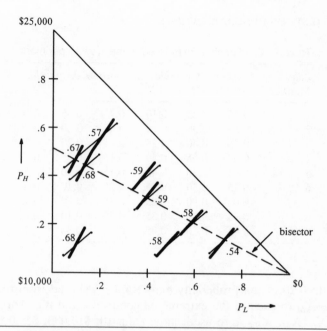

Figure 9-3. Between-subjects data, large gains gambles. (Fractions indicate percentage of subjects choosing the less risky gamble in each pair.)

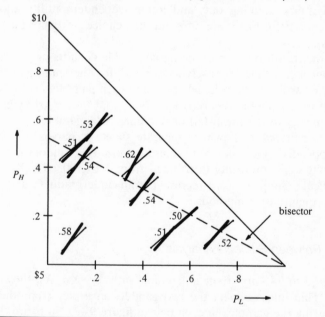

Figure 9-4. Between-subjects data, small gains gambles.

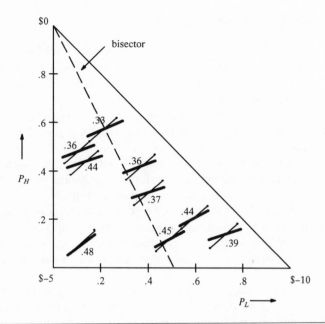

Figure 9–5.   Between-subjects data, small loss gambles.

The fraction of subjects choosing the less risky gamble in each pair is written next to each thick line.[8] For example, figure 9–3 shows that 68 percent of the subjects chose the less risky gamble in pair 7 (near the lower left corner).

The slope of the thick line at each pair is a linear function of the fraction of subjects who chose the less risky gamble. The slope of each line simply provides a visual index of the fraction written next to it. Like iron filings that show the direction of a magnetic field on paper when a magnet is held beneath them, the thick lines suggest underlying patterns (but have no formal meaning).

EU predicts that the thick lines will be parallel, which is approximately true in figures 9–3 to 9–5. (Equality of fractions cannot be rejected by chi-squared tests). The violations of parallelism observed in many other studies—evidenced by common ratio and common consequence effects, for instance—are gone.

Within-subject Results; Betweenness

Figures 9–3 to 9–5 express between-subject tests. Within-subject tests are generally better. They use several choices by one subject to test that subject's adherence to an axiom. The test statistics are the fraction of subjects violating an axiom.

Betweenness was tested this way by giving subjects pairs of gambles of the sort $G = (p_L, p_M, p_H)$ versus $H = (p_L + 0.10, p_M - 0.20, p_H + 0.10)$ and H versus $I = (p_L + 0.20, p_M - 0.40, p_H + 0.20)$. Since $H = 0.5G + 0.5I$ (assuming reduction of compound lotteries), if subjects obey betweenness the only permissible preference pairs are $(G > H, H > I)$ and $(H > G, I > H)$. For instance, in pairs 5–6 there are four possible patterns of choice: *LL* (the less risky gamble in both pairs), *LM* (the less risky gamble in pair 5 and the more risky gamble in pair 6, indicating quasi-convexity, or dislike of randomization), *ML* (quasi-concavity, preference for randomization), and *MM*. The betweenness axiom predicts *LL* and *MM*.

The fractions of subjects choosing each possible pattern for the new pairs 5–6 and 9–2 are shown in table 9–3. Data from Camerer (1989) are shown for comparison. About 70 percent of subjects obey betweenness (*LL* + *MM*), in both the new and old data. (This number should be compared to a benchmark of 87 percent, the fraction making the same choice twice in a row.) But the old data indicate systematic quasi-convexity (*LM*) for pairs near the hypotenuse, quasi-concavity (*ML*) for pairs near edges, and the opposite patterns for loss gambles. Violations in the new data are about equally distributed among the *LM* and *ML* patterns. Thus, *systematic* betweenness violations largely disappear when gambles are pulled off the edges.

Within-subject Tests: Parallelism and Fanning

Parallelism can be tested using gamble pairs in different parts of the triangle. The data are shown in table 9-4. Consider the bisector pairs 4, 3, and 1. Since subjects choose a less risky (*L*) or more risky (*M*) gamble in each pair, there are $2^3 = 8$ possible patterns of choices. Patterns *LLL* and *MMM* are consistent with EU.[9] Pattern *LLM*—choosing the less risky gamble in pairs 4 and 3 and the more risky gamble in pair 1, which is stochastically dominated by pairs 3 and 4—is consistent with fanning out; *LMM* is too. *MLL* and *MML* are consistent with fanning in.

If violations were due to chance, the fraction of choices consistent with

Table 9–3. Within-subject Tests of Betweenness

theories:	large gains (n = 84)			small gains (n = 79)			small losses (n = 86)		
	EU	quasi-convex	quasi-concave	EU	quasi-convex	quasi-concave	EU	quais-convex	quasi-concave
choices:	LL + MM	LM	ML	LL + MM	LM	ML	LL + MM	LM	ML
new: pairs 5–6	0.69	0.20	0.11	0.78	0.10	0.13	0.79	0.12	0.09
old: edge	0.84	0.02	0.14	0.68	0.18	0.14	0.66	0.29	0.05
old: hypotenuse	0.73	0.25	0.02	0.81	0.11	0.08	0.69	0.09	0.22
new: pairs 9–2	0.71	0.14	0.14	0.66	0.18	0.16	0.70	0.14	0.16
old: edge	0.53	0.03	0.43	0.46	0.10	0.44	0.73	0.15	0.12
old: hypotenuse	0.65	0.21	0.14	0.73	0.21	0.06	0.70	0.10	0.20

Table 9–4. Within-subject Tests of Parallelism

| | | | fraction choosing each pattern | | | |
| | | | hypotenuse | | edges | |
choices	consistent theories	bisector 4-3-1	6-8-2	old	5-7-9	old
Large Gain Gambles		n = 134	n = 84	n = 132	n = 84	n = 137
LLL	EU	0.36	0.32	0.36	0.38	0.21
MMM	EU	0.19	0.18	0.14	0.14	0.10
LLM	fanning out	0.12	0.11	0.19	0.18	0.36
LMM	fanning out	0.10	0.07	0.09	0.06	0.18
MLL	fanning in	0.07	0.10	0.07	0.08	0.03
MML	fanning in	0.04	0.10	0.02	0.07	0.04
LML		0.08	0.07	0.12	0.05	0.00
MLM		0.04	0.06	0.04	0.04	0.09
Small Gain Gambles		n = 130	n = 79	n = 134	n = 79	n = 138
LLL	EU	0.29	0.29	0.38	0.27	0.14
MMM	EU	0.25	0.23	0.11	0.20	0.20
LLM	fanning out	0.14	0.09	0.13	0.11	0.18
LMM	fanning out	0.07	0.09	0.04	0.08	0.17
MLL	fanning in	0.08	0.08	0.16	0.09	0.08
MML	fanning in	0.10	0.06	0.04	0.10	0.07
LML		0.05	0.06	0.07	0.05	0.06
MLM		0.03	0.10	0.07	0.10	0.11
Small Loss Gambles		n = 96	n = 79	n = 137	n = 79	n = 134
LLL	EU	0.16	0.14	0.12	0.20	0.10
MMM	EU	0.39	0.41	0.33	0.35	0.30
LLM	fanning out	0.07	0.05	0.10	0.08	0.05
LMM	fanning out	0.11	0.06	0.15	0.06	0.10
MLL	fanning in	0.05	0.09	0.06	0.10	0.09
MML	fanning in	0.08	0.12	0.13	0.10	0.20
LML		0.07	0.07	0.04	0.01	0.04
MLM		0.06	0.06	0.07	0.09	0.11

EU (*LLL* or *MMM*) would be 76 percent,[10] but only 50 percent to 60 percent of the choices are consistent. However, the distribution of inconsistent choices is split about evenly between fanning out, fanning in, and other patterns. The old data from Camerer (1989) have more inconsistencies and show systematic fanning out in gain gambles (and some fanning in for losses). As with betweenness, *systematic* violations of parallelism are smaller in the new data, with pairs inside the triangle.

Contrary to prospect theory, choices are no more consistent with EU for the bisector pairs (4-3-1) than for other pairs (6-8-2 or 5-7-9). However, since there are relatively few violations in *any* of the new pairs (and the sample sizes are modest), the test lacks the power to detect bisector parallelism even it existed. A more powerful test would be useful.

Stylized Facts and New Paradoxes

The new data in the last section are one example of several recent studies in which carefully chosen gamble pairs are used to test a variety of theories simultaneously. The implications of these studies can be roughly summarized in several stylized facts. The stylized facts express what we have *learned* from the new studies, not all that we know about choices.

While the studies are all recent, they are more voluminous and methodologically varied then the initial demonstrations of paradoxes by Allais and others. If the original data were enough to provoke two dozen researchers to rethink EU, the new data should set a hundred to work.

Stylized Fact #1: EU is Not Violated Inside The Triangle

In Camerer (1989) large EU violations usually occurred when subjects chose between an edge gamble and an inner gamble. Figure 9–6 reproduces some of those data, which strongly violate parallelism of indifference curves. Comparing figure 9–6 with figure 9–3 from above (using only inner gambles), it is clear that moving gambles inside the triangle reduces EU violations dramatically, making indifference curves nearly parallel.

Others have observed the same reduction in EU violations from moving inside the triangle. Figure 9–7 illustrates data from Conlisk (1989). (As in figures 9–3 to 9–6, thin lines connect the two gambles in a pair and the number next to each line is the fraction of subjects choosing the less risky (southwestern) gamble in the pair.)

In a replication of the Allais common consequence effect, 51 percent choose the $1 million instead of (0.10, $5 m; 0.89, $1 m) (in the southwest corner) but only 14 percent choose (0.11, $1 m) over (0.10, $5 m) (in the southeast corner). When the pairs are slid inside the triangle, the same fraction (47 percent) pick the less risky gamble in both pairs.

In Gigliotti and Sopher (1990), only 22 percent of the patterns of

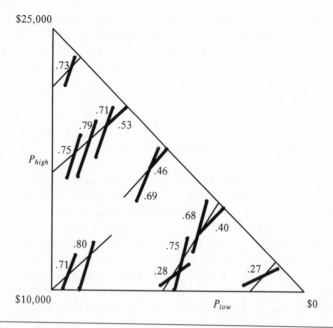

Figure 9–6. Fraction of subjects choosing the less risky gamble in each pair, large gains (from Camerer, 1989).

choice involving edge gambles satisfied EU. Fanning-out patterns outnumbered fanning-in patterns by nearly 10 to 1. But when choices were among inner gambles, the number of EU patterns doubled and fanning out fell by half. Harless (in press) found relatively fewer EU violations inside the triangle too, and the frequencies of fanning in and out were roughly equal.

EU violations inside the triangle are still too high to be considered random error (see Harless and Camerer, 1991), but they are not very systematic. Much as Newtonian mechanics is an adequate working theory at low velocities, EU seems to be an adequate working theory for gambles inside the triangle. Why?

Corner gambles have two of the probabilities (p_L, p_M, p_H) equal to zero, edge gambles have one probability equal to zero, and inner gambles have no probabilities equal to zero. Therefore, an inner gamble (like (0.1, $0; 0.2, $5; 0.7, $10)) has a low probability on an outcome that has no chance of occurring in a nearby edge gamble (like (0, $0; 0.4, $5; 0.6, $10)). Disappearance of EU violations inside the triangle (and

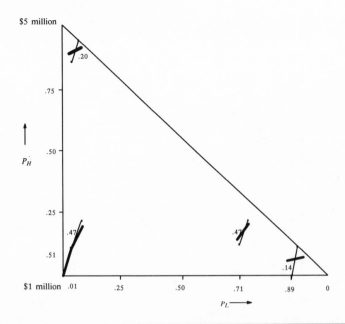

Figure 9–7.   Gamble pairs and results in Conlisk (1989). (Pairs always begin with one gamble and increase P_H by 0.10 and P_L by 0.01 to generate the second gamble. Fractions of less risky choices for each pair are shown next to the line connecting the gambles in that pair.)

other evidence)[11] suggests the crucial ingredients for EU violation are a difference in the number of outcomes between the gambles in a pair (cf. Neilson, 1989) and nonlinearity of the decision weighting function near zero.

Of course, there is much earlier evidence that probabilities are weighted nonlinearly (Preston and Baratta, 1948; Edwards, 1955; Mosteller and Nogee, 1951; Cohen, Jaffray and Said, 1985; De Neufville and Delquie, 1988). The novel observation here is how crucial overweighting of low probabilities is for accounting for many observed violations of EU.

Stylized fact #1 is consistent with nonlinear weighting theories (prospect theory and its kin, rank-dependent theories). Lottery-dependent utility is only consistent in a form more general than that proposed in (6) above. The stylized fact casts doubt on theories with linear indifference curves (EU, weighted utility, implicit EU and its variants).

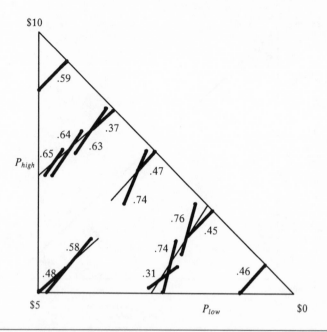

Figure 9–8.   Fraction of subjects choosing the less risky gamble in each pair, small gains (from Camerer, 1989).

Stylized Fact #2; Both Slopes and Shapes of Indifference Curves Reflect Around a Reference Point

Typical risk attitudes seem to reflect around a reference point, showing risk aversion for gains and risk preference for losses.

But the general hypothesis of reflection must be qualified in several ways. Reflection is often hard to detect in within-subjects tests (Hershey and Schoemaker, 1980), and sometimes shows only less risk aversion for losses than for gains, rather than risk seeking for losses (Fagley and Miller, 1987). Choices over low-probability gambles often show the opposite reflection, risk *preference* for gains and risk *aversion* for losses (gambling on and insuring against unlikely events are familiar examples). And people are often risk-preferring over gambles with strictly positive outcomes. For example, 80 percent preferred the gamble (0.7, $10; 0.3, $30) to a certain $16 (a mean-decreasing spread) in Battalio, Kagel and Komain (1990). Similarly, people are less risk-seeking over gambles with strictly negative outcomes (Payne, Laughhunn and Crum, 1981).

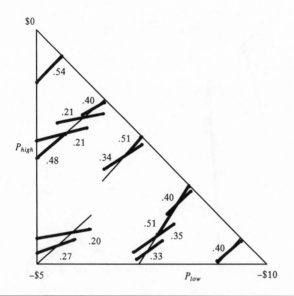

Figure 9–9. Fraction of subjects choosing the less risky gamble in each pair, small losses (from Camerer, 1989).

Since risk aversion is manifested in steeply sloped indifference curves, reflection implies indifference curves slopes will be steeper in gains triangles and flatter in loss triangles. They are (see figures 9–4 and 9–5).

Prospect theory predicts reflection of the *shape* of curves too:[12] Curves in a gain triangle will look like curves in a loss triangle, reflected around the 45-degree line. None of the other theories (besides the nonlinear-weighting kin of prospect theory) generally predicts such a reflection of shape.

Curves do appear to reflect in shape. For instance, figures 9–8 and 9–9, reproducing data from Camerer (1989) for gambles involving small gains and losses, look remarkably like reflections of each other. Curves also reflect in shape in the middle of the triangle (Chew and Waller, 1986).

Figure 9–10 illustrates data from Battalio, Kagel and Komain (1990) that show reflections of slopes and shapes in the corners of a triangle diagram (their table 8, sets 1 and 3). For gains gambles (X_M = \$18 and X_H = \$27), 61 percent preferred the less risky gamble in the pair of edge triangles (shown connected by a line cutting through the triangle) but only 28 percent and 47 percent preferred the less risky gamble in the two

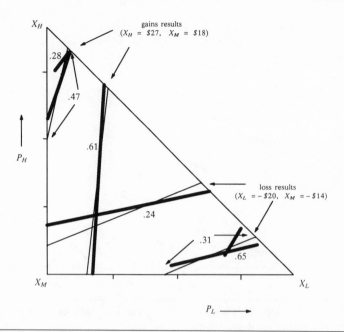

Figure 9–10.   Gamble pairs and results in Battalio, Kagel and Jiranyakul (1990).
(Two sets of results are shown. The steeper, upper left corner pairs were gains
gambles. The flatter, lower right corner pairs were loss gambles.)

pairs lying to the northwest.[13] For loss gambles $(X_L = -\$27, X_M = -\$14)$, also shown in figure 9–10, the pattern is roughly opposite. A minority (24 percent) preferred the less risky gamble in the mid-triangle pair, but many more preferred the risky gambles in the two pairs in the southeast corner. Indifference curves drawn to illustrate these two sets of preferences are rough reflections of each other around the 45-degree line.

The inability to explain the empirical reflection of curve shape is a weakness in theories, like rank-dependent EU, which assume that weights depend only on the *rank* of outcomes. However, except for reflection, the general patterns predicted by rank-dependent EU are much like those of prospect theory. Therefore, a modification of rank-dependent theory in which weights are assigned to losses, according to the rank of their *magnitudes*, will generate reflection of curves[14] and might account for the data nicely. Such a modification also smoothly generalizes prospect theory to many outcomes (Starmer and Sugden, 1989b; Tversky and Kahneman, in press).

Stylized fact #2 is only consistent with theories that permit reflection of risk attitudes around a reference point, and take individual probabilities and weight them nonlinearly (thus excluding standard rank-dependent theories). Prospect theory and related nonlinear weighting theories are consistent; no other theories are unless they are amended to permit reflection around a reference point.

Stylized Fact #3: The Fanning Out Hypothesis is Violated

Machina's (1982) fanning out hypothesis was an ingenious attempt to explain several kinds of paradox with a single principle that was both behaviorally appealing and formal. It is a good characterization of behavior in previously explored areas of the triangle (especially the southeast corner). But in studies of newer areas it is reliably violated.

Figure 9–7 (based on Conlisk, 1989), gives one such violation. Subjects are more risk-preferring (only 20 percent choose the less risky gamble) in choosing near the northwest corner than in choosing among stochastically dominated gambles near the southwest and southeast corners (where 47 percent choose less risky gambles), that is, their indifference curves appear to get flatter as they move northwest, fanning *in* rather than fanning out. Fanning in in the northwest corner is also observed by Starmer and Sugden (1989b), Camerer (1989, table 7, pairs 1–2), and Battalio, Kagel and Komain (1990, shown in figure 9–10).

Figure 9–10 also shows fanning in to the southeast for losses (a reflection of northwest fanning in for gains). In gambles over gains, Prelec (forthcoming) and Starmer (1989) observed fanning in toward the southeast.

Prospect theory and rank-dependent theory can account for fanning in along the left edge, and to the northwest, by nonlinear weighting of probabilities. Weighted utility cannot, but variants with more flexibility can (Dekel, 1986; Chew, 1985; Gul, 1991; Neilson, press).

Fanning out is also badly violated by risk preference for gambles involving guaranteed gains (Battalio, Kagel, Jiranyakul, 1990; Thaler and Johnson, 1990). If people are risk averse when choosing between $10 and (0.5, 0; 0.5, $20), then fanning out predicts even more risk aversion in choosing between the better gambles $20 and (0.5, $10; 0.5, $30). But people become more risk-seeking instead. Fanning out is also violated in an interesting portfolio experiment conducted by Loomes (1991).

Stylized fact #3 is inconsistent with theories that predict exclusive fanning out (weighted utility, Machina's hypothesis). Theories with

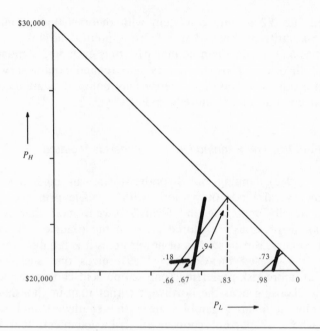

Figure 9–11.   Gamble pairs and results in Prelec (1990).

convex probability weighting functions (such as prospect theory), and some variants of rank-dependent theory can account for fanning in toward the northwest.

Stylized Fact #4: Betweenness is Systematically Violated

There is a lot of evidence that betweenness is violated. A dramatic violation is reported by Prelec (1990), and illustrated in figure 9–11. When choosing between $A = (0.66, 0; 0.34, \$20\,k)^{15}$ and $C = (0.67, 0; 0.32, \$20\,k; 0.01, \$30\,k)$ subjects overwhelmingly (82 percent) prefer C. (Only 18 percent prefer the less risky gamble A.) But when choosing between $A = (0.66, 0; 0.34, \$20\,k)$ and $B = (0.83, 0; 0.17, \$30\,k)$, almost all (94 percent) choose A. Since C is a probabilistic mixture of the gambles A and B, (16/17, A; 1/17, B), betweenness requires C to be between A and B in preference (either $A > C > B$ or $A < C < B$). The pattern $C > A$ and $B > A$ is a violation.

Intuitively, subjects don't mind increasing the chance of getting

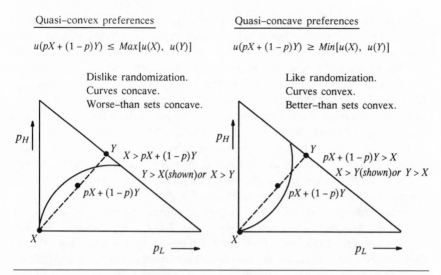

Figure 9–12. Possible violations of betweenness.

nothing from 0.66 to 0.67 in exchange for an extra 0.01 chance of winning \$30 k (so $C > A$). But the same increase sixteen more times is unappealing (so $A > B$).

Put more formally, betweenness requires utility to be linear in the probabilities *along an indifference curve*: if an incremental change in probabilities is acceptable, multiples of the incremental change should be too. Independence requires the incremental change to be acceptable throughout the triangle.

Figure 9–10 shows betweenness violations similar to Prelec's in the data of Battalio, Kagel and Jiranyakul (1990). In the southeast corner, 69 percent of subjects prefer small increments in p_L and p_H from the edge gamble to an inner gamble, but only 35 percent like increments twice as large.

There is lots of other evidence of betweenness violations that are similar in nature but less frequent. There are two possible directions of betweenness violations (illustrated in figure 9–12). People with "quasi-convex" preferences dislike randomization. They will order choices $Y > X > pX + (1 - p)Y$ or $X > Y > pX + (1 - p)Y$ and have concave indifference curves in the triangle. People with "quasi-concave" preferences like randomization. They will order choices $pX + (1 - p)Y > X > Y$ or $pX + (1 - p)Y > Y > X$ and have convex indifference curves.

Consider gambles over gains first. A rough composite of the evidence suggests that along the lower edge, indifference curves are convex, corresponding to quasi-concavity, or randomization-preference. In the southwest corner, Chew and Waller, 1986; Gigliotti and Sopher, 1990; to the southeast, Prelec, forthcoming (see figure 9–11); Camerer, 1989 (see figure 9–6). Along the left edge and hypotenuse, curves appear concave, that is, quasi-convex, randomization-averse (Battalio, Kagel and Jiranyakul, 1990, see figure 9–10; Camerer, 1989, see figure 9–6).

For losses, the patterns of quasi-concavity and quasi-convexity reflect around a reference point as mentioned in stylize fact #2, (see Chew and Waller, 1986; Battalio, Kagel and Jiranyakul, 1990 (see figure 9–10); Camerer, 1989 (compare figures 9–8 and 9–9)).

Betweenness violations also largely disappear when gambles are all inside the triangle. (Starmer, 1989, pairs 1-6-7; Gigliotti and Sopher, 1990; Camerer, 1989 and above (see figures 9–3 to 9–5). That stylized fact suggests the violations are due to nonlinear weighting of probabilities.

There are two subtle methodological qualifications to these data. First, in most experiments transitivity must be assumed for betweenness to be clearly violated. There is a simple way to test for transitivity and betweenness separately, but as far as we know only Coombs and Huang (1976) and Camerer and Ho (1991) have used it.[16] They and Bernasconi (1991) all find substantial betweenness violations even after controlling for intransitivity.

Second, betweenness is most compelling when the probability mixture $pA + (1 - p)B$ is a compound gamble, but most experiments present the mixture in a reduced form where probabilities in two stages are multiplied out. As with apparent violations of compound independence, it could be that betweenness holds for compound gambles but violations of reduction lead to apparent betweenness violations in the domain of reduced gambles. This hope appears to be dashed, since Camerer and Ho (1991) found equal numbers of betweenness violations using both compound and reduced versions of the mixture $pA + (1 - p)B$.

Stylized fact #4 is consistent with some theories in which probabilities are weighted nonlinearly. Theories assuming betweenness (weighted utility, implicit utility and its variants) are inconsistent.

Stylized Fact #5: The Degree of EU Violation Depends on Outcomes

The *frequency* of EU violation appears to depend on the size of gamble payoffs. Figures 9–6, 9–8, and 9–9 (from Camerer, 1989) illustrate the outcome-dependence of violations. There are more violations when payoffs are large in magnitude (see also MacCrimmon and Larsson, 1979; Hogarth and Einhorn, 1990; compare Chew and Waller, 1986). Edwards (1955) also reported a *sign*-dependence of probability weights. Theories which explain EU violations simply by nonlinear weighting of probabilities (prospect theory and EU with rank-dependent probabilities) cannot explain the connection between frequency of violations and stakes.

For example, in prospect theory the slope of an indifference curve is given by $dp_H/dp_L = \pi'(p_M)v(X_M) / [\pi'(p_H)v(X_H) - \pi'(p_M)v(X_M)]$. Notice that slopes are determined by two kinds of quantities: (1) values $v(X_H)$ and $v(X_M)$ that don't change within a triangle; and (2) the derivatives of $\pi(p)$ that do change within the triangle as p_M and p_H change. (The nonlinearity of $\pi(p)$ implies $\pi'(p)$ is not constant.) Changes in slope within a triangle therefore are determined solely by $\pi'(p)$. Points in two different triangles with the same values of p_M and p_H, and different values of X_H and X_M, should therefore have roughly the same degree of change in slopes—that is, the same amount of EU violation—but they don't (Starmer and Sugden, 1989a).

Stylized fact #5 is consistent with theories that allow outcome dependence of the degree of fanning out (weighted utility, implicit EU, lottery-dependent EU) and inconsistent with theories that posit non-linear probability weighting independently of outcomes (prospect theory, rank-dependent theory). Within the class of theories, which weight probabilities nonlinearly, payoff dependence suggests, $\pi(\cdot)$ is more nearly linear for low payoffs than for higher payoffs. Hogarth and Einhorn's (1990) "venture theory" allows precisely such a payoff dependence of $\pi(\cdot)$ and reports evidence supporting their theory.

Stylized Fact #6: Violations of EU Show Cross-species Robustness

It is a startling fact that all attempts to find human patterns of EU violation with rats have replicated them. Battalio, Kagel and MacDonald (1985), observed common ratio effects; Kagel, Battalio and MacDonald (1990) observed fanning in in the northwest corner for gains and in the southeast corner for losses (time delays).

These data are remarkable because rats are sluggish to respond to incentives, compared to humans, and must learn the probabilities and amount of reward through experience. The animals are also highly motivated because their choices determine most of what they actually eat.

Either the cross-species robustness of results is an amazing coincidence, or it suggests a common underlying explanation, perhaps rooted in misperception of probabilities. Any alternative theory of choice that cannot explain why animals and humans violate EU and fanning out in the same way has a strike against it.

Some Other Studies

There are many other important recent studies that do not fit neatly into the triangle diagram paradigm. I will survey some of them all too briefly.

Regret: If preferences can be represented by a utility function over individual gambles (for example, $A > B$ if $u(A) > u(B)$), then changing the correlation between the gambles' outcomes should not matter. But changes in the statistical correlation do matter (Loomes, 1988a,b, 1989a; Loomes and Sugden, 1987b; Starmer and Sugden, 1987a) in a way consistent with regret theiories in which preferences are represented by $u(A, B)$ (such as "skew-symmetric bilinear utility," Fishburn, 1984; or the regret theories of Bell, 1982; Loomes and Sugden, 1982, 1987). Regret effects also seem to depend heavily on the nature of the gamble display (Battalio, Kagel and Jiranyakul (1990, table 6) and Harless (1992) use displays that elicit no regret).

Since the correlation between gamble outcomes is sometimes unstated in experiments, it is possible that many violations of EU can also be explained by regret. Studies suggest some violations are due to regret, but not all (Camerer, 1989; Battalio, Kagel and Jiranyakul, 1990; Harless, 1992; Loomes and Sugden, 1987b; Loomes, 1988a; Starmer and Sugden, 1989a).

Eliciting indifference curves: Hey and Strazzera (1989) estimated subjects' indifference curves directly using "lottery-equivalents" (cf. McCord and De Neufville, 1986): Subjects were shown an initial gamble on an edge, and asked to name a hypotenuse point equivalent in preference (a point on the same indifference curve). Subjects then named equally good interior points until three to five points on an indifference curve were found. Most subjects' curves were reasonable, but some crossed or had negative slopes. The fitted lines appear roughly parallel, but there are too few points on each curve to conduct statistical tests with much power.

Fitting parameters to individual subjects: A few researchers have estimated functional parameters for individual subjects (Currim and Sarin (1989) for prospect theory and Daniels and Keller (in press) for lottery-dependent utility). These initial results are not encouraging. Alternative theories always fit initial choices better than EU, since they have extra degrees of freedom, but they are not much better than EU predicting new pairwise choices, getting only 60 percent right.

Studies of framing: Efforts to establish the principles people use in choosing prospect-theoretic reference points are mostly discouraging. Fischhoff (1983) used simple pairwise choices that could be framed several ways. Subjects' ratings of which frames seemed most natural were uncorrelated with the frames they appeared to use in making choices.

Thaler (1985) proposed a "hedonic editing" rule for choosing reference points. For example, people should segregate two $50 gains (resetting their reference point to absorb the first gain before valuing the second one) because $v(50) + v(50) > v(100)$ if $v(\cdot)$ is concave for gains.

But Thaler and Johnson (1990) found that hedonic editing didn't explain choices in two-stage settings where a prior gain or loss was followed by a choice. People use a variety of rules instead. For example, a prior loss −$7.50 is apparently segregated from a second-stage choice between $0 and (0.5, $2.25; 0.5, −$2.25), producing risk-aversion (60 percent of subjects rejected the gamble). But the −$7.50 loss is apparently integrated when subjects could break even, since 71 percent preferred a second-stage gamble (0.33, $7.50; 0.67, $0) to $2.50. Framing principles appear to be a long list of such rules.

Conclusions

Data from several recent experimental studies suggest an unhappy fact: All the new theories designed to explain violations of expected utility are themselves violated in other ways. I summarized the new violations in several stylized facts.

Here is a rough scorecard (see also table 9-5). Theories based on betweenness (weighted utility, implicit EU, et al.) cannot explain facts 1 and 4. Theories that assume constant "fanning out" or "fanning in" of indifference curves (the fanning out hypothesis, weighted utility) are contradicted by fact 3. Theories that operate on final wealth positions, or weight outcomes according to their rank without regard to the *sign* of outcomes (such as rank-dependent theories), cannot explain fact 2. Theories in which probability weights are independent of outcomes (prospect theory, and its precursors and variants) cannot explain fact 5. Robustness of EU violations across species, fact 6, is posed as a challenge for all theories.

Table 9–5. Recent Evidence Summarized as Stylized Facts

		Evidence		Is the theory consistent with the evidence?						
Stylized facts	Authors (dates/details)	Text figures	EU	Weighted utility	Implicit EU	Disappointment (semi weighed)	Fanning out	Lottery dependent	Prospect theory	Rank-dependent utility
1. EU is not violated inside the triangle.	Camerer (this chapter) Conlisk (1989, section IV) Gigiliotti & Sopher (1990) Harless (in press)	3–5 7	Yes	No	No	No	Yes	No	Yes	Yes
2. Slope *and* shape of indifference curves reflect around a reference point.	Battalio, Kagel & Jiranyakul (1990, Table 8) Camerer (1989, Figs. 10–11) Chew & Waller (1986, contexts, 1a, 1c)	10 8–9	No	No	No	No	No	No	Yes	No
3. Fanning out is systematically violated	Battalio, Kagel & Jiranyakul (1990, Table 8) Camerer (1989, pairs 1–2) Conlisk (1989, section V) Loomes (1991) Prelec (1990) Starmer (1989) Starmer & Sugden (1989b)	10 8 7 11	No	No	Yes	Yes	No	Yes	Yes	Yes

No.	Proposition	References	Expt.								
4.	Betweenness is systematically violated	Battalio, Kagel & Jiranyakul (1990, Table 8) Camerer (1989, Table 6) Chew & Waller (1986, pairs O-I) Gigliotti & Sopher (1990, pairs AB-JK) Prelec (1990)	10 6 11 	No	No	No	No	Yes	Yes	Yes	Yes (Yest)
5.	EU violations depend on outcomes (size & sign).	Camerer (1989) Edwards (1955) Hogarth & Einhorn (1990) MacCrimmon & Larsson (1979) Starmer & Sugden (1989b)	6, 8–9	No	Yes	Yes	Yes	Yes	Yes	No	No
6.	EU violations are robust across species.	Battalio, Kagel & MacDonald (1985) Kagel, Battalio & MacDonald (1990)		No	No	?	?	No	?	?	?

I interpret the evidence as most favorable to prospect theory[17] because facts 1 to 4 can be explained by (1) valuing gains and losses (rather than integrating them into wealth) and (2) weighting probabilities nonlinearly. These two tendencies are built directly into prospect theory; they could be grafted onto other theories too (at some mathematical cost). Lottery-dependent utility, and other theories not considered here, may be able to account for many of the facts too (except perhaps facts 1 and 2).

What one learns from the data depends on what one does with utility theory. Defenders of the faith (like Howard, 1992) may be pleased and unsurprised to learn that alternatives to EU are also sometimes violated. However, they should note that all the stylized facts except #1 point to *new* ways in which EU is violated.

Decision analysts may not learn much from the experiments because they do not shake the normative foundation of EU. One implication may be useful in practice, however. Facts 1 and 5 together suggest that substantial overweighting of rare, high-consequence events is a big source of intuitive violations of the normative theory. Analysts will want to take extra care (and usually do) in eliciting preferences and beliefs about such events.

Those who search for better descriptions of choices can learn from the data which directions have the most empirical promise (nonlinear weighting theories) and the least (betweenness-based theories).

Economists and others need tractable theories to lay individual-level mathematical foundations for production of aggregate-level theories of markets (in finance, insurance, labor economics, game theory, auction theory, etc.).[18] They learn from the data that rank-dependent and betweenness-based theories both have empirical shortcomings. Since both classes of theory appear analytically useful, some attention should shift to the rank-dependent theories because they are less badly violated.

Acknowledgments

I am grateful for helpful comments from Ward Edwards, John Kagel, an anonymous referee, and participants in the Santa Cruz conference and seminars at the University of Minnesota, Harvard University, the Johns Hopkins University, the University of Pennsylvania, and the University of Pittsburgh. Lisabeth Miller and Brian Schwartz helped run the experiments.

Notes

1. The studies reviewed all use probabilities that are objective (or, as objective as experimenters can make them), so they test variants of EU (von Neumann and Morgenstern, 1947) rather than *subjective* expected utility, or SEU (Savage, 1954). Some studies of SEU are reviewed in Camerer and Weber (in press).

2. Many interesting theories have been left out. Notable are moments-based theories (Payne, 1973; Allais, 1979; Hagen, 1979), theories based on insufficient discrimination (Leland, 1990; cf. Rubinstein, 1988) or dimensional comparisons (Payne, 1973; Shafir, Osherson and Smith, 1989); and theories which integrate security, expectation, and aspiration (Lopes, 1987; Jaffray, 1988; Gilboa, 1988; Encarnacion, 1987). Tests that put these theories on an equal footing with other theories described here would be extremely useful.

3. If Z is a gamble too, the gambles in the second inequality are compound gambles and must be reduced further.

4. Most studies report few violations of compound independence (Kahneman and Tversky, 1979, on "isolation effects"; Conlisk, 1989, Bernasconi, 1990, Camerer and Ho, 1991). Others report some violations of the analogous "sure-thing principle" (Keller, 1985) or just as many violations of compound and reduced-gamble independence (Carlin, in press). Subtle differences in displays may explain the variation in results.

5. In the triangle diagram, a gamble X (first-order) stochastically dominates a gamble Y if $p_L(X) \leq p_L(Y)$ and $p_H(X) \geq p_H(Y)$. That is, X has less chance of the worst outcome and more chance of the best outcome; X will lie to the northwest of Y in the triangle.

6. In such theories, the slope of an indifference curve for gambles over gains is given by $dp_H/dp_L = \pi'(p_M)v(X_M)/(\pi'(p_H)v(X_H) - \pi'(p_M)v(X_M))$ (if $v(X_L) = 0$; otherwise the result doesn't hold; Camerer, 1989, p. 75). It follows that the slope is constant along the line $p_H = p_M$, which is the bisector $p_H = (1 - p_L)/2$.

7. Gambles were purely hypothetical because playing one randomly-chosen gamble made little difference in earlier work (Camerer, 1989), except for losses (actual losses from an initial stake were different than both hypothetical losses and equivalent hypothetical gains). Others have found differences, usually more risk-aversion when choice are actually played (Feather, 1959; Slovic, 1969; MacDonald and Wall, 1989; Battalio, Kagel, Jiranyakul, 1990; Hogarth and Einhorn, 1990; cf. Edwards, 1953), but differences were never large enough to overturn clear conclusions drawn from hypothetical-choice data.

8. Sample sizes are 134, 130, and 97 for high, low and negative bisector pairs (1,3,4) and 84, 79, and 87 for other pairs.

9. Here we assume preferences are deterministic and people make no errors in expressing them. The simplest model, assuming random errors, is tested by looking for *systematic* patterns of EU violation. More sophisticated studies would be useful (see Harless and Camerer, 1991).

10. Since 87 percent of the subjects made exactly the same choice twice in a row, presumably (0.87) (0.87), or 76 percent, made the same choice three times in a row. This is the natural benchmark for judging frequency of violations in three pairwise choices.

11. In the common ratio problem (figure 9–1i), all gambles are located on an edge but EU is still violated. However, the southwestern gamble is in a corner and has less support (one outcome) than the edge gamble subjects compare it to. Therefore, EU violation also seems to depend on a difference in support. In common ratio problems where none of the gambles are located in a corner, EU violations are substantially smaller. Figure 10, from Battalio, Kagel & Jiranyakul (1990) gives two examples.

12. The argument is subtle. In prospect theory, the gamble over gains $(p_L, X_L; p_M, X_M; p_H, X_H)$ has weighted value $\pi(p_M)v(X_M) + \pi(p_H)v(X_H)$ (assuming X_L is zero, X_M and X_H are positive, and $p_L > 0$). Then indifference curves have slope $dp_H/dp_L = \pi'(p_M)v(X_M)/(\pi'(p_H)v(X_H) - \pi'(p_M)v(X_M))$. When the gambles involve only losses, X_L and X_M are negative and the best outcome X_H is zero. Loss gambles have weighted value $\pi(p_L)v(X_L) + \pi(p_M)v(X_M)$ and their indifference curves have slope $dp_H/dp_L = (\pi'(p_L)v(X_L) - \pi'(p_M)v(X_M))/\pi'(p_M)v(X_M)$. Reflecting a line $p_H = a + bp_L$ around the 45-degree line $p_H = P_L$ requires interchanging (p_L, p_M, p_H) with (p_H, p_M, p_L) and taking the reciprocal of the slope. That is precisely the difference between the loss-curve slope and the gain-curve slope. Indifference curves derived from rank-dependent probability weights will not reflect because the weights depend only on the rank of outcomes, not their sign.

13. In other experiments with losses, MacDonald and Wall (1989) observed the opposite pattern—a standard common ratio effect—when the initial gamble pair was $-\$8$ (a certain loss) versus $(0.25, -\$1; 0.75, -\$14)$.

14. That is, weight outcomes by differentials of a transformed *de*cumulative distribution of gains (one minus the cumulative distribution) but use the cumulative distribution for losses. In gambles with all positive or all negative outcomes, this yields

$$u(X_L)\{1 - g(p_M + p_H) + u(X_M) \{g(p_M + p_H) - g(p_H)\} + u(X_H)g(p_H)$$
$$u(X_L)g(p_L) + u(X_M) \{g(p_M + p_L) - g(p_L)\} + u(X_H) \{1 - g(p_M + p_L)\}$$

for gains and for losses. Then it is tedious but direct to show that indifference curve shapes will reflect. When gambles involve both gains and losses a more elaborate "splicing" procedure is needed (Tversky and Kahneman, in press).

15. Where \$20k denotes \$20,000, etc.

16. In most experiments, subjects only made choices for two of the three pairs (A, B), $(A, pA + (1 - p)B)$ and $(B, pA + (1 - p)B)$. Suppose subjects choose $A > B$ and $pA + (1 - p)B > A$. One can show betweenness is violated by *observing* it using the third pair (subjects choose $pA + (1 - p)B$ over B) or by assuming transitivity and inferring it. But if transitivity is violated, subjects might choose $A > B)$, $pA + (1 - p)B > A$, and $B > pA + (1 - p)B$, thus satisfying betweennes (the mixture is between A and B in preference). The proper test is to ask all three pairwise-choice questions rather than only two. Then some would-be betweenness violations are chalked up to intransitivity $(B > pA + (1 - p)B$ in the third choice), but a roughly equal number of invisible betweenness violations not apparent in the two-choice test arise (when $B > A$ and $pA + (1 - p)B > A$, then $pA + (1 - p)B > B$ too).

17. One is tempted to conclude that prospect theory survives best because it has the most degrees of freedom and is hardest to falsify. But the only properties required to explain facts 1 to 4 are convexity of $\pi(p)$ (except near the endpoints), overweighting of low probabilities, and reflection around a reference point which is assumed to be a subject's initial wealth. Other theories are just as imprecise and are contradicted by more stylized facts. Indeed, prospect theory is not immune either: fact 5 contradicts it and other evidence does too (Battalio, Kagel and Komain, 1990, pp. 40–41).

18. Some recent efforts by economists are reviewed by Epstein (1990). They include: Work on auctions (Chew, 1985; Karni and Safra, 1989; Engelbrecht-Wiggans, 1989); labor economics (Beenstock, 1988); equilibrium in games (Crawford, 1990; Dekel, Safra, and Segal, 1990; Fishburn and Rosenthal, 1986); macroeconomics (Epstein and Zin, 1989, 1990; Weil, 1990); finance (Shefrin and Statman, 1984, 1985; Dekel, 1989; Neilson, in press); and marketing (Thaler, 1985).

References

Allais, M. (1953). "Le Comportement de L'homme Rationel Devant le Risque, Critique des Postulates et Axiomes de L'ecole Americaine," *Econometrica*, 21, 503–546.

Allais, M. (1979). "The So-called Allais Paradox and Rational Decisions Under Uncertainty." In M. Allais and O. Hagen (Eds.), The Expected Utility Hypothesis and the Allais Paradox. Reidel, Dordrecht the Netherlands.

Battalio, R.C., Kagel, J.H., and D.N. MacDonald (1985). "Animals' Choices Over Uncertain Outcomes: Some Initial Experimental Evidence," *American Economic Review*, 75, 597–613.

Battalio, R.C., Kagel, J.H., and K. Jiranyakul (1990). 'Testing Between Alternative Models of Choice Under Uncertainty: Some Initial Results." *Journal of Risk and Uncertainty*, 3, 25–50.

Becker, J.L., and R. Sarin (1987)." Lottery Dependent Utility." *Management Science*, 33, 1367–1382.

Beenstock, M. (1988). "Regret and Jubilation in Union Wage Bargaining." *Oxford Economic Papers*, 40, 296–301.

Bell, D. (1982). "Regret in Decision Making Under Uncertainty." *Operations Research*, 30, 961–981.

Bernard, G. (1964). "Reduction du Paradoxe de Saint Petersbourg par la Theories de L'utilite." *Comptes-Rendus de l'Academie des Sciences*, 259, 3168–3170.

Bernasconi, M. 1991, "Nonlinear Preference and Atemporal Dynamic Consistency: An Experimental Study." Working paper. University of York Centre for Experimental Economics.

Bernasconi, M. (in press). "Different Frames for the Independence Axiom: An Experimental Investigation in Individual Decision Making Under Risk." *Journal of Risk and Uncertainty*.

Bordley, R., and G. Hazen (1991). "SSB and Weighted Linear Utility as Expected Utility with Suspicion." *Management Science*, 37, 396–408.

Camerer, C.F. (1989). "An Experimental Test of Several Generalized Utility Theories." *Journal of Risk and Uncertainty*, 2, 61–104.

Camerer, C.F., and T. Ho (1990). "Violations of Compound Lottery Reduction: Evidence and Interpretation. Working paper. Department of Decision Sciences, University of Pennsylvania.

Camerer, C.F., and T. Ho (1991). "Violations of the Betweenness Axiom and Nonlinearity in Probability." Working paper. Department of Decision Sciences, University of Pennsylvania.

Camerer, C.F., and M. Weber (in press). "Recent Developments in Modelling Preferences: Uncertainty and Ambiguity." *Journal of Risk and Uncertainty*.

Carlin, P.S. (in press). "The Reduction of Compound Lotteries Axiom and the Allais Paradox." *Journal of Economic Behavior and Organization*.

Chew, S.H. (1983). "A Generalization of the Quasilinear Mean with Applications to the Measurement of Income Inequality and Decision Theory Resolving the Allais Paradox." *Econometrica*, 51, 1065–1092.

Chew, S.H. (1984). "An Axiomatization of the Rank Dependent Quasilinear Mean Generalizing the Gini Mean and the Quasilinear Mean." Working paper. Department of Political Economy, Johns Hopkins University.

Chew, S.H. (1985). "Implicit-weighted and Semi-weighted Utility Theories, M-estimators, and Non-demand Revelation of Second-price Auctions for an Uncertain Auctioned Object." Working paper #155. Department of Political Economy, Johns Hopkins University.

Chew, S.H. (1989). "Implicit Weighted Utility Theory: The Betweenness Approach to Decision Making Under Risk." *Annals of Operations Research*, 19, 273–298.

Chew, S.H., and L.G. Epstein L.G. (In press). "The Structure of Preferences and Attitudes Towards the Timing of the Resolution of Uncertainty." *International Economic Review*.

Chew, S.H., and K.R. MacCrimmon (1979). "Alpha-nu Choice Theory: An Axiomatization of Expected Utility." Working paper #669. University of British Columbia Faculty of Commerce.

Chew, S.H., and W.S. Waller (1986). "Empirical Tests of Weighted Utility Theory." *Journal of Mathematical Psychology*, 30, 55–72.

Cohen, M., Jaffray, J.Y., and T. Said (1985). "Individual Behavior Under Risk and Under Uncertainty: An Experimental Study." *Theory and Decision*, 18, 203–228.

Conlisk, J. (1989). "Three Variants on the Allais Example." *American Economic Review*, 79, 392–407.

Coombs, C., and L. Huang (1976). "Tests of the Betweeness Property of Expected Utility." *Journal of Mathematical Psychology*, 13, 323–337.

Crawford, V. (1990). "Equilibrium Without Independence." *Journal of Economic Theory*, 50, 127–154.

Currim, I., and R. Sarin (1989). "Prospect Versus Utility." *Management Science*, 35, 22–41.

Daniels, R.L., and L.R. Keller (in press). "An Experimental Evaluation of the Descriptive Validity of Gamble Dependent Utility Theory." *Journal of Risk and Uncertainty*.

De Neufville, R., and P. Delquie (1988). "A Model of the Influence of Certainty and Probability 'Effects' on the Measurement of Utility." In B.R. Munier (Ed.), *Risk, Decision and Rationality*. Reidel, Dordrecht, Holland.

Dekel, E. (1986). "An Axiomatic Characterization of Preferences under Uncertainty: Weakening the Independence Axiom." *Journal of Economic Theory*, 40, 304–318.

Dekel, E. (1989). "Asset Demands Without the Independence Axiom." *Econometrica*, 57, 163–169.

Dekel, E., Safra, Z., and U. Segal (1990). "Existence and Dynamic Consistency of Nash Equilibrium with Non-expected Utility Preferences." Working paper. Department of Economics, University of California, Berkeley.

Edwards, W. (1953). "Probability-preferences in Gambling." *American Journal of Psychology*, 66, 349–364.

Edwards, W. (1954a). "Probability Preferences Among Bets with Differing Expected Values." *American Journal of Psychology*, 67, 56–67.

Edwards, W. (1954b). "The Reliability of Probability Preferences." *American Journal of Psychology*, 67, 68–95.

Edwards, W. (1954c). "The Theory of Decision Making." *Psychological Bulletin*, 51, 380–417.

Edwards, W. (1955). "The Prediction of Decisions Among Bets." *Journal of Experimental Psychology*, 51, 201–214.

Encarnacion, J. (1987). "Preference Paradoxes and Lexicographic Choice." *Journal of Economic Behavior and Organization*, 4, 231–248.

Engelbrecht-Wiggans, R. (1989). "Effect of Regret on Optimal Bidding in Auctions." *Management Science*, 35, 685–692.

Epstein, L.G. (1990). "Behaviour Under Risk: Recent Developments in Theory and Applications." Working paper. Department of Economics, University of Toronto.

Epstein, L.G., and S.E. Zin (1989). "Substitution, Risk Aversion and the Temporal Behavior of Consumption and Assert Returns: A Theoretical Framework." *Econometrica*, 57, 937–969.

Epstein, L.G., and S.E. Zin (1990). "Substitution, Risk Aversion and the Temporal Behavior of Consumption and Assert Returns: An Empirical Analysis." Working paper 8718, Department of Economics, University of Toronto.

Fagley, N.S., and P.M. Miller. (1987). "The Effects of Decision Framing on Choice of Risky vs Certain Options." *Organizational Behavior and Human Decision Process*, 38, 264–277.

Feather, N.T. (1959). "Subjective Probability and Decision Under Uncertainty." *Psychological Review*, 66, 150–164.

Fischhoff, B. (1983). "Predicting Frames." *Journal of Experimental Psychology: Learning, Memory, and Cognition*, 9, 103–116.

Fishburn, P. (1984). "SSB Utility Theory: An Economic Perspective." *Mathematical Social Science*, 8, 63–94.

Fishburn, P., and R. Rosenthal (1986). "Noncooperative Games and Nontransitive preferences." *Mathematical Social Sciences*, 12, 1–7.

Gigliotti, G., and B. Sopher (1990). "A Test of Generalized Expected Utility Theory." Department of Economics, Rutgers University.

Gilboa, I. (1988). "A Combination of Expected Utility and Maxmin Decision Criteria." *Journal of Mathematical Psychology*, 32, 405–420.

Green, J., and B. Jullien (1988). "Ordinal Independence in Nonlinear Utility Theory." *Journal of Risk and Uncertainty*, 1, 355–387. (erratum in 2, 119.)

Gul, F. (1991). "A Theory of Disappointment in Decision Making under Uncertainty." *Econometrica*, 59, 667–686.

Handa, J. (1977). "Risk, Probabilities, and a New Theory of Cardinal Utility." *Journal of Political Economy*, 85, 97–122.

Harless, D.W. (in press). "Predictions About Unit Triangle Indifference Curves Inside the Unit Triagle: A Test of Competing Decision Theories." *Journal of Economic Behavior and Organization.*

Harless, D.W. (1992). "Actions Versus Prospects: The Effect of Problem Representation on Regret." American Economic Review, 82, 634–649.

Harless, D.W., and C.F. Camerer (1992). "The Predictive Utility of Generalized Utility Theories." Working paper, October, Center for Decision Research, University of Chicago.

Hershey, J.C., and P. Schoemaker (1980). "Prospect Theory's Reflection Hypothesis: A Critical Examination." *Organizational Behavior and Human Decision Processes,* 25, 395–418.

Hey, J.D. (1984). "The Economics of Optimism and Pessimism: A Definition and Some Applications." *Kyklos,* 37, 181–205.

Hey, J.D., and E. Strazzera (1989). "Estimation of Indifference Curves in the Marschak-Machina Triangle: A Direct Test of the 'Fanning Out' Hypothesis." *Journal of Behavioral Decision Making,* 2, 239–260.

Hogarth, R., and H. Einhorn (1990). "Venture Theory: A Model of Decision Weights." *Management Science,* 36 (7), 780–803.

Howard, R. (1992). "In Praise of the Old Time Religion." In W. Edwards (Ed.), *Utility Theories: Measurements and Applications.* Kluwer Academic Publishers. Boston, MA.

Jaffray, J. (1988). "An Axiomatic Model of Choice Under Risk Which is Compatible with the Certainty Effect." In B. Munier (Ed.), *Risk, Decision and Rationality.* Reidel Dordrecht, the Netherlands.

Kagel, J.H., Battalio, R.C., and D. McDonald (1990). "Tests of 'Fanning out' of Indifference Curves for Random Prospects: Results from Animal and Human Experiments." *American Economic Review.* Vol. 80 (4), p. 912–921.

Kahneman, D., and A. Tversky (1979). "Prospect Theory: An Analysis of Decision Under Risk." *Econometrica,* 47, 263–291.

Karmarkar, U.D. (1978). "Subjectively Weighted Utility: A Descriptive Extension of the Expected Utility Model." *Organizational Behavior and Human Performance,* 21, 61–72.

Karni, E., and Z. Safra (1989). "Dynamic Consistency, Revelations in Auctions and the Structure of Preferences." *Review of Economic Studies,* 56, 421–433.

Keller, L.R. (1985a). "The Effects of Problem Representation on the Sure-thing and Substitution Principles." *Management Science,* 31, 738–751.

Keller, L.R. (1985b). "Testing of the 'Reduction of Compound Alternatives' Principle." *OMEGA International Journal of Management Science,* 13, 349–358.

Leland, J.W. (1990). "Indiscriminability in Evaluation: An Approximate Expected Utility Theory Resolution to Expected Utility Violations." Working paper. Department of Social and Decision Sciences, Carnegie-Mellon University.

Loomes, G. (1988a). "Further Evidence of the Impact of Regret and Disappointment in Choice Under Uncertainty." *Economica,* 55, 47–62.

Loomes, G. (1988b). "When Actions Speak Louder than Prospects." *American Economic Review*, 78, 463–470.

Loomes, G. (1989a). "Predicted Violations of the Invariance Principle in Choice Under Uncertainty." *Annals of Operations Research*, 19.

Loomes, G. (1991). "Evidence of a New Violation of the Independence Axiom." *Journal of Risk and Uncertainty*, 4, 91–108.

Loomes, G., and R. Sugden (1982). "Regret Theory: An Alternative Theory of Rational Choice Under Uncertainty." *Economic Journal*, 92, 805–824.

Loomes, G., and R. Sugden (1987a). "Some Implications of a More General Form of Regret Theory." *Journal of Economic Theory*, 41, 270–287.

Loomes, G., and R. Sugden (1987b). "Testing for Regret and Disappointment in Choice Under Uncertainty." *Economic Journal*, 97, 118–129.

Lopes, L.L. (1987). "Between Hope and Fear: The Psychology of Risk." *Advances in Experimental Social Psychology*, 20, 255–295.

Luce, R.D. (1988). "Rank-dependent, Subjective Expected-utility Representations." *Journal of Risk and Uncertainty*, 1, 305–332.

MacCrimmon, K.R., and S. Larsson (1979). "Utility Theory: Axioms Versus Paradoxes." In M. Allais and O. Hagen (Eds.), *The Expected Utility Hypothesis and the Allais Paradox*. Reidel, Dordrecht.

Machina, M. (1982). "Expected Utility Analysis Without the Independence Axiom." *Econometrica*, 50, 277–323.

Machina, M. (1987). "Choice Under Uncertainty: Problems Solved and Unsolved." *Journal of Economic Perspectives*, 1, 121–154.

MacDonald, D.N., and J.L. Wall. (1989). "An Experimental Study of the Allais Paradox Over Losses: Some Preliminary Evidence." *Quarterly Journal of Business and Economics*, 28, 43–60.

Markowitz, H. (1952). "The Utility of Wealth." *Journal of Political Economy*, 60, 151–158.

Marschak, J. (1950). "Rational Behavior, Uncertain Prospects, and Measurable Utility." *Econometrica*, 18, 111–141.

McCord, M., and R. De Neufville (1986). "Lottery Equivalents: Reduction of The Certainty Effect Problem in Utility Assessment." *Management Science*, 32, 56–60.

Mosteller, F., and P. Nogee (1951). "An Experimental Measurement of Utility." *Journal of Political Economy*, 59, 371–404.

Neilson, W.S. (in press). "Fanning Hypotheses in Behavior Toward Risk." *Journal of Economic Behavior and Organization*.

Neilson, W.S. (1989). "Prospect Theory's Discontinuities Without Probability Weights." Texas A&M Department of Economics.

Payne, J.W. (1973). "Alternative Approaches to Decision Making Under Risk: Moments Versus Risk Dimensions." *Psychological Bulletin*, 80, 439–453.

Payne, J.W., Laughhunn, D.J., and R. Crum (1981). "Further Tests of Aspiration Level Effects in Risky Choice Behavior." *Management Science*, 27, 953–957.

Prelec, D. (1990). "A Pseudo-endowment Effect and its Implications for Some

Recent Non-expected Utility Models." *Journal of Risk and Uncertainty*, 3, 247–259.

Preston, M.G., and P. Baratta (1948). "An Experimental Study of the Auction-value of an Uncertain Outcome." *American Journal of Psychology*, 61, 183–193.

Quiggin, J. (1982). "A Theory of Anticipated Utility." *Journal of Economic Behavior and Organization*, 3, 323–343.

Quiggin, J. (1985). "Subjective Utility, Anticipated Utility, and the Allais Paradox." *Organizational Behavior and Human Decision Processes*, 35, 94–101.

Roell, A. (1987). "Risk Aversion in Quiggin and Yaari's Rank-order Model of Choice Under Uncertainty." *Economic Journal*, 97, 143–159.

Rubinstein, A. (1988). "Similarity and Decision Making Under Risk: Is There a Utility Theory Resolution to the Allais Paradox?" *Journal of Economic Theory*, 46, 145–153.

Savage, L.J. (1954). *The Foundations of Statistics*. Wiley, New York.

Segal, U. (1987). "The Ellsberg Paradox and Risk Aversion: An Anticipated Utility Approach." *International Economic Review*, 28, 175–202.

Segal, U. (1989). "Anticipated Utility: A Measure Representation Approach." *Annals of Operations Research*, 19, 359–373.

Segal, U. (1990). "Two-stage Lotteries Without the Reduction Axiom." *Econometrica*, 58, 349–377.

Shafir, E.B., Osherson, D.N., and E.E. Smith (1989). "An Advantage Model of Choice." *Journal of Behavioral Decision Making*, 2, 1–23.

Shefrin, H., and M. Statman (1984). "Explaining Investor Preference for Cash Dividends." *Journal of Financial Economics*, 13, 253–282.

Shefrin, H., and M. Statman (1985). "The Disposition to Sell Winners too Early and Ride Losers Too Long: Theory and Evidence." *Journal of Finance*, 40, 777–790.

Slovic, P. (1969). "Differential Effects of Real Versus Hypothetical Payoffs on Choices Among Gambles." *Journal of Experimental Psychology*, 80, 434–437.

Starmer, C. (1989). "Testing New Theories of Choice Under Uncertainty Using the Common Consequence Effect." Discussion paper. Economics Research Centre, University of East Anglia, Norwich, UK.

Starmer, C., and R. Sugden (1987a). "Experimental Evidence of the Impact of Regret on Choice Under Uncertainty." Discussion paper no. 23. Economics Research Centre, University of East Anglia.

Starmer, C., and R. Sugden (1989a). "Violations of the Independence Axiom in Common Ratio Problems: An Experimental Test of Some Competing Hypotheses". Annals of Operations Research, 19, 79–102.

Starmer, C., and R. Sugden (1989b). "Probability and Juxtaposition Effects: An Experimental Investigation of the Common Ratio Effect." *Journal of Risk and Uncertainty*, 2, 159–178.

Starmer, C., and R. Sugden (in press-b). "Testing Prospect Theory." *Annals of Operations Research*, 19.

Sugden, R. (1986). "New Developments in the Theory of Choice Under Uncertainty." *Bulletin of Economic Research*, 38, 1–24.

Thaler, R.H. (1985). "Mental Accounting and Consumer Choice." *Marketing Science*, 4, 199–214.

Thaler, R.H., and E.J. Johnson (1990). "Gambling With the House Money and Trying to Break Even: The Effects of Prior Outcomes on Risky Choice." *Management Science*, 36 (6), 643–661.

Tversky, A., and D. Kahneman (in press). "Advances in Prospect Theory: Cumulative Representations of Uncertainty." *Journal of Risk and Uncertainty*.

Viscusi, K.W. (1989). "Prospective Reference Theory: Toward an Explanation of the Paradoxes." *Journal of Risk and Uncertainty*, 26, 235–264.

von Neumann, J., and O. Morgenstern (1947). *Theory of Games and Economic Behavior*, (2nd ed.). Princeton University Press, Princeton, NJ.

Weber, M., and C.F. Camerer (1987). "Developments in Modeling Preferences Under Risk." *OR Spektrum*, 8, 139–151.

Weil, P. (1990). "Non-expected Utility in Macroeconomics." *Quarterly Journal of Economics*, 105, 29–42.

Yaari, M.E. (1987). "The Dual Theory of Choice Under Risk." *Econometrica*, 55, 95–115.

10 TOWARD THE DEMISE OF ECONOMIC MAN AND WOMAN; BOTTOM LINES FROM SANTA CRUZ

Ward Edwards

Introduction

Economic Man has been moribund for a long time now, as has been his rarely mentioned wealthier counterpart, Economic Woman. In 1954 I wrote a review paper that presented the principles of rational choice, as I then understood them, and summarized experimental and other literature bearing on the supposition that human beings behave rationally. I commented that "it is easy for a psychologist to point out that an economic man . . . is very unlike a real man." (Edwards, 1954, p. 382). I went on to offer rational models of human decision as interesting and appropriate to test experimentally.

Experimenters responded. Their response was richer and more hopeful because in 1954 L.J. Savage had proposed his version of the notion of personal probability, and thus, had made the definition of rationality, and so of Economic Man, less restrictive. The central issue came to be: Do unassisted human decision makers choose among risky options in such a way as to maximize Subjectively Expected Utility? (SEU is Expected Utility calculated with personal probabilities.)

The debate has been lively, productive, and important. The claim of

W. Edwards (ed.), UTILITY THEORIES: MEASUREMENTS AND APPLICATIONS.
Copyright © 1992. Kluwer Academic Publishers, Boston. All rights reserved.

this chapter is that, after more than forty years of experimentation and debate, these issues are settled; it is time to go on to other topics. In support of this claim, I offer a summary of two key events that took place in Santa Cruz, California, on June 12, 1989. These events occurred at the Conference that gave rise to this book.

The Conference and Its Two Bottom Lines

The Conference on "Utility: Theories, Measurements, and Applications" met in Santa Cruz, California, from June 11 to 15, 1989. The attendees were an all-star cast. I need not list them here; all attendees except Soo Hong Chew and Amos Tversky (neither of whom had yet arrived when the votes described below were taken) are also authors of chapters in this book or else co-authors of the discussion chapter, and so are listed in the Table of Contents.

The motivation that had led me to write the proposal to NSF that led to the Conference was straightforward. A number of distinguished theoreticians have proposed various vesions of models for decision making under uncertainty that are more relaxed than the SEU model, though closely resembling it. Several chapters of this book are devoted to explication of such models. I found myself unclear about the extent, if any, to which their authors saw these new decision models as normative, that is, as specifying how people *should* go about making decisions under uncertainty. The issue seemed important because the technology called decision analysis is built around SEU maximization as its principle of how choices should be made. If the wisest available basis for choices is something other than maximization of SEU, why should decision analysts try to help decision makers maximize SEU? The original goal of the conference, therefore, was to bring some of the theorists proposing weaker SEU-like choice models and some experimenters who test these models as descriptions of human decision making together with some of the decision analysts who use the strong version, to explore conflicts of point of view about SEU.

I opened the conference by saying what you have just finished reading and then asked for a show of hands on the following question:

Do you consider SEU maximization to be the appropriate normative rule for decision making under risk or uncertainty?

Every hand went up!

Scarcely believing my good fortune, I decided to press it hard. So I asked for a show of hands on a second question:

Do you feel that the experimental and observational evidence has established as a fact the assertion that people do not maximize SEU; that is, that SEU maximization is not defensible as a descriptive model of the behavior of unaided decision makers?

Again, every hand went up, including my own!

For me, anything that could possibly happen at the Santa Cruz Conference after that (and a lot did happen, as this book shows) was sheer gravy. The conferees, leaders of contemporary thinking about decisions under risk and uncertainty, had declared that they were not trying to supplant SEU as the appropriate normative model, and therefore, that they were not challenging the decision analytic technology that implements that model. In addition, they had expressed a unanimous view on the topic of the debate that has dominated behavioral decision theory since it began, well before 1954: whether or not SEU maximization is defensible as a descriptive decision theory. Their answer, and mine, is no.

Science is better at asking theoretical questions than at recognizing agreed-upon answers. A show of hands, no matter how distinguished the people to whom they are attached, is not easy to defend as the basis for declaring a scientific debate over. But no other procedure suggests itself for declaring that further debate on these two questions is not worth while. I therefore propose that decision scientists take these two conclusions as bottom lines. Like all scientific conclusions, they are provisional, subject to reexamination if new thought or new evidence warrants. But, I propose, a significant burden of proof should lie on anyone who wishes to continue debate about either to show that there is new reason to do so.

This chapter attempts to assess the implications of this dramatic pair of conclusions for decision science.

Implication for Decision Theorists

The most obvious implication of this pair of conclusions is that two different, but perhaps not very different, kinds of theories are needed. SEU maximization is already available as a normative theory, endorsed in this vote. A number of candidate descriptive theories are available, none of which has a long lead over its competitors.

This implication is not likely to appeal to all decision theorists with descriptive interests. Some, including a referee of this chapter, hope to find a single theory that is both normative and descriptive, but acknowledge that they have not yet found it. I cannot imagine a successful descriptive theory that does not allow some systematic violations of transitivity and that does not permit an experimenter to trick subjects into violating ordinal dominance. And I cannot imagine a normative theory that permits either kind of violation. SEU maximization as a normative theory, in my opinion, needs to be extended to cover issues on which it is silent, but does not need revision at its core. So I have no hope for a single theory that successfully serves both purposes.

Why do we want or need such a theory? Would descriptive success strengthen the normative status of SEU? No. If some minor revision of SEU would make it fully descriptive, should that revision therefore be incorporated into the normative theory? No. The main advantage I can see of finding a theory that would serve both purposes, if that were possible, is that such a revised definition of Economic Man and Economic Woman might be a powerful tool of economic theory, which aspires to be descriptive. That would clearly be a gain (if economic theorists could be persuaded to take the revision seriously), but not one for which normative power should be sacrificed. The other advantage is that it might be ego-boosting to provide strong support for the notion that people are rational. Such a pat on the back to the human race might be pleasant, but should not be sought by redefining rationality to mean "what people do."

I think behavioral decision theorists have pursued this chimera long enough; it is time to admit that it is not attainable. My thought about economic theory is a little more complicated, and comes at the end of this chapter.

Implications for Normative Work

Rejection of SEU as the appropriate normative model, it seems to me, would have had dramatic implications for normative theory and practice. Acceptance has quite modest implications; it simply encourages the decision analysts to continue with the technology development that has been their main preoccupation for the last twenty years or more. It also encourages theoreticians to explore more deeply how to go about applying the basic SEU maximization idea to contexts in which it is difficult to apply, such as those in which equity issues are of concern, those that arise in games, and those that arise when decision makers with nonidentical values must agree on a choice.

I have proposed elsewhere (von Winterfeldt and Edwards, 1986; Edwards, 1990) an agenda for behavioral research oriented toward the needs of decision analysis. Elicitation technology and validation both need attention. At present, no equivalent of the medical research tool called *clinical trials* exists for decision analysis; it is needed. Above all, to be effective as a tool for increasing the incidence of rational thought, decision analysis needs to be do-able without a decision analyst. Promising approaches to the automation of decision analytic procedures are under development (see Horvitz, Breese, and Henrion, 1988; Edwards, in press); I believe that making them effective and readily usable is the most important task now facing researchers on decision analysis.

There is plenty of research to be done, ranging from very experimental to very formal. But none of it represents a revolutionary change in the way that normative decision theorists think about their subject.

Keeney (1992) and others at Santa Cruz emphasized a helpful distinction between normative and prescriptive theory. As I understand it, prescriptive theory adds to the requirements of normative theory additional specifications of a more operational nature needed to apply normative ideas to real decision contexts. The specifications of elicitation technology are an obvious example. Keeney notes that a decision analyst must be concerned with structuring the problem and with communicating the results of the analysis effectively, topics about which normative theory is silent. The behavioral research relevant to decision analysis affects prescriptive theory, not normative theory.

Implication for Descriptive Work: No More Demonstration Experiments

The most obvious implication of the conclusion that people do not maximize SEU for descriptive research is that we no longer need studies the objective of which is to establish or reinforce that conclusion. We know it already.

The importance of the task of establishing that people to not maximize SEU has led to a predominant experimental style for the field that serves that task well, but serves the more constructive task of modeling how people do in fact make risky decisions much less well. The style is that of demonstration experiments. The tasks and the experimental circumstances in which they are performed are not designed to exhibit the sizes of effects or the variables that control behavior or (above all) the extent of individual differences. In typical demonstration experiments, the report of the data takes the rather emaciated form of noting that X percent of subjects made responses or patterns of responses that conform to predictions based on models of optimal behavior, while $(100 - X)$ percent of subjects did not. The experimental sessions thus reported often combined a number of tasks, all administered to the same subjects at the same time. Even in such circumstances, data reporting is as though each task was distinct, though the data would support exploration of whether a subject who violates an optimal-model prediction in one task is or is not more likely to violate a different optimal-model prediction in a different task. Such questions are rarely asked.

Demonstration experiments have not, in my opinion, provided a strong empirical basis for a new quantitative approach to descriptive decision theory. They have identified a number of interesting phenomena, collectively called the cognitive illusions, that violate normative rules, but have not provided the measurements of these illusions that would be needed to develop quantitative models. That was never their purpose. But if a new approach is required, as I am claiming, then more detailed questions need to be answered. A number of categories of cognitive illusions are well recognized; chapter 13 of von Winterfeldt and Edwards (1986) provides a list. For each, we need answers to such questions as: How large is the effect? How consistent is it across tasks? How consistent is it across people? How robust is it to variations in instructions, in the cost-payoff structure of the task, and in display and task-content variables? How resistant is it to education and explanation? The literature of behavioral decision theory includes instances in which these questions have been asked and a number of papers, like this one, asserting that they should be asked, but includes very few instances of serious attempts to answer them.

Experiments intended to answer such questions are far harder to conceive and carry out than demonstration experiments. No obvious metric for the magnitude of suboptimality exists, though *dollars* is a natural suggestion. No simple set of dimensions to classify procedural variations of decision tasks exists. Even such an apparently straightforward question as, "What fraction of subjects consistently exhibit a particular cognitive illusion?" is hard to think about answering because we have good reason to believe that educational and experiential background will affect the answer, and we don't really have a target population in mind.

Behavioral decision theory has been an easy field in which to do experiments quickly. The issues not addressed in such demonstration experiments are crucial to development of new quantitative approaches to theory. It is time to accept the cost in experimental effort of not sweeping crucial questions under the rug.

A Non-experimental Observation

Behavioral decision theorists, and in particular the new utility theorists, have proposed a number of models of risky decision making intended to account for empirical phenomena such as the Allais paradox. Several of those theories are elaborated in this book. Examination of them exhibits a surprising fact: All are minor relaxations of SEU maximization—not identical with SEU, but close.

By "close" to SEU, I mean two things. First, the structure of such theories is formally much like the structure of SEU. There is a value measure and an uncertainty measure; they interact multiplicatively. Decisions are made by maximizing, and the quantity to be maximized typically has the flavor of a sum of value-uncertainty products. Second, "close" means that the difference in expected value (if that can be calculated) between the option predicted to be chosen by the new utility theories and the option predicted to be chosen by SEU will be fairly small. (Issues of scale arise in such comparisons. For a technical treatment see the discussion of relative expected loss on pp. 426–433 of von Winterfeldt and Edwards, 1986.) I am not aware of any new utility theories that are not close to SEU in both of those senses.

Why? An obvious explanation would be the theoretical charm of SEU. But that charm has not been so compelling to descriptive theorists in the last twenty years. I think a more likely explanation is that the data compel any theory of static risky choice to be much like SEU, and that the theorists respond to the data. That hypothesis leads to a further question: Why do unaided risky decisions approximate SEU but not fully conform to it? I consider this qustion seminal for a new approach to behavioral decision theory. What follows is a sketch of an approach toward answering it.

Descriptive Decision Theory: Points of Departure

I start with four assumptions.

1. People do not maximize SEU, but they come close—close enough so that models intended to be descriptive must inevitably resemble SEU.
2. No inborn behavior patterns, rules, or instincts control risky choice except for one: people prefer more of desirable outcomes to less, and less of undesirable ones than more. (This sounds like a definition of "desirable," but is a bit more; it relates preference behavior to experiences of pleasure or displeasure.) Decision-making procedures, as applied to decisions that the decision maker is aware of and considers worth making with some care, are *entirely* the result of present analysis informed by past learning. (I do not include such

inputs to decisions as values and probability assessments in this assumption. The inputs are much more fundamentally linked to the inborn givens of human perception and motivation than are the processing rules by means of which they are combined.)

3. In the course of a lifetime of experience with our own decisions and their outcomes, with reports and evaluations of decisions by others, and with instruction in how decisions should be made, we have learned that decisions can be good or bad, and that it is better to make a good decision than a bad one, especially if the stakes are significant. We have also learned that good decisions are made by good decision makers; bad decisions are made by everyone else. We therefore have two reasons to make good decisions: they are inherently preferable to bad ones, and the ability to make them says something pleasant about us as people. Consequently, we make a conscientious effort to make good decisions, if the stakes are significant and often even if they are not.

4. An adult aware that he or she must make a decision and trying to make a good one will summon from memory the Principles of Decision Making that he or she has distilled from precept, experience, and analysis and will try to apply them to the decision at hand. These principles are not necessarily cogent or correct and are typically inconsistent with one another. Few adults note and correct inconsistencies or errors in such principles, mainly because they almost never formalize and critique the entire list.

From this point of view, much of the task of behavioral decision theory consists of identifying such principles and specifying how they interact to control decisions.

Three sources of such principles are available: past education and training, as originally vaguely understood and now dimly remembered; past experience with decisions and their outcomes; and analysis of the decision problem at hand.

The following list of twelve principles is certainly incomplete. Moreover, different people will have different lists, depending on past training and experience and on skill at self-criticism. But it is enough to illustrate the idea and to make a start at enumeration of the needed Principles. Figuring out how they combine with one another to control decision making is a task for another day.

Guidance From Analysis

Analysis offers three broad principles for use in the decision task at hand. They are:

1. More of a good outcome is better than less.
2. Less of a bad outcome is better than more.
3. Anything that can happen, will happen.

Principles 1 and 2 together are responsible for most of the resemblance of human behavior of SEU. They embody the key principle of *ordinal dominance*. Though it is possible to trick subjects into choosing dominated options by devices that conceal the fact that they are dominated, it is not possible to get people to prefer an option or outcome identified by them as dominated to the options or outcomes that dominate it. Ordinal dominance is both the most intuitively compelling and the most rarely violated of the axioms of rationality.

Principle 3 simply means that decision makers do consider the states on which the outcome of a decision depends. It hints that they may give undue consideration to rare outcomes, but the principle does not require that.

Analysis obviously goes farther; the point of this discussion is only to single out these three features of every analysis.

Guidance (Mis)learned From Past Training

No one can reach adulthood without extensive exposure to the views of others about how decisions should be made. I shall call this source of principles *training*, though explicit training in how to make decisions is rare. Such training is to be found in the popular press, in courses on topics ranging from history to statistics, in second- or third-hand precepts originating in business schools, etc. Introspection and casual inquiry enable me to list five principles of decision making to which I and others have been exposed in that way; your own experience or inquiry will surely suggest others. My five are:

4. Good decisions require variation of behavior. "Don't be rigid; be creative."
5. Good decisions require stereotypy of behavior. "Do the right thing. Don't play around."

6.   All values are fungible.
7.   Good decisions are made by good decision makers and are based on good intuitions; what distinguishes a good decision maker from a bad one is the quality of his or her intuitions.
8.   Rick aversion is wise; in general, the future is good to those who avoid risks. "Look before you leap."

The antinomy between Principles 4 and 5 is obvious but seldom noticed. The principles come from different sources; the notion that creativity is the opposite of rigidity and that it requires variation of behavior comes from both the experimental and the hortatory literature on creativity, while the notion that good decisions are stereotyped comes from management science. The notion that good decisions are made by good decision makers and are based on good intuitions comes mainly from history and from biographies of political and military leaders; it is more compatible with variability than with stereotypy. The sources of this principle never tell us what "good intuitions" are. Their point is that, whatever intuitions are, they are not analyses. I cannot recall an instance from nontechnical literature in which the success of a good decision maker was attributed to good analysis. The notion that values are fungible comes from both the front and the financial pages of any newspaper, and indeed, from even very modest understanding of tort law and financial reparations in civil cases.

Risk aversion, a principle for which normative theorists assert no normative justification, is routinely taught in business schools. It percolates outward from them to our general understanding of how decisions should be made. (If you question the assertion that business schools teach risk aversion, try to find a business school text that treats risk aversion and risk-seeking as equally appropriate deviations from risk neutrality, and gives equal page space to each.) The relation between it and social experience is seldom pointed out. If the alternative to taking a risk is to do nothing, then the merit of risk-taking depends on the merit of doing nothing. If society routinely rewards those who do nothing (for example, by paying interest to those who deposit excess funds in savings accounts; by providing social safety nets), a good case for risk aversion as wise policy can be made. In a less beneficent society, risk aversion has less merit. If your society is out to ruin you, only by taking risks and being lucky can you avoid being ruined. Most business schools are sited in beneficent societies.

Guidance (Mis)induced From Past Decision-making Experience

Four final principles of good decision making are, I assert, so easy to induce from our own past experience with decisions and their outcomes that all of us have induced them.

  9.   Good decisions frequently, though not always, lead to good outcomes.
10.   Bad decisions never lead to good outcomes.[1]
11.   The merit of a decision is continuous in its inputs.
12.   It is far better to be lucky than wise.

Principle 9 is not symmetric with Principle 10 because we routinely explain away bad outcomes, but never good ones; good outcomes of decisions obviously show that the decisions that produced them were good. An explicit implication of these principles together is that most decisions (at least most of those I make) are good. These principles together suggest, but do not establish, another: to identify a good decision maker, observe the outcomes of his or her decisions. If they are good, the person may be a good decision maker, if not, he or she is not. From this secondary principle it follows that in order to consider yourself to be a good decision maker, or to be so considered by others, you should avoid actions that have bad outcomes—another argument for risk aversion.

Principle 10, though dangerously incorrect, is strongly supported by (inadequately cirtiqued) experience and analysis. Ex ante, we do not knowingly make bad decisions when the stakes are significant. Ex post, a good outcome simply confirms our prior belief that the decision leading to it was good, as our decisions usually are, since we do not knowingly make bad decisions. Only if we experience a bad outcome do we second-guess the decision that led to it, and thus, perhaps, come to realize that it might have been bad.

Principle 11 applies only to decisions that have recognizably continuous inputs. I have here listed it as derived from experience; I could have classified it as derived from analysis instead. Its importance arises from its interaction with ordinal dominance. These ideas, jointly, come closer than does ordinal dominance alone to simulating SEU. For example, the ideas jointly imply an orderly array of switchover points as any input to an initially less-preferred option is increased; such arrays cannot exhibit much divergence from SEU. Awareness of Principle 11, if explicit, implies understanding of the notion of degrees of difference in merit among options; such an understanding comes close to a representation of strength of preference. I believe that most people do have an intuitive understanding of strength of preference and find such judgments easy to make.

Principle 12, to which I subscribe, would be a fully adequate prescriptive theory of decisions is one only knew how to apply it. Little wonder that most of us spend much time and effort trying to figure out how to do so! Its main implication for the present discussion is that it invites the decision maker to turn attention away from critical analysis of the decision at hand—an invitation that most decision makers are only too willing to accept. As every loser in Las Vegas should know, but doesn't, the environment always supplies cues on which pursuit of luck can be pinned (for example, runs of wins or losses); attempts to reduce uncertainty by using such cues are *always* available as alternatives to acceptance of uncertainty and analysis of the resulting decision task. Bad luck also offers a convenient explanation of bad outcomes, consistent with the well-understood notion that they can arise from good as well as from bad decisions.[2]

Next Steps

My assertion is that these twelve principles, and others like them, are the tools that educated adults bring to the taks of decision making, and therefore, the raw materials out of which behavioral decision theories must be made. Some principles contradict others; some make sense and some do not; most are relevant to most or all risky decisions, but they do not combine easily to specify what those decisions should be. The tasks of behavioral decision theory, from this point of view, include the following:

1. Amplify, detail, and further specify the principles of good decision making. Trace them to their roots in our training and experience. Find out about the variability in the principles produced by the variability in our backgrounds and experiences.
2. Specify how these principles combine to control decisions. In particular, what happens when they have conflicting implications for a particular decision? Is such a conflict helpful in inducing a decision maker to critique the conflicting principles? Do such conflicts recur, showing that the clashing and/or inappropriate principles have not been revised?
3. Use the results of Task 2 to develop a fully specified behavioral decision theory for adults. Use the results of Task 1, along with

whatever we know or can learn about decision making by children, to explain how the theory becomes decriptive.

4. Use the results of Tasks 2 and 3 to design better approaches to decision aiding and the training of human beings as decision makers.
5. Meanwhile, be careful to use normative tools if you have a decision to make and want it to be wise.

Caveat From Experimental Economics

I have argued that the theory of individual choice behavior contained in von Neumann and Morgenstern (1947) and Savage (1954) is dead as a descriptive theory of real choices, and have examined the implications of that demise. But that theory is not coextensive with Economic Man. The experimental economists have been conducting extremely ingenious and sophisticated experiments on buying and selling behavior in laboratory markets, testing a variety of predictions from economic theory. The remarkable finding is: the economic models frequently work well. Human beings may not make risky choices rationally, but they perform in accordance with rational models in experimental markets. Similar findings, from the same laboratories, come from group bargaining experiments.

Why? I am not aware of any proposed explanations of this inconsistency in the evidence available to us about rationality, and I have none to offer. The experimental economists do offer highly sophisticated discussions of the relevant issues; works like Plott (1986), Smith (1991), and Smith and Walker (1990) are required reading for decision scientists. I do note four differences between the experiments done by experimental economists and those on which conclusions about human irrationality are based. (1) Most of the findings from experimental economics have to do with the environmental consequences of sequences of decisions, not with individual decisions themselves. *Environmental consequences* typically means that the dependent variables of the experiments are prices and quantities, perhaps even asymptotic prices and quantities, rather than individual decisions to buy, sell, or offer to buy or sell. (2) Singificant payoffs to the subject are typically used. Smith and Walker (1990), reviewing the literature on amount of payoff as an independent variable in decision experiments (mostly those done by behavioral decision theorists), persuasively argue that larger payoffs routinely lead to more nearly optimal behavior. (3) The decision task that confronts subjects in such experiments is not one of making a single decision or set of decisions in a hypothetical context, but rather one of making a sequence of decisions such that the outcome of each is appropriately an information input to the next. (4) The experimental outcome that is predicted by the economic model is based on the behavior of several or many individuals, not just one. This is of course especially true of bargaining experiments. In most experiments done by experimental economists, the procedures must and do permit the subjects to interact with one another, typically indirectly, through the mechanisms of the market, auction, or other task, and often directly by talking with one another as well. (In a few experiments the interaction is with a computer, not with other subjects.) So the *relevant* information on which later decisions can be based always includes the results of earlier ones and often includes other information from or about other participants in the task. The data argue that subjects exploit such relevant information well.

The fact that the task calls for a sequence of informationally linked decisions, jointly leading to an aggregate outcome, seems especially important to me. It suggests an analogy to a control task. If compelled to specify steering angles, accelerator and brake pedal forces, and the like, ahead of time, a driver world find it a major challenge to get a car out of a garage. Since we can iteratively adjust these input variables on the basis of observation of consequences of the current control settings, we find driving easy. The tasks of experimental economics are iterative in just this sense; the tasks studied by behavioral decision theorists are not. Since human beings design markets, presumably they do so in a fashion that exploits readily accessible human abilities and skills. (One message I get from cursory reading of this literature is that our important real markets are rather well designed, given that the designers did not in any abstract sense know what they were doing.) Iterative adjustment of control variables based on feedback information is clearly a highly practiced human skill; rational analysis of a decision task based only on pre-decisional information seems not to be.

The previous paragraph might contain a germ of the explanation of the inconsistency between the findings of behavioral decision theory and those of experimental economics, but a far more detailed explanation of the experimental market and bargaining results is needed. Only when that detailed explanation is available can we either lay Economic Man and Economic Woman to well-earned rest, or else resuscitate them in some hard-to-imagine new avatar to triumph over behavioral decision theory at last. My money is on the former outcome.

Notes

1. A reader of an earlier draft of this chapter commented that this principle is simply false; *somebody* wins the lottery! The comment misses the point of the principle. The person who won the lottery made a good decision, by definition. It is the rest of us lottery participants whose decisions were, or at least may have been, bad.

2. A referee suggested yet another Principle that, if included in such a list, would probably belong here: Losses loom larger than gains. I have not included it for two reasons. I do not find it in my own thought or behavior, and am unsure about how widespread it is. More important, disentangling operation of such a Principle from the phenomena of gambler's ruin and quasiruin (see von Winterfeldt and Edwards, 1986, pp. 21, 324–325) and the actions appropriate to those phenomena is difficult. Most people clearly do not accept even quite favorable gambles if they can lead to large losses. But is that because of risk aversion, or rational considerations based on ruin, or some special Principle about the relative importances of losses and gains? I don't know.

References

Edwards, W. (1954). "The Theory of Decision Making." *Psychological Bulletin*, 41, 380–417.

Edwards, W. (1990). "Unfinished Tasks: A Research Agenda for Behavioral Decision Theory." In R. Hogarth (Ed.), *Insights in Decision Making: A Tribute to Hillel J. Einhorn*. University of Chicago Press, Chicago, IL.

Edwards, W. (1991). "Influence Diagrams, Bayesian Imperialism, and the Collins Case: An Appeal to Reason." *Cardozo Law Review*. 13 (2–3), Cardozo School of Law, New York.

Horvitz, E.J., Breese, J.S., and M. Henrion (1988). "Decision Theory in Expert Systems and Artificial Intelligence." *Journal of Approximate Reasoning*, 2, 247–302.

Keeney, R.L. (1991). "On the Foundations of Prescriptive Decision Analysis." In W. Edwards (Ed.), *Utility Theories: Measurements and Applications*. Kluwer Academic Publishers, Boston, MA.

Plott, C.R. (1986). "Rational Choice in Experimental Markets." *Journal of Business*, 59, S301–S327.

Savage, L.J. (1954). *The Foundations of Statistics*. Wiley, New York.

Smith, V.L. (1991). "Rational Choice: The Contrast Between Economics and Psychology." *Journal of Political Economy*, 99 (6).

Smith, V.L., and J.M. Walker (1990). "Monetary Rewards and Decision Cost in Experimental Economics." Economic Science Laboratory, University of Arizona.

von Neuman, J., and O. Morgenstern (1947). *Theory of Games and Economic Behavior*. Princeton University Press, Princeton, NJ.

von Winterfeldt, D., and W. Edwards (1986). *Decision Analysis and Behavioral Decision Theory*. Cambridge University Press, New York.

V DISCUSSION

11 OLD AND NEW ROLES FOR EXPECTED AND GENERALIZED UTILITY THEORIES

Thomas Eppel, David Matheson, John Miyamoto,
George Wu and Stuart Eriksen

Introduction

In organizing the conference on utility theory, Ward Edwards had what was for us the happy thought of inviting a group of graduate students and recent PhDs to serve as discussants of the invited presentations. As Ward had anticipated, this was both a learning experience for us and an opportunity to introduce our own views to an eminent collection of decision scientists. We have chosen to write a joint discussion chapter of the conference presentations, rather than separate discussions of individual contributions, because we felt that a joint discussion would help to bring out points of contact among the conference papers. We do not pretend, however, that our collaboration has yielded a unified perspective or critique of the conference papers. Rather, differences and even inconsistencies in point of view persist in this discussion, reflecting our diverse intellectual backgrounds and also the diversity of issues raised at the conference. What we have attempted to achieve is a kind of local consistency, in which contiguous segments of the discussion are internally consistent, without achieving perfect consistency across different segments of the discussion. Our goal is to articulate issues

W. Edwards (ed.), UTILITY THEORIES: MEASUREMENTS AND APPLICATIONS.
Copyright © 1992. Kluwer Academic Publishers, Boston. All rights reserved.

and record general themes that emerged from the somewhat disputatious interactions at the conference and to notice points of conflict or agreement in these discussions.

From its inception, it was clear that a central issue at the conference would be the merits and deficiencies of expected utility (EU) theory and its subjective counterpart, subjective expected utility (SEU) theory.[1] Of course, the complement to this issue was an evaluation of the merits and deficiencies of generalized utility theories that are being developed as alternatives to the old time religion. It was also clear that the critique of alternative utility theories could not be undertaken without clarifying whether the critique was from the standpoint of normative, descriptive, or prescriptive considerations. We have chosen to separate these three standpoints in our discussion, for they constitute the natural framework of the discourse. Before beginning our discussion, however, we should mention one last qualification. Most of our comments derive from the intellectual contributions of other participants at the conference. We cite the originator of these contributions when the attribution was particularly clear, but in many cases the ideas grew out of interactions for which no definite scorecard was kept. Suffice it to say that we do not claim to originate ideas in this discussion so much as to record and present in an orderly fashion a critical discussion of important points made by others.

This chapter is organized as follows. Section two discusses the normative status of utility theories and describes some situations that challenge the old time religion as the accepted normative standard. Section three summarizes empirical findings reported elsewhere in this volume and compares the old time religion with generalized utility theories from a descriptive point of view. Section four is our longest and most controversial contribution, in which we examine the role of utility theories in prescriptive applications. We approach this issue from various perspectives: the consideration of psychological concerns when advising clients, the potential role of generalized utility theories in prescriptive work, the problem of how to manage the discourse about a decision problem, and which problem elements to analyze with computational tools. We conclude our chapter with a summary of the major themes that we developed in the discussion.

The Normative Role of Utility Theories

A normative utility theory characterizes principles of rational decision making, in other words, principles to which one would always want to conform in any decision or choice. A deviation from a rational norm is regarded as an error of reasoning. Howard (1992) defends the old-time religion, that is, EU and SEU theory, against alternative normative theories that have come to be called generalized utility theories. Whether or not any of the generalized utility theories provide a viable alternative to the old time religion was one of the central topics of the conference. For Howard, the so-called paradoxes that inspired the development of generalized utility theories are not flaws in the old time religion, any more than temptations to sin and weakness of flesh justify the rejection of a Deity and holy precepts. Rather, the paradoxes provide evidence that some decision makers need to be educated and assisted. Howard (1992) formulates a set of normative principles, or desiderata, that he is prepared to defend and from which SEU theory follows as a logical consequence. Thus, rejection of SEU theory implies rejection of one or more of Howard's desiderata. Howard openly challenged the conference participants to describe a realistic situation in which a decision maker would want to violate one or more of his desiderata.

It was the consensus of the conference participants that the most likely contexts in which departures from Howard's list of desiderata might be found are decision situations involving regret, equity, or ambiguity. Keeney (1992), for example, argues that the axioms of EU theory are not always adequate for prescriptive decision theory when equity is an issue. Whether EU theory could provide an adequate analysis if an additional "equity dimension" were added to the analysis, was not resolved during the discussion. It was also suggested that ambiguity might pose difficulties for an SEU analysis since, in such a situation, the utility of an outcome could depend on second-order probabilities. Such probability-dependent utilities are not allowed in the old time religion.

Camerer drew an analogy to the situation that led Bernoulli to the formulation of expected utility theory: The St. Petersburg paradox provided a pattern of preference that was paradoxical from the standpoint of expected value theory. The question was raised whether the current challenges to EU theory are equally strong, compelling the replacement of EU and SEU theory by a generalized utility theory. Is the old time religion on the way out as the normative standard? We walked away from the conference with a tentative "No" to this question, but as some doubts remained, we asked the conference participants to read through Howard's list of desiderata (see table 11–1), and to indicate whether there were any desiderata with which they disagreed. The following quote from one participant is quite representative of the general tenor of responses: "From a normative perspective, the list (except for 4, *Practical*

Table 11–1. Howard's List of Desiderata

1.	**Note: All follow from the old time religion.**

2.   Essential properties:
2.1.   Applicable to any decision
2.2.   Must prefer deal with higher probability of better prospect
2.3.   Indifferent between deals with same probabilities of same prospects
2.4.   Reversing order of contemplating uncertain distinctions should not change
        any inference or decision
    2.4.1. Order of receiving a given body of information should not change
    any inference or decision
    2.4.2. Sometimes called "invariance to data order"
2.5.   "Sure Thing" principle satisfied
2.6.   Independence of immaterial alternatives
2.7.   New alternatives cannot make an existing alternative less desirable
2.8.   Clairvoyance cannot make decision situation less attractive
2.9.   Sequential consistency
    2.9.1. At this epoch, the choices you make in thought are consistent
2.10. Equivalence of normal and extensive form analysis

3.   Essential properties with measures of prospects
3.1.   No money pump possibilities
3.2.   Certain equivalents of deals exist
3.3.   Value of a new alternative must be non-negative
3.4.   Value of clairvoyance exists and cannot be negative
3.5.   No materiality of sunk costs
3.6.   No willingness to pay to avoid regret
3.7.   Stochastic dominance satisfied

4.   Practical considerations
4.1.   Individual evaluation of prospects possible
4.2.   Tree rollback possible

Considerations) is compelling and determines SEU many times over. The fact is that people, even experienced decision makers, do not automatically abide by all of these conditions, in part no doubt for the practical reasons alluded to in 4." Some of the more general comments suggested that Howard's desiderata should be violated only for specific problems where a strong rationale exists, based on problem characteristics or the decision maker's preferences. One participant argued that the most severe challenge to Howard's list might be the fact that most people perceive some consequences as gains and some as losses, which strongly influences choice behavior. This distinction does not fit into the old-time religion and turned out to be one of its major descriptive failures. But it is questionable how easy it is to convince decision makers not to make this distinction.

We now paraphrase some of the more detailed comments to specific items in Howard's list. This summary is based on the discussion during the conference as well as on the responses to our mailing of Howard's list. The comments differ widely in their generality and with respect to the central question about the normative status of the old time religion. We still feel that the old time religion provides a compelling normative standard in general; however, the following comments give an impression about what the major areas of concern are.

Violations of item 2.3. (*Indifference Between Deals With Same Probabilities of Same Prospects*) show that people need a lot of help in seeing through compound gambles. Of course, this might be a prescriptive issue rather than a normative one. One participant claimed that none of the generalized utility theories, if applied holistically (to the decision in normal form), violates item 2.4. (*Reversing Order of Contemplating Uncertain Distinctions Should Not Change Any Inference or Decision*). Item 2.4.1. should include the qualifier that there be no decisions within any of the possible resolution sequences. Another respondent argued in favor of "liberal" usage of items 2.4 and 2.10 (*Equivalence of Normal and Extensive Form Analysis*) in prescriptive work: if decision makers persist in violating 2.4 in a prescriptive setting, indicating that two supposedly identical problem frames (by changing order of states) are not identical, the analyst might have to accept this and proceed to help the clients solve their problem, rather than forcing them to accept the analyst's model of reality. In the same spirit, if a person does not believe that normal and extensive forms of a tree are identical, the analyst should use the tree structure as the person sees it and not force consistency.

Concerning 2.6. (*Independence of Immaterial Alternatives*) and 2.7. (*New Alternative Cannot Make an Existing Alternative Less Desirable*) it was mentioned that in real life, a new alternative could change the evaluation of an existing alternative due to learning and clarification of preferences. However, these two items express the desirable property that rankings of alternatives by preference should not be altered by the discovery or creation of a new alternative. In other words, a new alternative might be better than the highest ranked so far, or it might be worse than the lowest ranked so far, or it might be inserted into an intermediate position. But it should not change the relative rankings of the existing alternatives.

Item 2.8. (*Clairvoyance Cannot Make Decision Situation Less Attractive*) invites the question of whether knowledge is always better than ignorance. One of the respondents wondered whether a person is better off knowing that he or she has cancer, instead of merely contemplating the possibility. This issue was already discussed by Savage (1972). Note, however, that item 2.8. refers to the quality of the decision not to the quality of life.

Item 2.9. (*Sequential Consistency*) was criticized for the nonstandard terminology of "epoch" and the vagueness in saying that "the choices you make in thought are consistent." We were also reminded about Machina's (1989) argument that non-SEU preferences are not necessarily subject to money-pump manipulations. We will come back to this argument in our discussion of dynamic consistency and consequentialism.

The underlying assumption needed for "yes" to item 3.2. (*Certain Equivalents of Deals Exist*) requires a continuous and monotone measure of value, such as money. Item 3.4. (*Value of Clairvoyance Exists and Cannot Be Negative*) implies that one should not be willing to pay in order to prevent a clairvoyant from telling us the future. One respondent wishes that such principles would leave a bit of room in which to be a gambler. While one might be willing to pay a consultant to resolve a 50:50 uncertainty with $1,000 at stake, one might not for a 99:1 uncertainty. The same respondent regarded 3.5. and 3.6. as wonderful principles but wondered whether anybody could live by them. Another participant regarded 3.5., 3.6., and 3.7. as corollaries of consequentialism (*No Materiality of Sunk Costs, No Willingness to Pay to Avoid Regret, Stochastic Dominance Satisfied*). It was also suggested that regret or awareness of sunk costs are valid human experiences and should be considered when creating a model. For example, hair-rising experiences in the past (risks assumed that did not materialize) may be partly to blame for risk-averse postures regarding new risky prospects. Finally, it was pointed out that 4.2. (*Tree Rollback Possible*) might be much more than a practical consideration. While tree rollback is always possible (except perhaps in the absence of 4.1., *Individual Evaluation of Prospects Possible*), the real question is whether the solution it yields agrees with solutions obtained by other methods, since lack of such agreement provokes controversy as to which of the putative solutions is the real one.

This concludes our summary and discussion of Howard's list of desiderata and the participants' reactions to it. In reporting these detailed reactions, we obviously did not intend to resolve the issues that were raised. Rather, we wanted to give the reader a flavor of the discussion about the normative status of the old time religion. We now turn to a more general review of key concepts in the normative domain.

Machina's (1989) defense of generalized utility theories against money-pump possibilities deserves further attention because it allows us to discuss the important concepts of dynamic consistency and consequentialism. LaValle's chapter (1992) on small worlds and sure things argues that these concepts play a central role for the normative interpretation of utility theories. A decision maker is dynamically inconsistent if a clever opponent can offer a series of choices such that the decision maker is certain to lose some money. Machina points out that demonstrations of the dynamic inconsistency of non-EU theories assume that choice behavior is consequentialist in the following sense: if the strategies available to the decision maker are represented in a decision tree, preferences are consequentialist if the preference at any decision node is a function only of the subtree that temporally follows the given node (Hammond, 1988; Machina, 1989). In particular, if two decision nodes are followed by identical subtrees, the preferences at these nodes must be identical even if they have different histories of prior decisions and chance outcomes. Machina (1989) reviews arguments, due to Raiffa (1968), Yaari (1985), Green (1987), Wakker (1988), and others, showing that preference behavior will be dynamically inconsistent if it is non-EU maximizing and consequentialist. Machina (1989) also shows that the force of these arguments can be diminished by dropping the assumption of consequentialism and by indexing the strategies available at a decision node by the risks and opportunities that were encountered at preceding positions in the decision tree.

From this perspective we can discuss the broader implications of LaValle's derivation of consequentialist preference behavior from normatively plausible assumptions (see LaValle, 1992). If he is right, non-EU theories are doomed to be dynamically inconsistent, and hence, their potential as normative theories is extremely doubtful. Proponents of non-EU theories will naturally look closely for a point to mount a counterattack against LaValle's analysis. LaValle bases his analysis on four assumptions: existence of preferences (connectedness of the preference relation), invariance (no framing paradoxes), sure-thing dominance, and horizon flexibility. Thus, a central question concerns the normative appeal of these assumptions. In our opinion, these assumptions are reasonable normative principles and do not provide a likely target for criticism.

A more likely criticism, we believe, is directed at the underlying concept of a consequence that LaValle so painstakingly develops. A consequence for LaValle is defined by the risks and decisions that remain possible at a position in a decision tree. Consequences may be construed as unanalyzed wholes (for example, receiving a prize or paying a penalty), or as decision subtrees in which the risks and decisions made possible by receiving an outcome are spelled out in greater detail. Thus, consequences are not fundamentally different from gambles. Whether a consequence is described as an unanalyzed whole or as a decision subtree is a pragmatic concern, depending on the merits of simplicity versus detail that arise when conceptualizing or communicating a decision analysis. LaValle's characterization of a consequence explicitly treats as irrelevant the history of risks and decisions that precedes the position of the consequence in a decision tree.

LaValle defends his conception of a consequence by pointing to the complications that arise if one attempts to take account of the paths not taken in the decision tree. In his colorful terminology, he prefers to initiate the decision tree at the current point, "Now," rather than from the perspective of some previous time, "Back Then," because the accurate recreation of a past perspective is extremely difficult to carry out. Regardless of whether or not proponents of non-EU normative theories will be discouraged by LaValle's pessimistic views, or challenged by them, the point we want to make is that a commitment to consequentialism is made whenever one defines the primitive objects of the preference theory (the consequences) in the technical sense of the given theory. Consequentialism is presupposed in the definition of these primitive objects if positions in a decision tree do not carry information regarding the prior history of risks and decisions that brought one to the positions. If we accept LaValle's interpretation of what consequences must be and the normative status of his assumptions (existence of preferences, invariance, sure-thing dominance, and horizon flexibility) we have no logical alternative but to adopt EU theory as the normative standard.

In summary, although the normative analysis of some situations continues to pose difficulties for the old time religion, not one of the conference participants was willing to offer a generalized utility theory as an alternative normative theory. Some of the difficulties and "paradoxes" are more concerned with issues of implementing the normative ideals in a prescriptive setting. We will discuss such issues in more detail in section four.

The Descriptive Role of Utility Theories

In general, the purpose of descriptive theories is to "describe the world as it is" (see Howard, 1992). The purpose of a descriptive theory of decision making is to describe actual preferences and actual decision behavior. To understand actual preferences, however, we may also need to develop psychological models of the mental representations and cognitive processes that underlie preference behavior. Kahneman and Tversky's (1979) prospect theory, for example, has representational assumptions (framing) and process assumptions (editing of outcomes). The appraisal of a normative theory focuses upon the issue of whether the behavior implied by the theory is indeed rational, whereas a descriptive theory is mainly judged by the degree that it correctly predicts observable decision behavior. Keller (1989) offers a more elaborate list of criteria by which descriptive models can be evaluated, including "predictive ability, face validity, psychological insights into choice behavior, enhancement of understanding of cognitive processes, elegance, parsimony, etc." (pp. 259–260).

It is well known that preferences and choices observed in controlled experiments do not always follow the predictions of expected utility theory. In fact, it was the discovery of such discrepancies (sometimes called "paradoxes") between actual behavior and the normative standards of expected utility theory that gave rise to the development of alternative models. The participants of the conference agreed that, for descriptive purposes, generalized utility theories can play an important role if they predict observed behavior more accurately than expected utility theory. On the other hand, such an improvement comes as no surprise since generalized utility theories were primarily developed with this descriptive purpose in mind, whereas, the old time religion started out as a normative theory. Furthermore, as generalizations of expected utility theory, generalized utility theories impose fewer restrictions on the observations. Better agreement between theory and empirical observations is a necessary consequence. Thus, a tradeoff emerges between empirical accuracy and parsimony of model assumptions. The evaluation of expected utility theory and generalized utility theories as competing descriptive theories depends on how one weighs these two criteria against each other.

Camerer (1992) presents data and analyses that compare predictions from expected utility theory, prospect theory, and several generalized utility theories. Using the Marschak triangle diagram (Marschak, 1950) to describe the construction of the gambles used in his experiment, Camerer shows that expected utility performs reasonably well as a descriptive theory as long as the gambles are not too close to the edges of the triangle. However, alternative theories (generalized utility theories, prospect theory) outperform expected utility theory if the gambles involve small probabilities and/or large payoffs. The fact that many real-life decision situations (e.g., medical, investment, public policy) fall into this category emphasizes the descriptive value of generalized utility theories and prospect theory in such situations. While no theory can account for all the observed empirical phenomena, prospect theory seems to be the most accurate descriptive theory, overall. Camerer also alludes to the above mentioned tradeoff between accuracy of the model and parsimony of the model. He questions whether further generalizations will fulfill a fruitful purpose. Mere data fitting, with no improvement of our conceptual understanding of decision behavior, would be the extreme of such an approach. We mentioned before that our conceptual understanding could be enhanced by considering process models. Gaining insight into the processes that influence choice behavior is a first step toward designing effective tools needed in prescriptive applications.

Two of Camerer's stylized facts seem especially noteworthy to us: "Slope and shape of indifference curves both reflect around a reference point" and "the reduction of compound lotteries axiom is violated, directly and indirectly." Luce (1992) also argues that seeing through compound gambles and reference point effects are probably the most pervasive empirical phenomena that challenge the descriptive and maybe even prescriptive status of expected utility theory.

In summary then, it is obvious that in some situations generalized utility theories offer better descriptions of actual behavior than the old time religion. However, this improvement in empirical accuracy is bought at the price of increased model complexity. How some of the most pervasive empirical findings (reference point effects, dynamic aspects in compound lotteries) affect prescriptive work will be discussed in the next section.

The Prescriptive Role of Utility Theories

The central problem in prescriptive work is how normative and descriptive considerations, decision methodology, and practical experience can be integrated to produce quality decisions in real-world contexts. It is the prescriptive role of utility theories that created the most controversy during the conference. In particular, the potential role of generalized utility theories in this prescriptive context remained largely unresolved. At the same time, even though the old time religion provides an acceptable normative standard in the abstract, the implementation of this standard in a concrete situation involves many problems. As questions of prescriptive theory turned out to be the most controversial during the conference, this final section contains the most conflict in the views expressed and, consequently, is longer and more complex than the previous sections. Our discussion of the prescriptive role of utility theories will cover the special status of psychological concerns (like regret, anxiety, etc.), the role of generalized utility theories in a prescriptive context, how to manage the discussion about a decision problem, and how to balance computation and judgment.

The problem of prescriptive analysis can be stated as: How should a decision analyst advise a client, friend, or himself/herself on how to make a decision? Moreover, we would like to know what type of counsel is appropriate when the decision maker is subject to cognitive illusions and logical errors, has poorly defined or labile preferences, and suffers from a myriad of psychological concerns, including anxiety, disappointment, regret, and weakness of will. Working in this advisory context, it is important to discuss what types of problems an analyst might encounter. First, there are the various forms of logical and cognitive errors (Kahneman, Slovic and Tversky, 1982). In this case, it is rather uncontroversial that prescriptive analysis should not deviate from normative theory. A decision analyst does not abandon the axioms of probability simply because the client falls prey to the conjunction fallacy. Only slightly more difficult to deal with are violations of relatively transparent axioms such as first-order stochastic dominance and transitivity. MacCrimmon and Larsson (1979) have found that most people find these axioms extremely appealing normatively. When decision makers are shown such errors, they usually feel the pull of the axiom and wish to reconcile their choices to make them consistent with these axioms. Other types of violations of axioms, especially those involving psychological concerns, are more troublesome and will be discussed later.

Among the chapters in this book, Keeney's (chapter 3) discussion of prescriptive foundations of decision analysis is obviously the most relevant in this context. The concept of a "quality decision analysis" is fundamental to Keeney's formulation of prescriptive foundations. Keeney's table 3–1 describes the main, general characteristics of a quality decision analysis. Because the foundations of prescriptive decision analysis should provide a basis for producing quality decision analyses, we may regard these characteristics as objectives that guide the formulation of appropriate foundations. With this in mind, it is noteworthy that relative to the purposes of prescriptive decision analysis, expected utility theory is treated not as a normative ideal, but rather as a useful heuristic or working model. In Keeney's view, the decision to adopt the expected utility axioms as a framework for a given decision analysis may often be justified, but it is not a necessary requirement for a quality decision analysis. Keeney offers an example involving equity and a second example, where legal considerations have been omitted from the analysis, to illustrate situations in which one would not choose the act that has the highest expected utility.

One might object to Keeney's examples on the grounds that a more elaborate EU representation of these decision problems could be found. Incorporating attributes omitted from Keeney's representation, the actions that Keeney regards as preferred, but nonoptimal in an EU analysis, would be EU maximizing in the more elaborate EU analysis. We believe that such an argument misses Keeney's point. Even if a more elaborate EU analysis could be constructed that leads to the same conclusions as the non-EU reasoning, the prescriptive issue is whether the more elaborate EU analysis or a non-EU analysis better serves to achieve the objectives of the decision analysis listed in Keeney's table 3–1. If the EU analysis were difficult to formulate, difficult to assess, or difficult to communicate, one might prefer a non-EU basis for the analysis. Moreover, a simple EU analysis might be worthwhile, even if the action that is ultimately chosen is not the action that is formally EU maximizing within the simple analysis, because the simple EU analysis yields important insights into the structure of the decision problem (compare Keeney's example pertaining to omitted legal issues). The decision to construct an analysis within the framework of the EU axioms and the decision to choose the action that is formally optimal in an EU analysis are themselves subordinate means to achieving a quality decision analysis, and there may be instances in which non-EU analyses better serve to achieve this purpose. The fact that a more elaborate EU analysis can be constructed for these situations is of some theoretical interest, but it need not affect the prescription to adopt non-EU methodology in the actual conduct of the decision analysis.

Including Psychological Concerns

In his discussion of why people violate the substitution principle, Sarin (1992) refers to the special status of psychological concerns such as anxiety, regret, and fear. He suggests that such concerns play a valid role in decision analysis, but that "the economic costs for avoiding psychological concerns should be pointed out to the decision maker." We agree with this prescription, but not with the underlying assumption that normative theory assumes a dispassionate decision maker who suppresses or otherwise avoids the influence of emotional responses to decision making. A person who reflects on what course of action to take should take all of his or her concerns into account. Some of these concerns, if real to the person, could be quite passionate. Normative theory is silent about the content of attributes that the decision maker wants to consider. It is the reflection about what action to take that requires a certain detachment from emotions.

Violations of normative rules due to psychological concerns are very troublesome and deserve considerable attention. For example, if a client announces that he or she wants to make Allais-type choices, we might offer one of the many arguments for satisfying the independence axiom. If he or she persists in the original choices, even after understanding our arguments, is there anything we can do? He or she might argue that the independence axiom seems like a reasonable principle, but *in this case* the $0 outcome in one option is not the same as the $0 outcome in another option. For in the first case, if one were to gamble for the potential $5 million and receive the $0 outcome, the $0 would be accompanied by an implicit psychological consequence, namely, intense regret for having passed up a sure $1 million. In the other case, even if one were to gamble for the potential $5 million and receive the $0 outcome, there would be much less regret because the unchosen option also possessed a substantial chance of receiving $0. Therefore, the $0 in the first case is $0 plus intense regret, and the $0 in the second case is $0 without intense regret. Let us suppose that our client reasons along these lines, thereby revealing that anticipations of regret strongly influence his or her choices. What should a prescriptive theory recommend in this case? Several approaches are suggested by Raiffa (1986) and Bell, Raiffa and Tversky (1988). The analyst can impress upon the client the difference between good decisions and bad outcomes. This might meet with some success, but the analyst may have other alternatives such as forcing the client to price out his or her regret. When framed differently, the client might suddenly be unwilling to pay such a high regret premium.

Perhaps you cannot alleviate all concerns for regret, but if it is a real source of disutility, is it then rational *not* to include it in the analysis? At this point, one could refine the consequence description and assess a utility function, $U(x, r)$, where x is a dollar amount and r is the level of regret. Of course, inclusion of regret as an attribute can lead to well-known problems of intransitivity. As a result, we must also advise our client on these *dynamic considerations* and emphasize the danger of making decisions myopically.

Regret is only one of many psychological complications that might hinder a general prescriptive application of expected utility theory. In the setting of lotteries with delayed resolution, the axiom of dynamic consistency might be violated. In this case, the psychological factor is no longer regret, but anxiety (see Wu, 1991, for a discussion of the prescriptive role of anxiety). In a standard setting of immediate resolution of uncertainty, expectation formation can lead to ex post feelings of elation or disappointment (Bell, 1985). In either case, a complete description of the consequences is necessary to do justice to the analysis. The carriers of value in this analysis include not only monetary utility, but psychological (dis)utility as well.

Why have we stressed these psychological effects? Many violations of expected utility theory can be interpreted as symptomatic of hidden psychological attributes. These psychological attributes can be explicitly represented within the domain of outcomes, and the utility function can be defined over the enriched domain that includes psychological consequences. When this is done, what were previously viewed as non-EU patterns of behavior are now seen to be EU maximizing. The key to this approach is that we are not rationalizing behavior, but prescribing decisions that maximize a more complicated (but more realistic) human welfare function.

A New Role for Generalized Utility Theories

We have just argued that one of the key roles of the prescriptive analysis is to uncover the hidden psychological carriers of value. Yet, even when the psychological attribute in question has been identified, the decision analyst must still evaluate the options available in a logically consistent framework. Take anxiety for example. Wu (1991) shows that under some behavioral assumptions, the effects of anxiety can be modeled with a rank dependent model (Quiggin, 1982). Similarly, a generalization of Bell's (1985) disappointment model has a rank dependent form. It is also known that skew-symmetric bilinear utility (SSB) (Fishburn, 1982) has a dual interpretation in the regret theory of Bell (1982) and Loomes and Sudgen (1982). These functional forms provide a direct method for evaluating options for decision makers who wish to include psychological concerns in their analysis.

Part of the difficulty with permitting psychological variables to enter the analysis is that decision makers do not have the ability to assess how large a premium they are paying for their feelings of regret, disappointment, or anxiety. These dual generalized utility models provide an easy way of assessing these premiums. In enlarging the consequence description to include psychological concerns, we have not completely abandoned our role as normativists. Earlier, we mentioned that the magnitudes of these concerns should satisfy some principles of consistency. Moreover, it is clear that emotions can seem *too salient* to a decision maker—the possibility of regret, anxiety, or disappointment might simply loom too large in his or her mind. By assessing the size of these premiums, the decision analyst can present the decision maker with an alternative frame. Hopefully, this new frame will prevent over-magnified paranoia induced by these emotions. See Raiffa (1986) for an example of how a decision analyst might combat excessive regret.

Discourse Management

As decision analysts we face a vague, ambiguous, and complex challenge. We know that people commit systematic errors when they make decisions. Our job is to assist in defining and structuring decisions and then to apply our tools in order to aid the decision maker. We need to manage discussions, engage in political struggles, and interact with many people in order to accomplish these aims and ultimately clarify the decision. Decision analysts must constantly be seeking to assist the client by developing the issues that are the most important and by applying their analytical skills in the areas where they will be most fruitful.

In accomplishing these tasks, the analyst faces two basic questions: how to manage an ongoing discussion about the decision; and how to determine what elements of the problem to model and what elements to leave up to judgment. This section will address the first problem, which we call "discourse management." The second issue will be discussed later.

The ability to further the discussion about the decision is an important feature of prescriptive decision analysis. LaValle (1992) testifies to this fact by saying that "the act of explicitly modeling a decision situation as a tree (or otherwise) has been found by many besides myself to be a creativity-stimulating and knowledge-fathoming aid." This usefulness comes from two sources. First, in order to have a clear discussion, one often needs to define the issues as clearly as in a decision tree. Second, describing a situation with a decision model enables a clear understanding of how the various problem elements relate to each other. These two features lead to insight and refined discussion about the decision situation. By examining how our decision technologies control this discussion, we can identify some important considerations for the normative theories.

These considerations provide a basis for judging the appropriateness of proposed models as the foundation for prescriptive analysis.

As Keeney (1992) points out, there are at least two types of technologies to consider in understanding the role of decision analysis in aiding decision makers. The first type are the theoretical assumptions. These assumptions (axioms) and their interpretations constitute the basis of the normative model. The second type are the operational assumptions. These assumptions establish a practical methodology for applying the theoretical assumptions to a real problem.

From the perspective of managing the discussion between analyst and client, the role of prescriptive analysis is to establish the terms of discourse for and to guide the flow of the discussion about the decision. It defines what one can talk about in the decision and how to talk about it. At the core of the decision analytic conception is a distinction between alternatives, uncertainties, and values, as well as a commitment to discuss decision situations in these terms. An analyst strives to identify, clarify, and quantify each of these aspects of a decision. Particular normative theories carry with them additional definitions and commitments. We build these theories on the basis of axioms, which we justify in terms of their interpretations. In many cases, this justification is mathematical, although it need not always be so. For example, Howard (1992) defines his axioms by their contribution to the decision discussion, rather than their mathematical form.

The methodology, on the other hand, guides the discussion and thus the analysis. These methodologies specify when and how to have conversations about uncertainties, values, alternatives, and other required elements. Keeney (1992) suggests five aspects that need to be addressed by these methodologies, from identifying the problem (having a discussion about what we want to examine with our decision models), to communication of the insights (having a discussion about what the analysis means).

Knowledge maps (Howard, 1989) provide an example of how methodologies can guide the discussion. In preparation for a probability assessment, one draws an influence diagram that shows all of the uncertainties that are relevant to the variable of interest. This exercise provides a structure for discussion about the factors contributing to uncertainty. Different views can be quickly represented and talked about. The analyst and the client eventually agree on some portion of the diagram to assess, leaving the remainder of the diagram to serve as a reminder of other considerations. When the assessments are made, the assessee needs to reflect on these other considerations as sources of uncertainty in determining his or her judgments. The decision of which portion to assess entails an explicit discussion of which elements of the problem will be addressed with computational methods, and which will be left up to the judgment of the assessee (see next section). Even after the assessment, the knowledge map can guide the discussion. Suppose that, after the assessment, a person disagrees with the range of uncertainty on a variable. By appealing to the knowledge map created earlier, the analyst can identify the issues that were considered at the time of the assessment. The challenger must come up with an explanation for why the current assessment should be improved. Whatever the challenger says, this explanation serves only to advance the discussion about the decision. If he or she claims that an important factor is left out, then the analyst has learned something. If he or she agrees that the right factors were considered, then he or she may realize that the assessment reflects the best available information. Either way, everyone is closer to a clear understanding of which decision to make. This clarity also helps to justify the decision to others.

In order to understand the appropriateness of various normative models to provide the foundation for prescriptive analysis, it is necessary to establish criteria. Unfortunately, considerations related to discourse management are absent from most sets of criteria suggested in this volume. We would ask the following questions of any model before using it as the foundation for a prescriptive analysis. Can the model express the decision maker's concerns? Does the technology tend to further the discussion or get in the way? Does the analysis obfuscate or clarify? Can we explain the results of the analysis in meaningful terms?

The last issue focuses our attention on how we understand the recommendations of the analysis. Based on the notion that people explain and talk about the analysis of a particular decision by making extractions of the model, Matheson proposes the "explanation principle" as a criterion for effective discourse management. The explanation principle states that the way an analyst explains a model should not change his recommendations. For example, suppose that an analyst has built a large decision tree model of a investment decision and has derived the recommendation to invest from it. Furthermore, suppose that the model is too complex to be understood in its entirety. In order to explain it to the client, the analyst must extract pieces of the model, small trees that represent key issues, and explain each of those. These extracted models will necessarily suppress some of the detail of the more complex model. However, at the level of abstraction of the extracted model, it must be a faithful representation of the complex one. The principle of explanation defines what we mean by a "faithful representation:" if the analyst computes an optimal policy on the extracted tree, then the results can be meaningfully interpreted in terms of the optimal policy computed on the complex tree.

Expected utility satisfies the principle of explanation. Any intermediate branches on a tree can be collapsed into distributions over the prospects given optimal suppressed decisions. If the analyst recalculates the optimal policies on the collapsed tree, they will be faithful to the complex model. Thus, extraction will not change the optimal policy of any of the remaining decisions. Any explanation of the complex model based on such an extraction will always result in consistent recommendations.

LaValle (1992) argues for the old time religion on the basis of what he calls "horizon flexibility" and "invariance." These concepts are related to the principle of explanation. By "horizon flexibility," LaValle means that changing the extent of a decision tree between larger and smaller worlds should not change the optimal policy. The larger world in LaValle's analysis corresponds to the complex model. The smaller world corresponds to an extraction of that model for the purpose of explanation. Horizon flexibility imposes consistency requirements on the various extractions, which imply the principle of explanation. By "invariance," LaValle means that the strategic and extensive forms of analysis should produce the same optimal policy. Strategic form and extensive forms are extractions of each other: Although the level of abstraction does not change, the mode of presentation does. The key issue in the invariance principle is that changing the style of explanation from the strategic to the extensive form of the model does not alter the decision recommendation.

Exploring the Balance Between Judgment and Computation

Another important issue for a decision analyst is to decide which elements of the problem deserve to be modeled in detail and which elements can be assessed by direct judgment. This question arises because mathematical models are useful to extend one's thinking. As Sarin (1992) points out, "the divide and conquer strategy employed in decision analysis to break the problem into simple parts is intended to reduce the cognitive burden on the decision maker." This ability to reduce cognitive burden through the application of computational techniques is an important feature of prescriptive decision analysis. An analyst can aid a decision maker by supplementing the decision maker's thinking with mathematical models. Unfortunately, it is easy to build models that overwhelm the most advanced computational methods. Thus, any analyst faces the practical question of how much and which cognitive burden should be reduced with computational methods.

One type of answer to this question is that the variables that are the most important for the decision should be addressed computationally. A sensitivity analysis helps focus the analyst's attention on these variables. Another type of answer says that when the decision is clear, the analyst can stop replacing direct judgments with judgments supported by computation. A third type of answer argues that the analyst should address with computation those judgments that are potentially unreliable representations of the client's beliefs and/or preferences.

Keller (1989) explains the sense of this last type of answer by stating that "analysts must meet design specifications (normative goals), based on descriptive constraints of human judgmental abilities" (p. 260). She points out that the extent to which an analyst can aid decision makers is constrained by the dependability of the judgments that go into the decision model. We should look to descriptive models to determine the dependability of various judgments. Sarin (1992) develops another twist on this type of answer. "It is apparent that a gap between descriptive theory and normative theory will always exist. This is because people's unaided judgment and choices are influenced by ignorance, cognitive limitations, and psychological concerns." He points out that computational methods are most valuable when unaided judgment is the least dependable. Again, we should consult descriptive models to identify situations in which this might be the case.

Descriptive models help us determine the proper balance between judgment and computation in two ways. They identify areas where people's judgments are suspect, revealing where decision modeling is the most valuable. They also identify the constraints of human judgmental ability, which indicates what types of judgments an analyst can expect people to make dependably. Descriptive models can be simply a collection of empirical results (for example, Camerer's list of stylized facts) or mathematical representations of certain empirical phenomena (for example, Luce's model).

We will take Camerer's (1992) list of stylized facts and turn them around to give guidance to the prescriptively-minded analyst. One of Camerer's stylized facts is: "Choices inside the triangle violate expected utility less often and systematically than choices on the edges." The edges of the triangles are places where gambles have prospects with small probabilities. Thus, the analyst should bring his or her analytical tools to bear on situations of this type. By conditioning on various events, the analyst should be able to frame the problem such that the deals on which assessments are made have intermediate probabilities. From these assessments, the analyst can compute the implications for small probabilities.

Similarly, the analyst should try to keep judgments focused on small values that the assessee is familiar with, since "the frequency of expected utility violations depends on the outcomes there are more violations when payoffs are large in magnitude" (Camerer, 1992). Probability assessments, using for example a probability wheel, can almost always be done with small outcomes. For value assessments, the analyst may be able to break the value into readily assessable components and then compute the overall values. Value judgments involving large outcomes that cannot be avoided in this fashion should be assessed especially carefully.

The dependability of assessments is influenced greatly by the reference point. Luce (1992) argues that "a major point of irrationality on the part of decision makers concerns gambles with mixed positive and negative outcomes." Camerer (1992) notes a similar result from his empirical work. That reference points are important is no surprise to an analyst. Assessment procedures generally incorporate debiasing techniques designed to avoid reference point effects. However, in determining which elements to attack with computation, an analyst should focus on judgments across reference points, other things being equal.

Two observations argue for making assessment in extensive form and computing recommendations from these. Camerer (1992) notes that "the reduction of compound lotteries axiom is violated, directly and indirectly." Additionally, Luce (1992) argues that people do not convolve distributions properly, rather that they have an additive notion of utility over joint receipt. Making judgments based on a strategic form amounts to forcing people to convolve and collapse complex trees in their minds. Therefore, assessments on the extensive form of a tree can be expected to be more dependable.

By identifying places where people's judgments are the least dependable, the analyst can better decide which elements of the decision he or she should focus upon with analytical tools. These descriptive insights supplement procedures for focusing on the most important decision elements, as determined by, for example, sensitivity analysis.

Descriptive theories of decision making are invaluable in developing assessment procedures for prescriptive analysis. By indicating what conditions produce dependable judgments, they guide an analyst in interpreting the answers to assessment questions. Descriptive theories also indicate that inconsistent judgments could be motivated by factors that are not in the current model of the decision. The careful analyst, therefore, needs to consider descriptive theories in order to determine how to ask assessment questions and in order to determine the possible implications of inconsistent answers.

It is well known that expressing problems in different ways, which are equivalent to each other by expected utility, can lead to different judgments. Keller (1989) points out that framing is also important for generalized utility models, "since the choice of the way to frame the current decision problem can alter the choice prescribed by generalized utility models, framing issues are of considerable practical concern (p. 269)." Additionally, the frame can invoke different judgments for substantive reasons. Sarin (1992) suggests that such "inconsistencies may occur due to cognitive limitations or psychological concerns invoked by the problem scenario." If cognitive limitations are responsible for inconsistencies, then the analyst should provide computational methods to overcome such burdens. However, for framing inconsistencies that are due to different psychological concerns, the analyst should identify them and make them explicit. Bringing these concerns to the surface generally leads to insight into the decision.

Conclusions

In this chapter, we tried to synthesize the major themes that emerged during the conference. All participants agreed that the distinction between normative, descriptive, and prescriptive issues is very important for the discussion of utility theories. We therefore chose to structure this chapter according to this distinction. From a normative perspective, the old time religion emerged as the commonly accepted norm for rational decisions. The most severe challenge arises from the interpretation of the consequences that a decision maker contemplates, especially the distinction between relative gains and losses from a status quo. Descriptively, it is well known that the axioms of expected utility theory are often violated. Even so, it still serves as a reasonable approximation in many cases. For purely descriptive purposes, generalized utility theories can play a valid and important role. In particular, for small probabilities and/or high stakes, they improve the descriptive accuracy at the expense of more complicated model assumptions. The prescriptive role of utility theories created the most controversy. The question of how to model violations of the accepted norms of decision behavior due to psychological concerns (regret, anxiety) remained largely unresolved. We showed how such concerns can create a new role for generalized utility theories in a prescriptive context. For example, generalized utility theories can be used to calculate preminums that a decision maker would be willing to pay in order to include psychological concerns in the analysis. On the other hand, we also discussed in some detail how the challenges for implementing the old time religion can be addressed in decision analytic work. From this more practical perspective, we emphasized the role of expected utility theory for facilitating the discussion about the decision and for identifying issues that should not be left to the unaided judgment of the decision maker.

Notes

1. At the conference, these theories were jointly referred to with affection as the "old time religion." As a matter of terminology, we will refer to EU theory when it is assumed that probabilities are stated numerically in the formulation of the decisions under discussion, and we will refer to SEU theory when at least some relevant probabilities are not explicitly stated, but rather must be assessed subjectively.

References

Bell, D.E. (1982). "Regret in Decision Making Under Uncertainty." *Operations Research*, 30, 961–981.

Bell, D.E. (1985). "Disappointment in Decision Making Under Uncertainty." *Operations Research*, 33, 1–27.

Bell, D.E., Raiffa, H., and A. Tversky (1988). "Descriptive, Normative, and Prescriptive Interactions in Decision Making. "In D.E. Bell, H. Raiffa and A. Tversky (Eds.), *Decision Making: Descriptive, Normative, and Prescriptive Interactions* (pp. 9–30). Cambridge University Press, New York.

Camerer, C. (1992). "Recent Tests of Generalizations of Expected Utility Theory." In W. Edwards (Ed.), *Utility Theories: Measurements and Applications*. Kluwer Academic Publishers, Boston, MA.

Fishburn, P. (1982). "Nontransitive Measurable Utility." *Journal of Mathematical Psychology*, 26, 31–67.

Green J. (1987). "Making Book Against Oneself: The Independence Axiom and Nonlinear Utility." *Journal of Economic Theory*, 4, 45–57.

Hammond, P.J. (1988). "Consequentialist Foundations of Expected Utility." *Theory and Decision*, 25, 25–78.

Howard, R.A. (1989). "Knowledge Maps." *Management Science*, 35, 903–922.

Howard, R.A. (1992). "In Praise of the Old-time Religion." In W. Edwards (Ed.), *Utility Theories: Measurements and Applications*. Kluwer Academic Publishers, Boston, MA.

Kahneman, D., Slovic, P., and A. Tversky (Eds.) (1982). *Judgment Under Uncertainty: Heuristics and Biases*. Cambridge University Press, New York.

Keeney, R.L. (1992). "On the foundations of Prescriptive Decision Analysis. In W. Edwards (Ed.), *Utility Theories: Measurements and Applications*. Kluwer Academic Publishers, Boston, MA.

Keller, L.R. (1989). "The Role of Generalized Utility Theories in Descriptive, Prescriptive, and Normative Decision Analysis." *Information and Decision Technologies*, 15, 259–271.

LaValle, I.H. (1992). "Small Worlds and Sure Things: Consequentialism by the Back Door." In W. Edwards (Ed.), *Utility Theories: Measurements and Applications*. Kluwer Academic Publishers, Boston, MA.

Loomes, G., and R. Sudgen (1982). "Regret Theory: An Alternative Theory of Rational Choice Under Uncertainty." *Economic Journal*, 92, 805–824.

Luce, R.D. (1992). "Rational Versus Plausible Accounting Equivalences in Preference Judgments. In W. Edwards (Ed.), *Utility Theories: Measurements and Applications*. Kluwer Academic Publishers, Boston, MA.

MacCrimmon, K.R., and S. Larsson (1979). "Utility Theory: Axioms Versus Paradoxes." In M. Allais & O. Hagen (Eds.), *Expected Utility Hypothesis and the Allais Paradox* (pp. 333–409). Reidel, Dordrecht, Holland.

Machina, M. (1989). "Dynamic Consistency and Non-Expected Utility Models of Choice Under Uncertainty." *Journal of Economic Perspectives*, 27, 1622–1668.

Marschak, J. (1950). "Rational Behavior, Uncertainty Prospects, and Measurable Utility." *Econometrica*, 18, 111–141.

Miyamoto, J.M. (1992). "Generic Analysis of Utility Models." In W. Edwards (Ed.), *Utility Theories: Measurements and Applications*. Kluwer Academic Publishers, Boston, MA.

Quiggin, J. (1982). "A Theory of Anticipated Utility." *Journal of Economic Behavior and Organization*, 3, 333–343.

Raiffa, H. (1968). *Decision Analysis: Introductory Lectures on Choices Under Uncertainty*. Addison-Wesley, Reading, MA.

Raiffa, H. (1986). "Back From Prospect Theory to Utility Theory." In M. Grauer, M. Thompson and A. Wierzbicki (Eds.), *Plural Rationality and Interactive Decision Processes* (100–113). Springer, Berlin.

Samuelson, P. (1952). "Probability, Utility, and the Independence Axiom." *Econometrica*, 20, 670–678.

Sarin, R.K. (1992). "What Now for Generalized Utility Theory?" In W. Edwards (Ed.) *Utility Theories: Measurements and Applications*. Kluwer Academic Publishers, Boston, MA.

Savage, L.J. (1972). *The Foundations of Statistics* (2nd ed.) Dover Publications, New York.

Wakker, P. (1988). "Nonexpected Utility as Aversion of Information." *Journal of Behavioral Decision Making*, 1, 169–175.

Wu, G. (1991). "Anxiety and Decision Making Among Gambles with Delayed

Resolution of Uncertainty." Unpublished doctoral dissertation. Harvard University, Cambridge, MA.

Yaari, M.E. (1987)."The Dual Theory of Choice Under Risk." *Econometrica*, 55, 95–117.

Author Index

295

Subject Index